THE
VALIANT

JEFF LEMIRE | MATT KINDT | PAOLO RIVERA | JOE RIVERA

CONTENTS

Collection Cover Art: Paolo Rivera
with Joe Rivera

Assistant Editor: Kyle Andrukiewicz
Editor: Warren Simons

VALIANT.

Peter Cuneo
Chairman

Dinesh Shamdasani
CEO & Chief Creative Officer

Gavin Cuneo
Chief Operating Officer & CFO

Fred Pierce
Publisher

Warren Simons
VP Editor-in-Chief

Walter Black
VP Operations

Hunter Gorinson
Director of Marketing, Communications
& Digital Media

Atom! Freeman
Matthew Klein
Andy Liegl
Sales Managers

Josh Johns
Digital Sales & Special Projects Manager

Travis Escarfullery
Jeff Walker
Production & Design Managers

Alejandro Arbona
Editor

Tom Brennan
Kyle Andrukiewicz
Associate Editors

Peter Stern
Publishing & Operations Manager

Chris Daniels
Marketing Coordinator

Ivan Cohen
Collection Editor

Steve Blackwell
Collection Designer

Rian Hughes/Device
Trade Dress & Book Design

Russell Brown
President, Consumer Products,
Promotions and Ad Sales

Jason Kothari
Vice Chairman

THE VALIANT

ETERNAL WARRIOR

For ten thousand years, the Eternal Warrior has walked the face of the Earth.
A master of ancient and modern weaponry, he's sworn his life to defend the
Geomancers, the long line of oracles born with the power to speak for the Earth itself.

GEOMANCER

The latest in a line of enigmatic mystics guided by the Earth, Kay McHenry
struggles in her new role as the Geomancer.

BLOODSHOT

A nanite-infused soldier, Bloodshot was once used–against his will–as a weapon
by Project Rising Spirit. While the rest of his past remains a mystery, he now fights
on behalf of the U.S. and British governments.

ARMSTRONG

The Eternal Warrior's brother, Armstrong has walked the face of the Earth for
more than ten millennia. He's been sober for at least four of them. Well-traveled
and a fan of poetry, he's a surprisingly wise and loyal confidant.

NEVILLE ALCOTT

The MI-6 liaison for the world's elite superteam Unity, little is known about the man who pulls the strings of the most powerful beings on Earth.

X-O MANOWAR

Aric of Dacia was a fifth-century Visigoth warrior and heir to the throne before he was stranded in our time with a sentient suit of powerful alien armor. After a difficult period of adjustment, Aric became an unlikely hero and Earth's greatest champion.

NINJAK

Calculating and mysterious, Ninjak is a combat and technology master. He pledges no allegiance to any country, preferring to work freelance for the highest bidder, but his personal ethics often align him with Neville Alcott and the Eternal Warrior.

COL. JAMIE CAPSHAW

Commanding officer of G.A.T.E—the Global Agency for Threat Excision. She works with her British counterpart, MI-6's Neville Alcott, to address unfolding crises around the world.

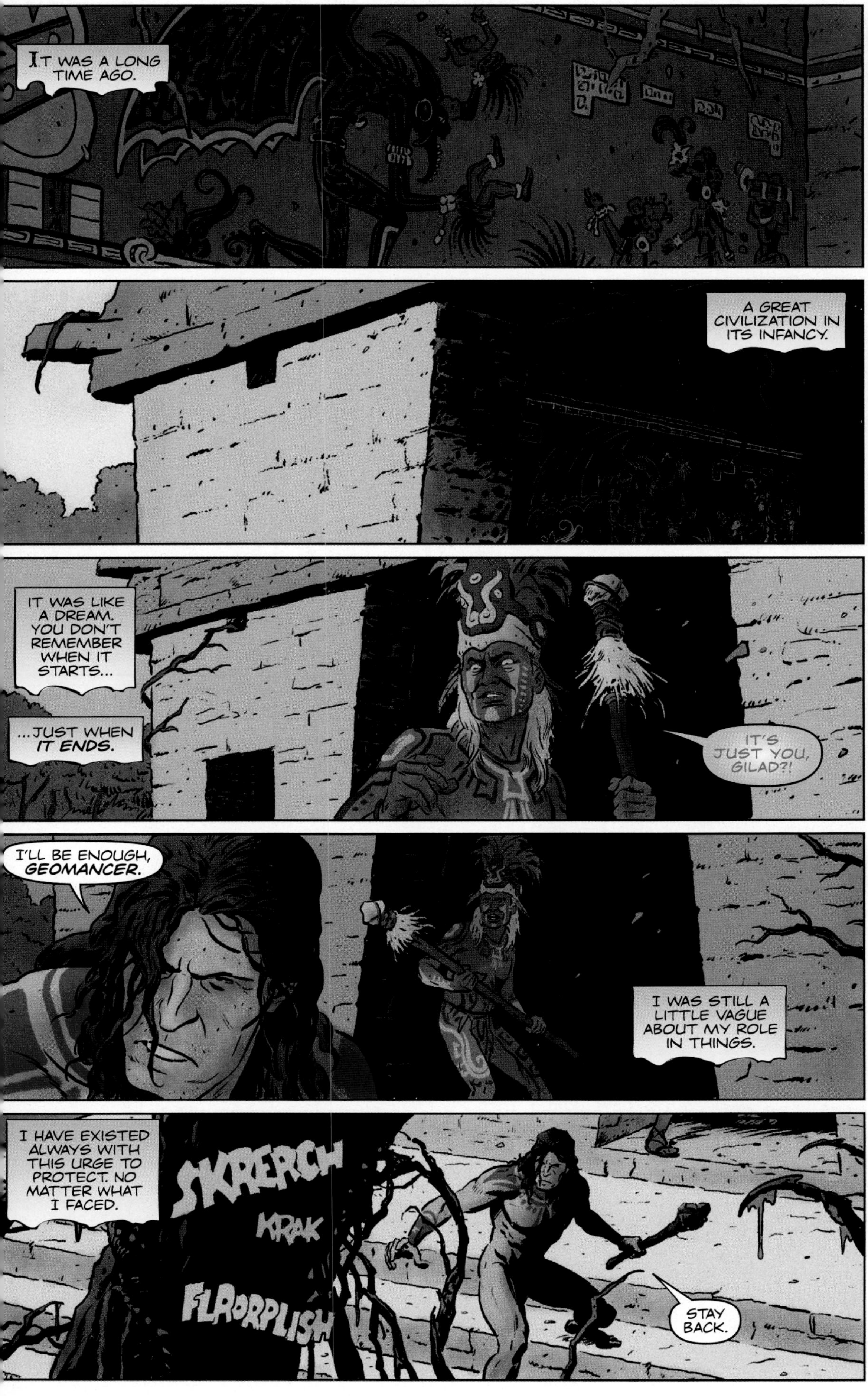
IT WAS A LONG TIME AGO.
A GREAT CIVILIZATION IN ITS INFANCY.
IT WAS LIKE A DREAM. YOU DON'T REMEMBER WHEN IT STARTS...
...JUST WHEN *IT ENDS.*
IT'S JUST YOU, GILAD?!
I'LL BE ENOUGH, *GEOMANCER.*
I WAS STILL A LITTLE VAGUE ABOUT MY ROLE IN THINGS.
I HAVE EXISTED ALWAYS WITH THIS URGE TO PROTECT. NO MATTER WHAT I FACED.
SKRERCH
KRAK
FLRORPLISH
STAY BACK.

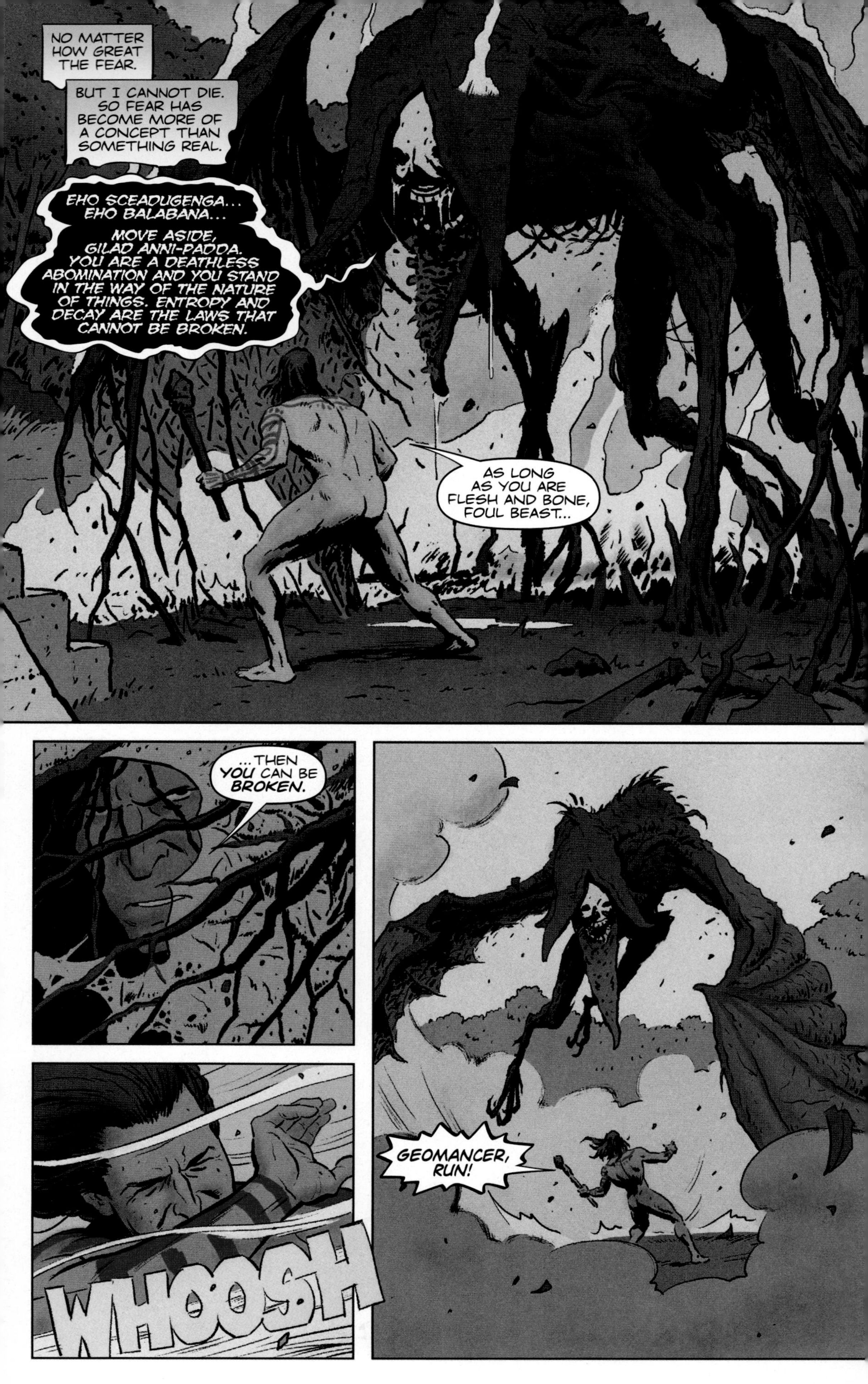
NO MATTER HOW GREAT THE FEAR.
BUT I CANNOT DIE. SO FEAR HAS BECOME MORE OF A CONCEPT THAN SOMETHING REAL.
EHO SCEADUGENGA... EHO BALABANA...
MOVE ASIDE, GILAD ANNI-PADDA. YOU ARE A DEATHLESS ABOMINATION AND YOU STAND IN THE WAY OF THE NATURE OF THINGS. ENTROPY AND DECAY ARE THE LAWS THAT CANNOT BE BROKEN.
AS LONG AS YOU ARE FLESH AND BONE, FOUL BEAST...
...THEN YOU CAN BE BROKEN.
WHOOSH
GEOMANCER, RUN!

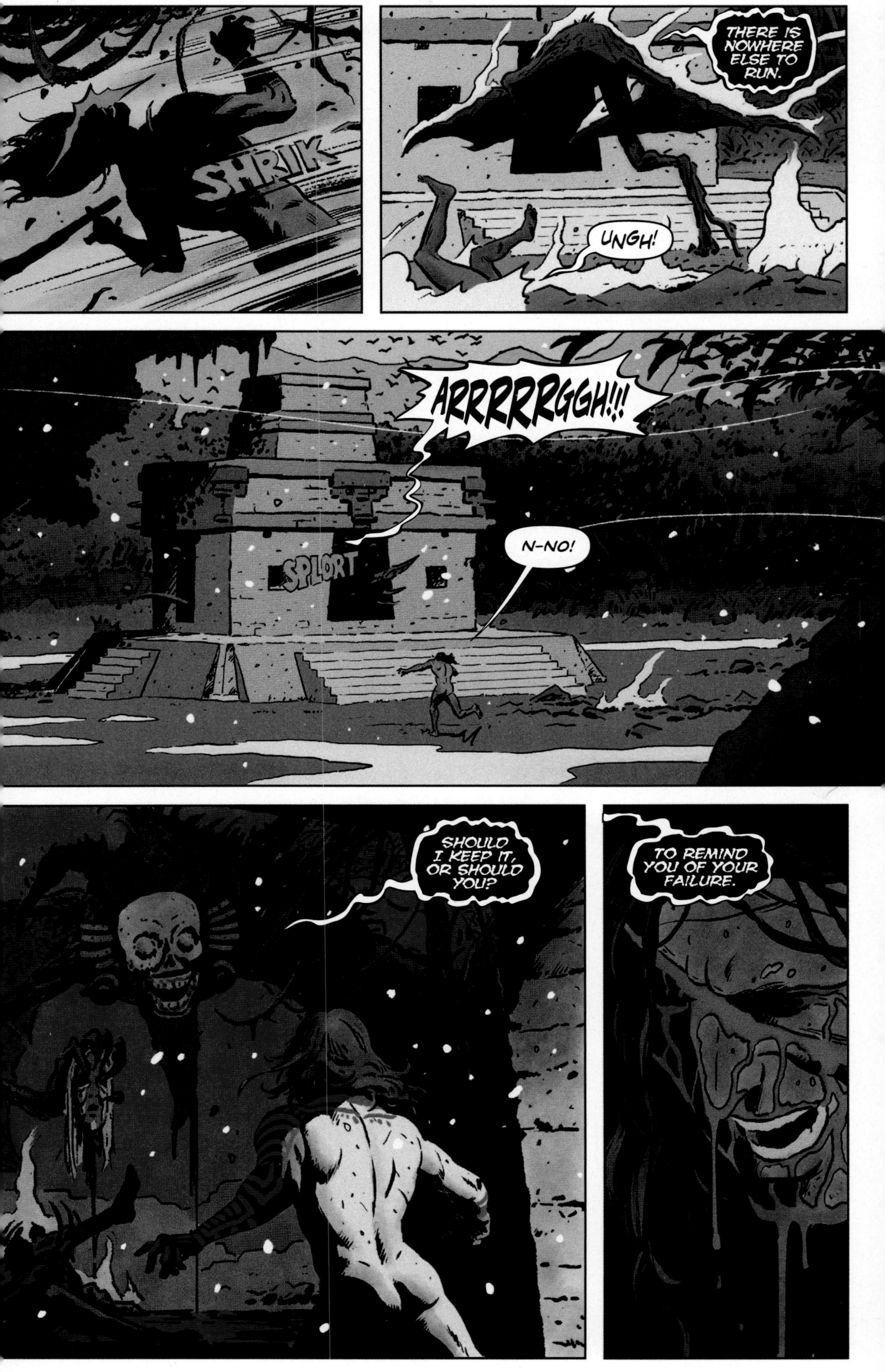
SHRIK
THERE IS NOWHERE ELSE TO RUN.
UNGH!
ARRRRRGGH!!!
SPLORT
N-NO!
SHOULD I KEEP IT, OR SHOULD YOU?
TO REMIND YOU OF YOUR FAILURE.

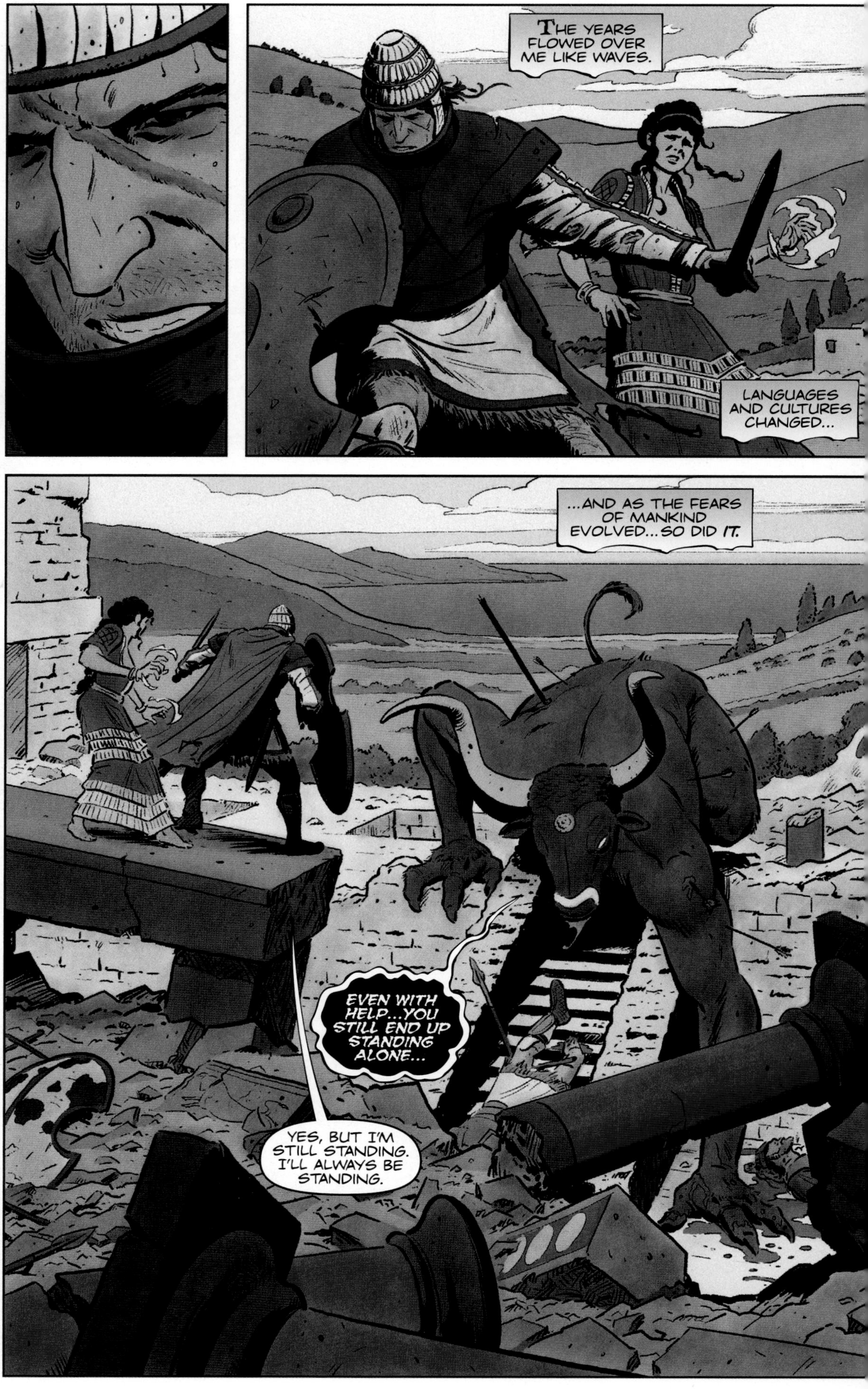
THE YEARS FLOWED OVER ME LIKE WAVES.
LANGUAGES AND CULTURES CHANGED...
...AND AS THE FEARS OF MANKIND EVOLVED...SO DID IT.
EVEN WITH HELP...YOU STILL END UP STANDING ALONE...
YES, BUT I'M STILL STANDING. I'LL ALWAYS BE STANDING.

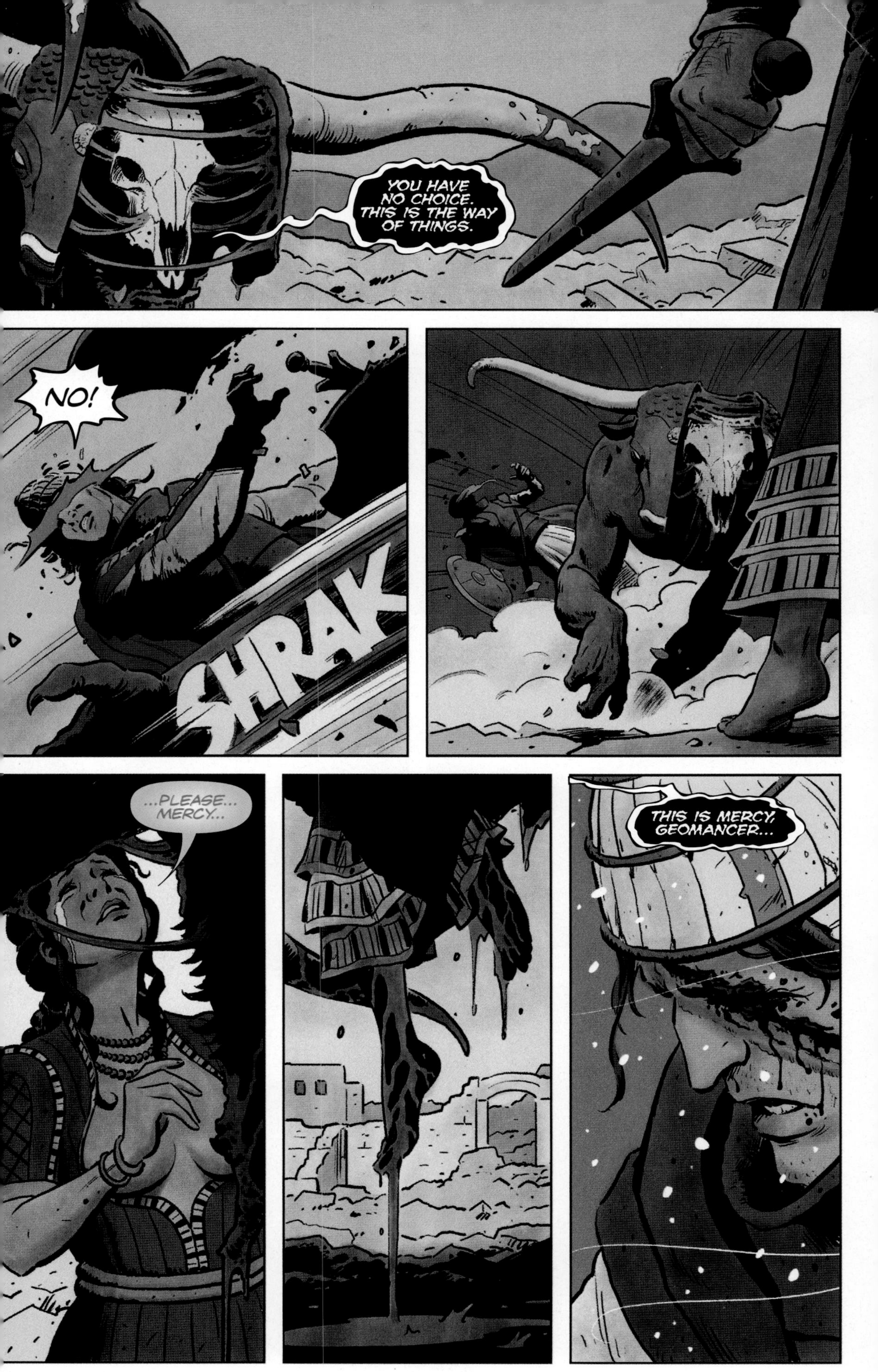
YOU HAVE NO CHOICE. THIS IS THE WAY OF THINGS.
NO!
SHRAK
...PLEASE... MERCY...
THIS IS MERCY, GEOMANCER...

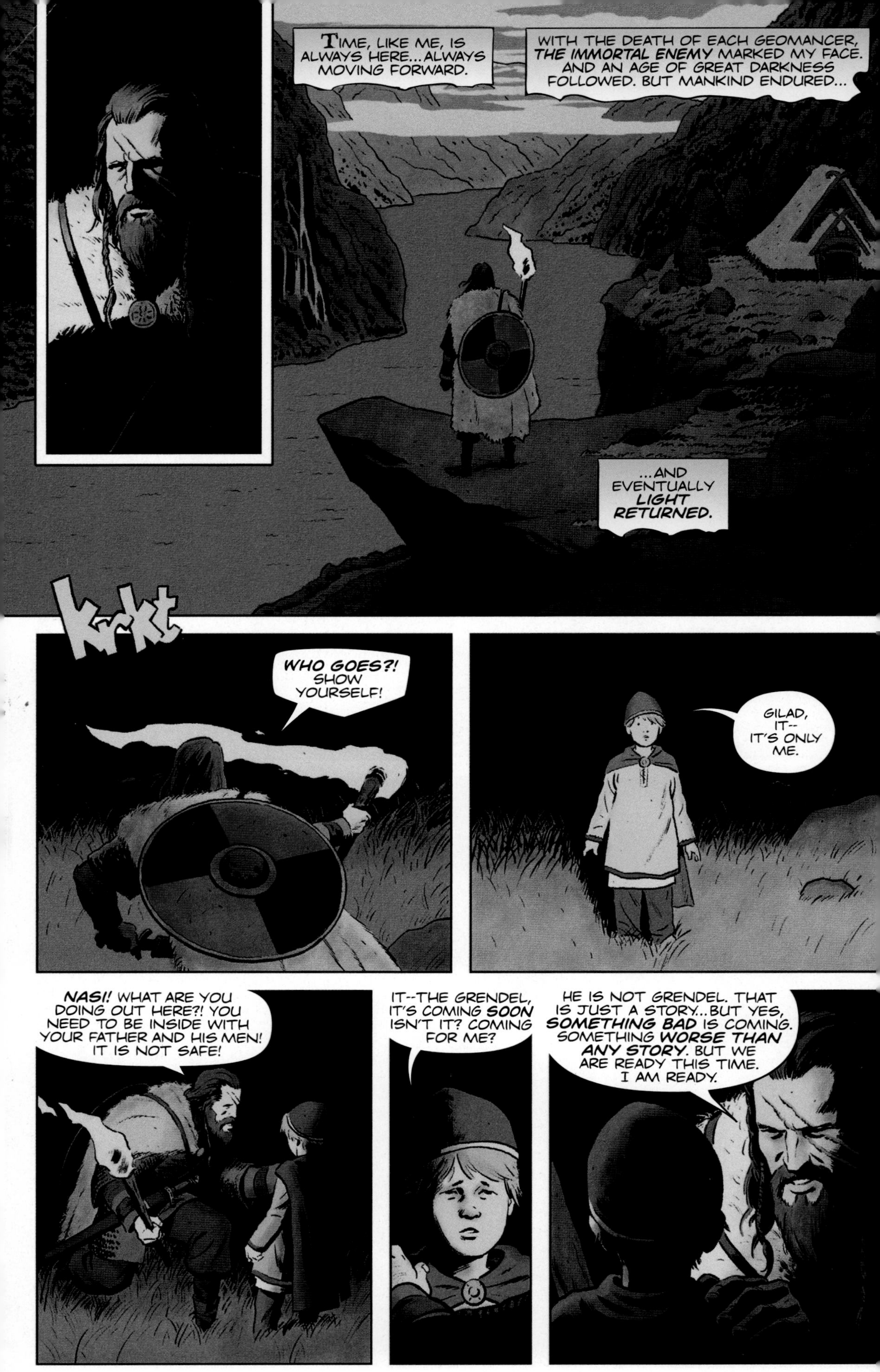
TIME, LIKE ME, IS ALWAYS HERE...ALWAYS MOVING FORWARD.
WITH THE DEATH OF EACH GEOMANCER, THE IMMORTAL ENEMY MARKED MY FACE. AND AN AGE OF GREAT DARKNESS FOLLOWED. BUT MANKIND ENDURED...
...AND EVENTUALLY LIGHT RETURNED.
krckt
WHO GOES?! SHOW YOURSELF!
GILAD, IT-- IT'S ONLY ME.
NASI! WHAT ARE YOU DOING OUT HERE?! YOU NEED TO BE INSIDE WITH YOUR FATHER AND HIS MEN! IT IS NOT SAFE!
IT--THE GRENDEL, IT'S COMING SOON ISN'T IT? COMING FOR ME?
HE IS NOT GRENDEL. THAT IS JUST A STORY...BUT YES, SOMETHING BAD IS COMING. SOMETHING WORSE THAN ANY STORY. BUT WE ARE READY THIS TIME. I AM READY.

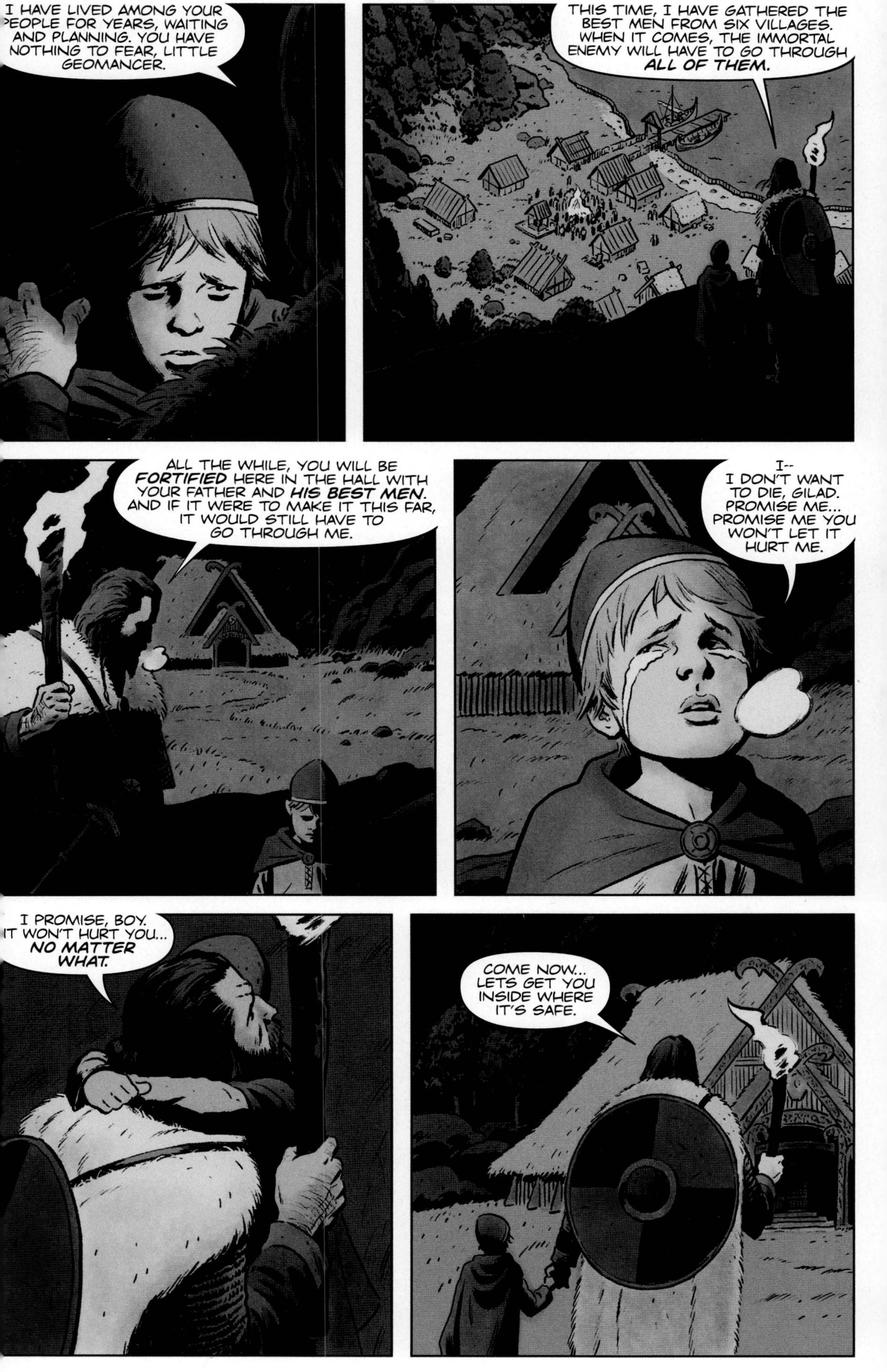
I HAVE LIVED AMONG YOUR PEOPLE FOR YEARS, WAITING AND PLANNING. YOU HAVE NOTHING TO FEAR, LITTLE GEOMANCER.
THIS TIME, I HAVE GATHERED THE BEST MEN FROM SIX VILLAGES. WHEN IT COMES, THE IMMORTAL ENEMY WILL HAVE TO GO THROUGH **ALL OF THEM.**
ALL THE WHILE, YOU WILL BE **FORTIFIED** HERE IN THE HALL WITH YOUR FATHER AND **HIS BEST MEN.** AND IF IT WERE TO MAKE IT THIS FAR, IT WOULD STILL HAVE TO GO THROUGH ME.
I-- I DON'T WANT TO DIE, GILAD. PROMISE ME... PROMISE ME YOU WON'T LET IT HURT ME.
I PROMISE, BOY. IT WON'T HURT YOU... **NO MATTER WHAT.**
COME NOW... LETS GET YOU INSIDE WHERE IT'S SAFE.

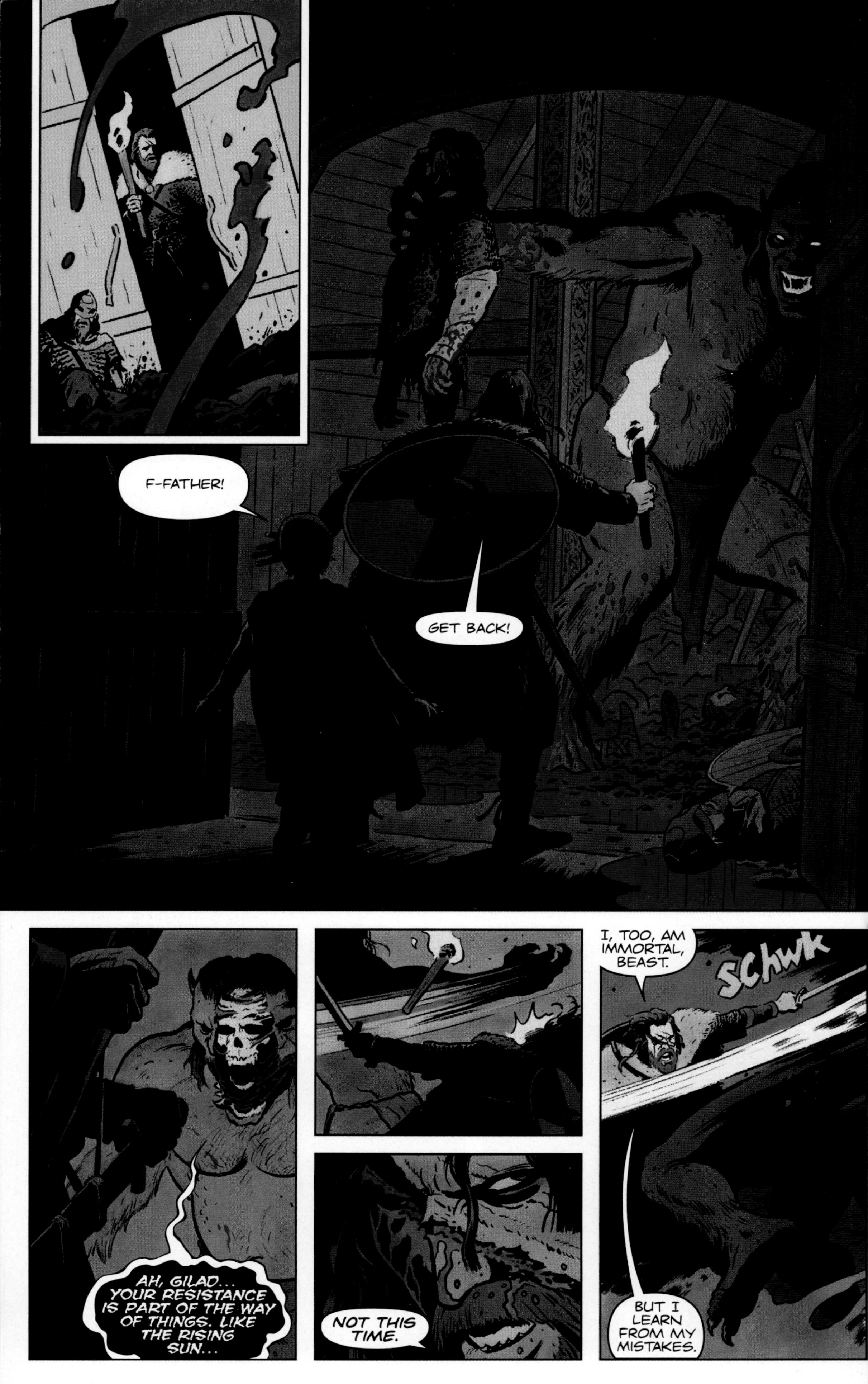
F-FATHER!
GET BACK!
AH, GILAD... YOUR RESISTANCE IS PART OF THE WAY OF THINGS. LIKE THE RISING SUN...
NOT THIS TIME.
I, TOO, AM IMMORTAL, BEAST.
SCHWK
BUT I LEARN FROM MY MISTAKES.

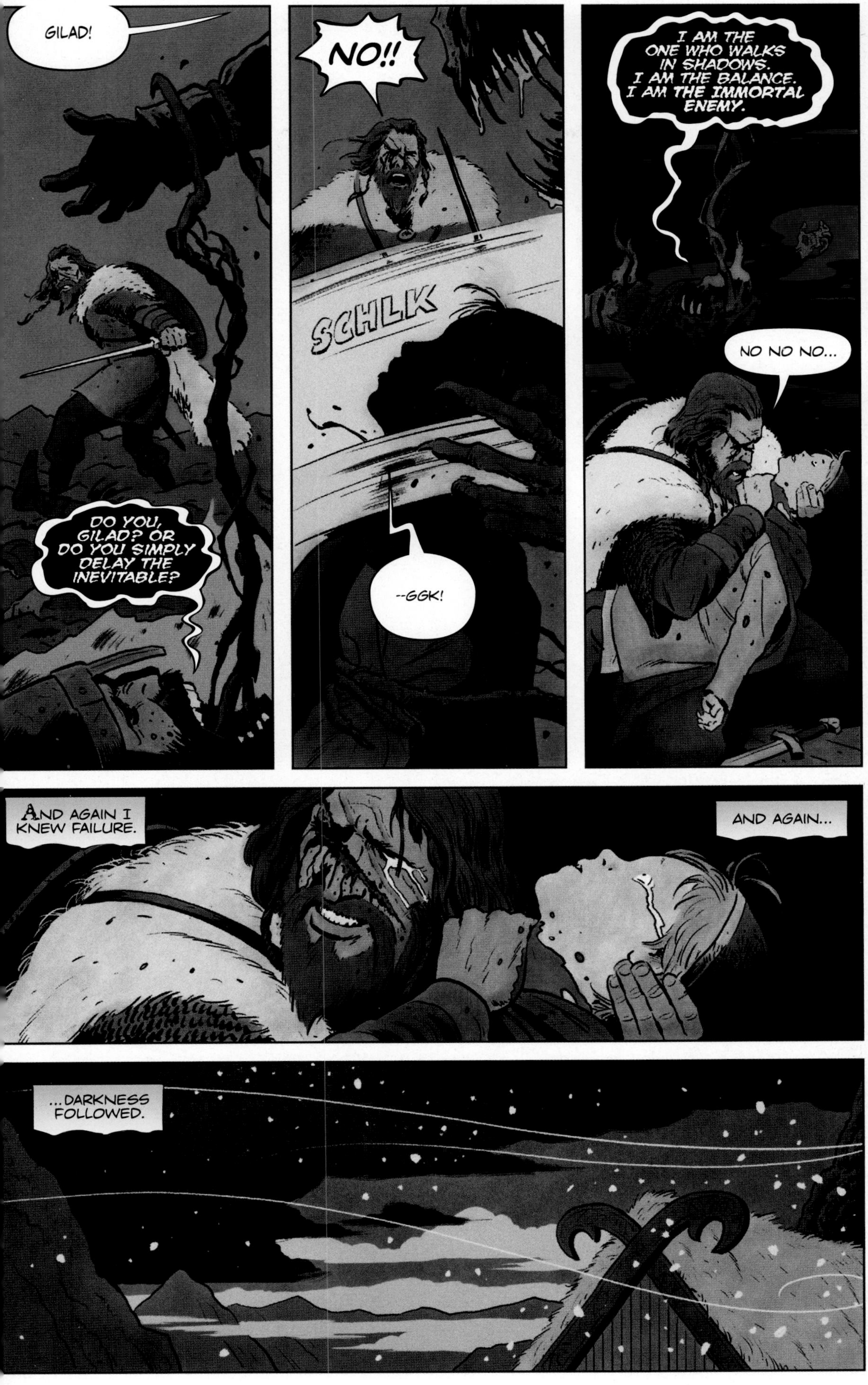
GILAD!
DO YOU, GILAD? OR DO YOU SIMPLY DELAY THE INEVITABLE?
NO!!
SCHLK
--GGK!
I AM THE ONE WHO WALKS IN SHADOWS. I AM THE BALANCE. I AM THE IMMORTAL ENEMY.
NO NO NO...
AND AGAIN I KNEW FAILURE.
AND AGAIN...
...DARKNESS FOLLOWED.

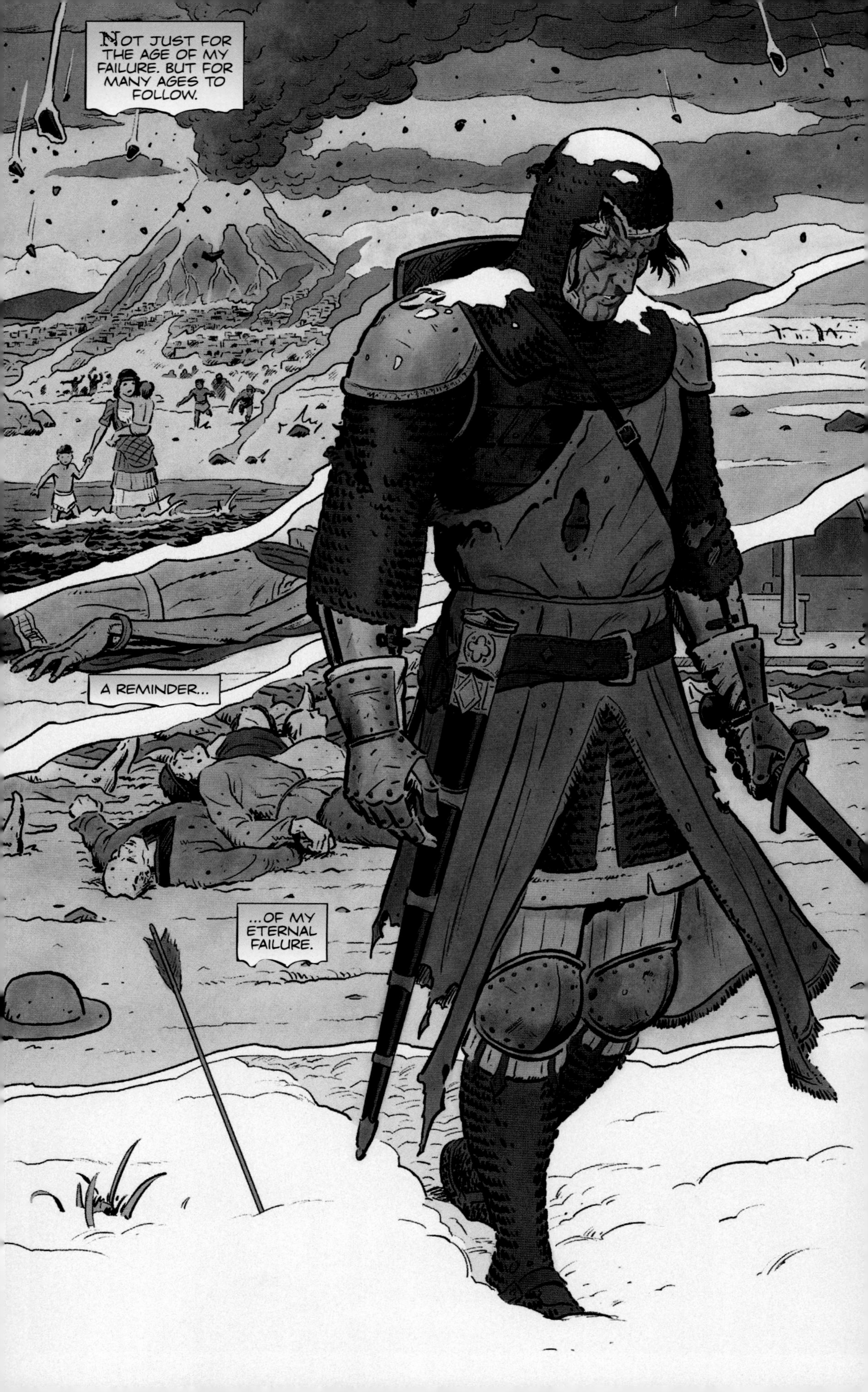
NOT JUST FOR THE AGE OF MY FAILURE. BUT FOR MANY AGES TO FOLLOW.
A REMINDER...
...OF MY ETERNAL FAILURE.

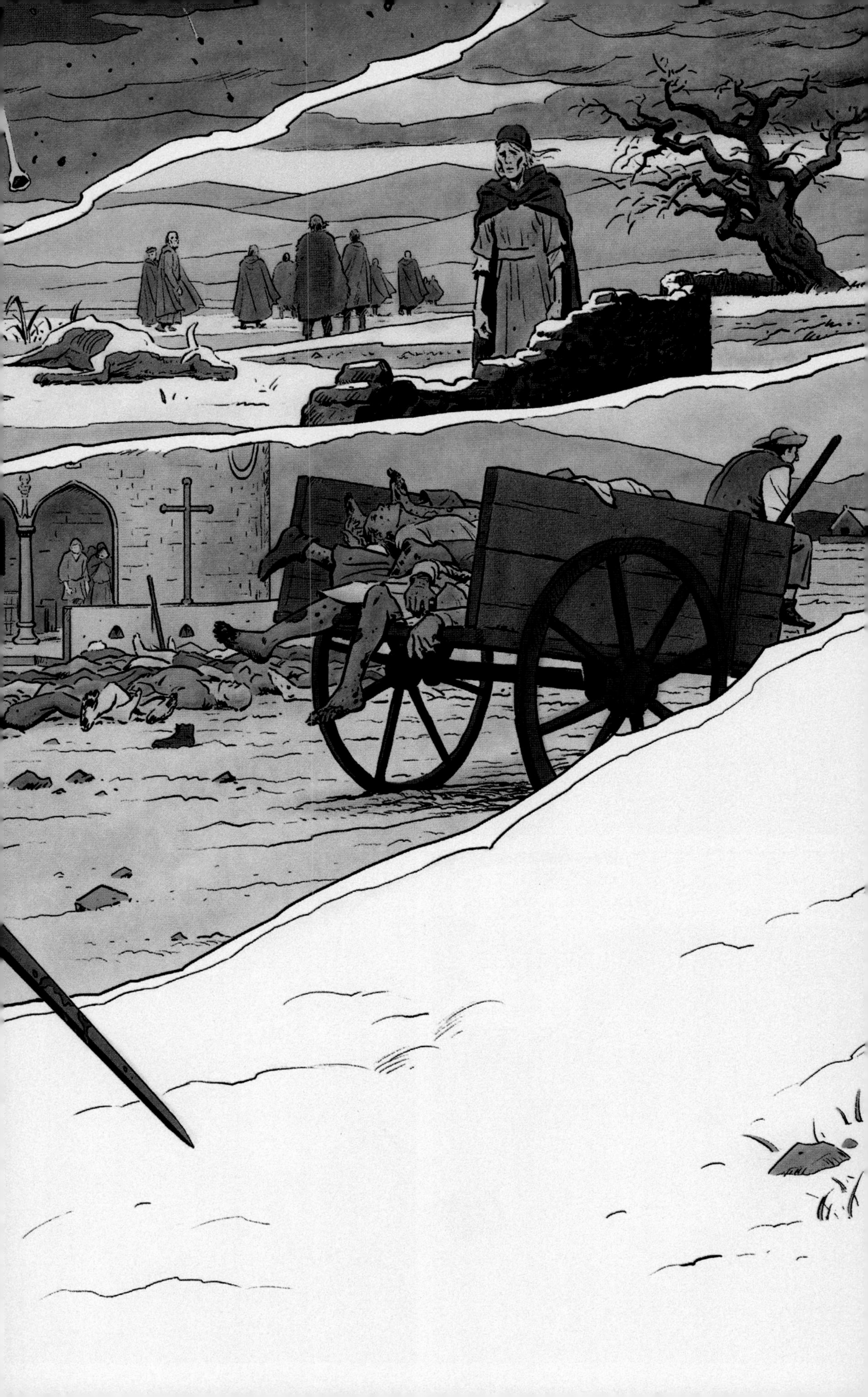

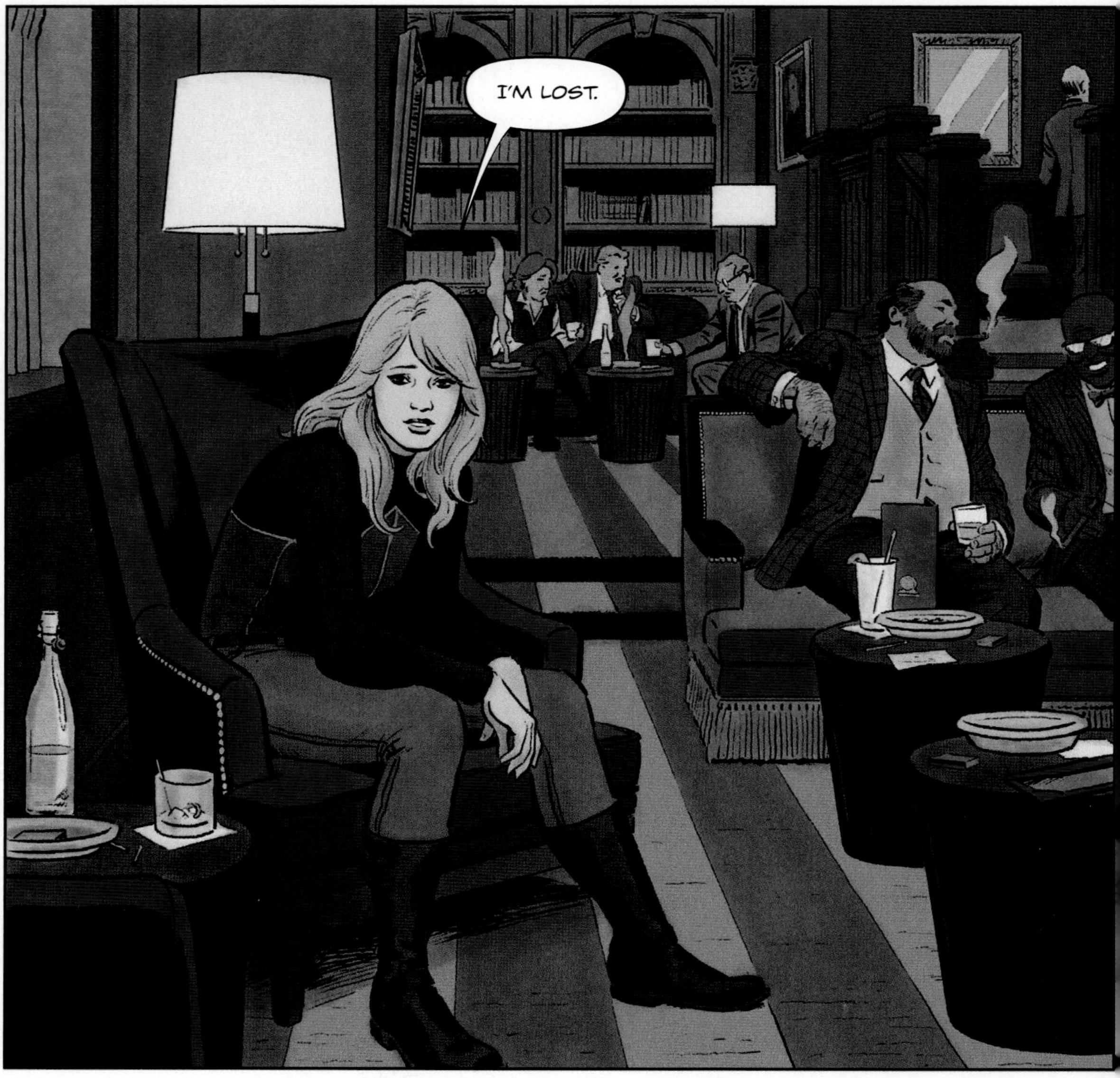
I'M LOST.

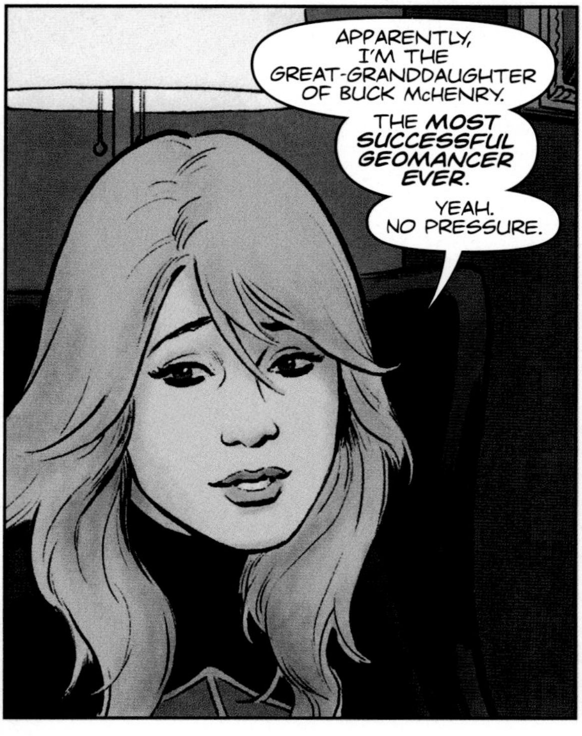
APPARENTLY, I'M THE GREAT-GRANDDAUGHTER OF BUCK McHENRY.
THE *MOST SUCCESSFUL GEOMANCER EVER*.
YEAH. NO PRESSURE.

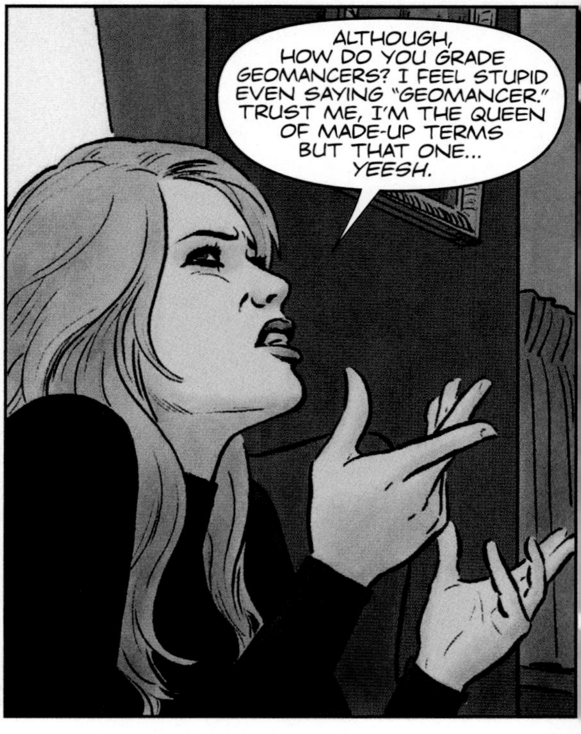
ALTHOUGH, HOW DO YOU GRADE GEOMANCERS? I FEEL STUPID EVEN SAYING "GEOMANCER." TRUST ME, I'M THE QUEEN OF MADE-UP TERMS BUT THAT ONE... YEESH.

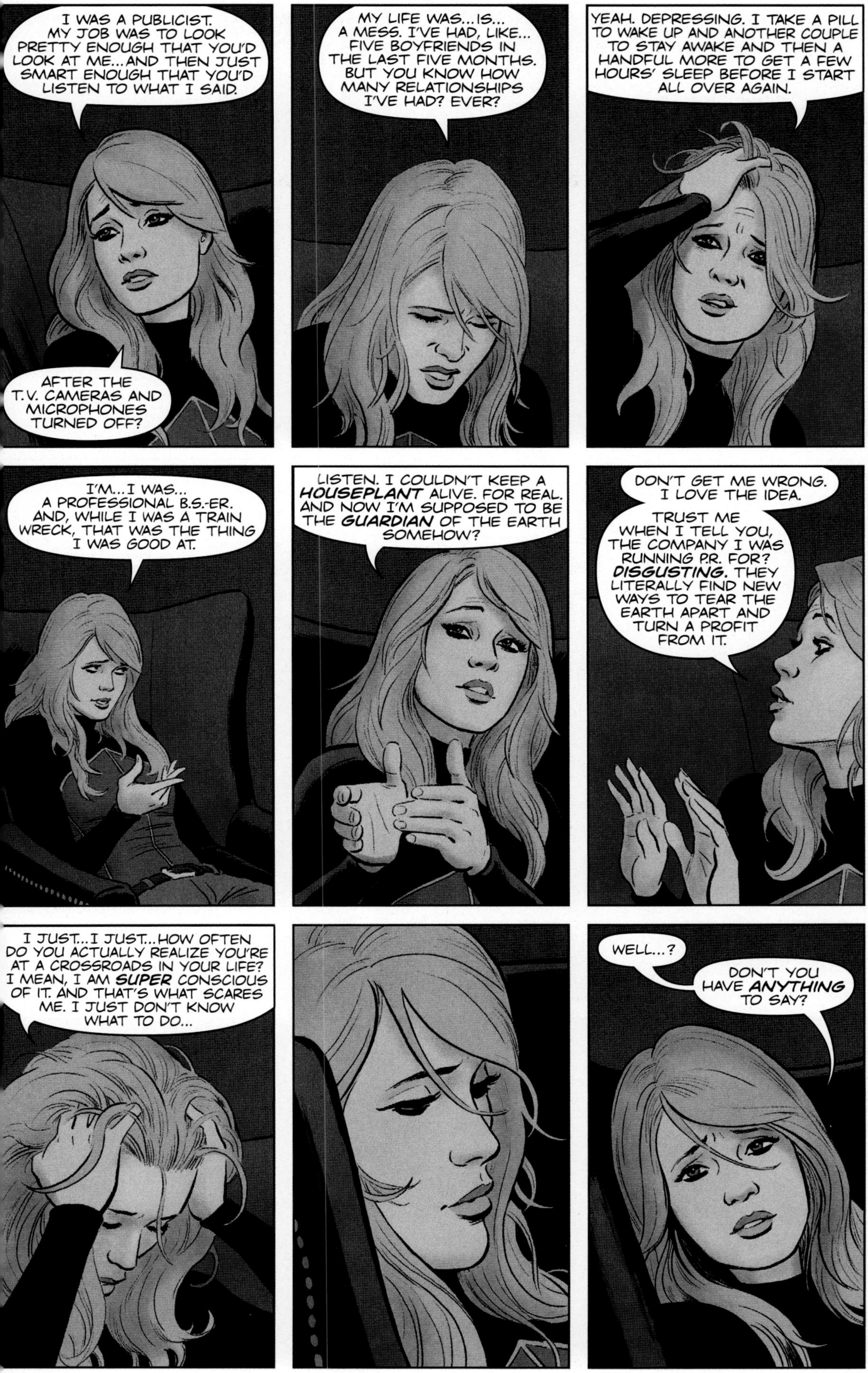
I WAS A PUBLICIST. MY JOB WAS TO LOOK PRETTY ENOUGH THAT YOU'D LOOK AT ME...AND THEN JUST SMART ENOUGH THAT YOU'D LISTEN TO WHAT I SAID.
AFTER THE T.V. CAMERAS AND MICROPHONES TURNED OFF?
MY LIFE WAS...IS... A MESS. I'VE HAD, LIKE... FIVE BOYFRIENDS IN THE LAST FIVE MONTHS. BUT YOU KNOW HOW MANY RELATIONSHIPS I'VE HAD? EVER?
YEAH. DEPRESSING. I TAKE A PILL TO WAKE UP AND ANOTHER COUPLE TO STAY AWAKE AND THEN A HANDFUL MORE TO GET A FEW HOURS' SLEEP BEFORE I START ALL OVER AGAIN.
I'M...I WAS... A PROFESSIONAL B.S.-ER. AND, WHILE I WAS A TRAIN WRECK, THAT WAS THE THING I WAS GOOD AT.
LISTEN. I COULDN'T KEEP A ***HOUSEPLANT*** ALIVE. FOR REAL. AND NOW I'M SUPPOSED TO BE THE ***GUARDIAN*** OF THE EARTH SOMEHOW?
DON'T GET ME WRONG. I LOVE THE IDEA.
TRUST ME WHEN I TELL YOU, THE COMPANY I WAS RUNNING P.R. FOR? ***DISGUSTING.*** THEY LITERALLY FIND NEW WAYS TO TEAR THE EARTH APART AND TURN A PROFIT FROM IT.
I JUST...I JUST...HOW OFTEN DO YOU ACTUALLY REALIZE YOU'RE AT A CROSSROADS IN YOUR LIFE? I MEAN, I AM ***SUPER*** CONSCIOUS OF IT. AND THAT'S WHAT SCARES ME. I JUST DON'T KNOW WHAT TO DO...
WELL...?
DON'T YOU HAVE ***ANYTHING*** TO SAY?

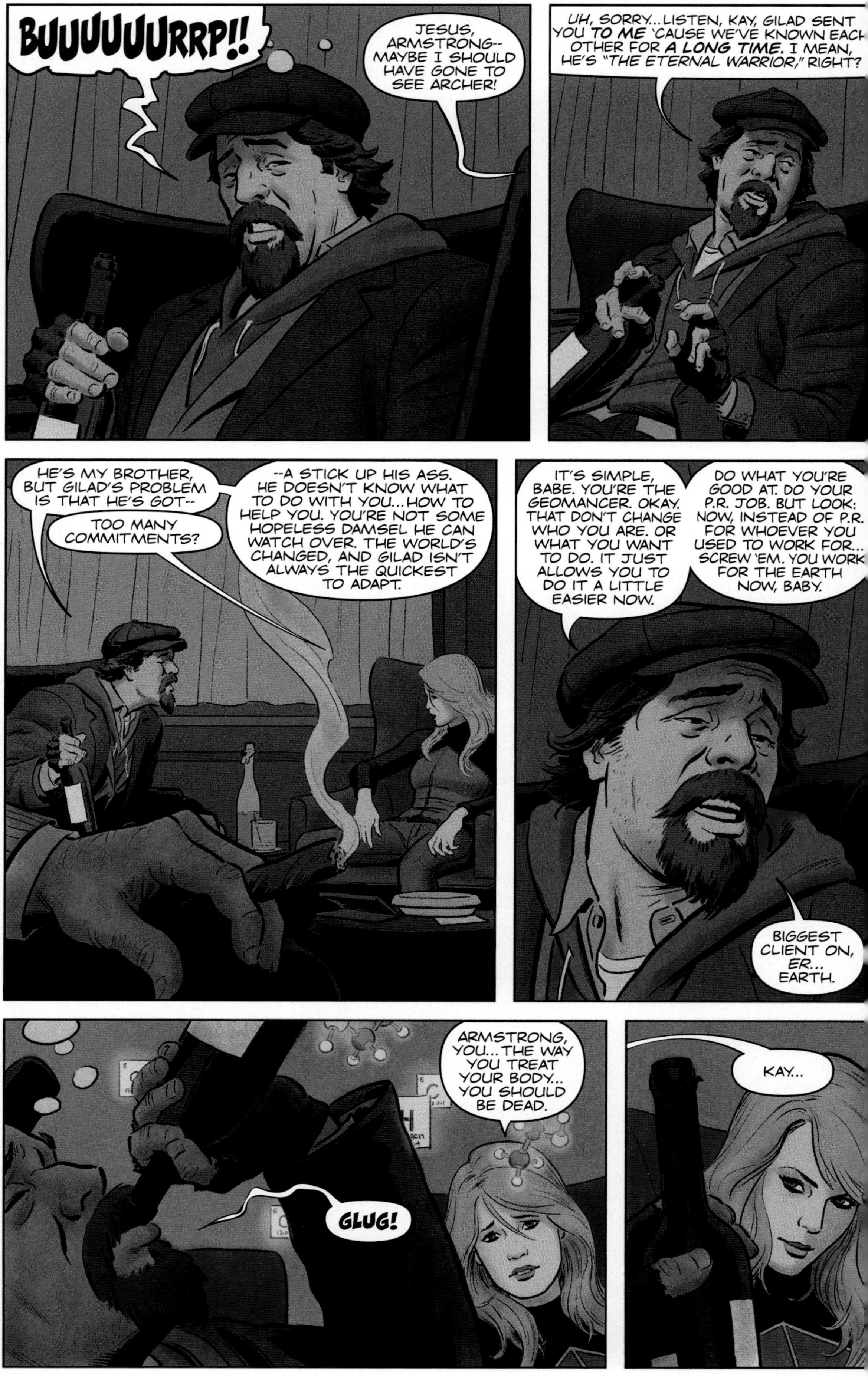
BUUUUUURRP!!
JESUS, ARMSTRONG-- MAYBE I SHOULD HAVE GONE TO SEE ARCHER!
UH, SORRY... LISTEN, KAY, GILAD SENT YOU **TO ME** 'CAUSE WE'VE KNOWN EACH OTHER FOR **A LONG TIME.** I MEAN, HE'S *"THE ETERNAL WARRIOR,"* RIGHT?
HE'S MY BROTHER, BUT GILAD'S PROBLEM IS THAT HE'S GOT--
TOO MANY COMMITMENTS?
--A STICK UP HIS ASS. HE DOESN'T KNOW WHAT TO DO WITH YOU... HOW TO HELP YOU. YOU'RE NOT SOME HOPELESS DAMSEL HE CAN WATCH OVER. THE WORLD'S CHANGED, AND GILAD ISN'T ALWAYS THE QUICKEST TO ADAPT.
IT'S SIMPLE, BABE. YOU'RE THE GEOMANCER. OKAY. THAT DON'T CHANGE WHO YOU ARE. OR WHAT YOU WANT TO DO. IT JUST ALLOWS YOU TO DO IT A LITTLE EASIER NOW.
DO WHAT YOU'RE GOOD AT. DO YOUR P.R. JOB. BUT LOOK: NOW, INSTEAD OF P.R. FOR WHOEVER YOU USED TO WORK FOR... SCREW 'EM. YOU WORK FOR THE EARTH NOW, BABY.
BIGGEST CLIENT ON, ER... EARTH.
ARMSTRONG, YOU... THE WAY YOU TREAT YOUR BODY... YOU SHOULD BE DEAD.
GLUG!
KAY...

"...YOU'RE NOT THE ONLY ONE WHO'S GOOD AT WHAT THEY DO."

AN UNDISCLOSED LOCATION IN THE PACIFIC RIM.

TELL ME AGAIN WHY I'M IN THE MIDDLE OF THE JUNGLE, NEVILLE?

BLAM BLAM

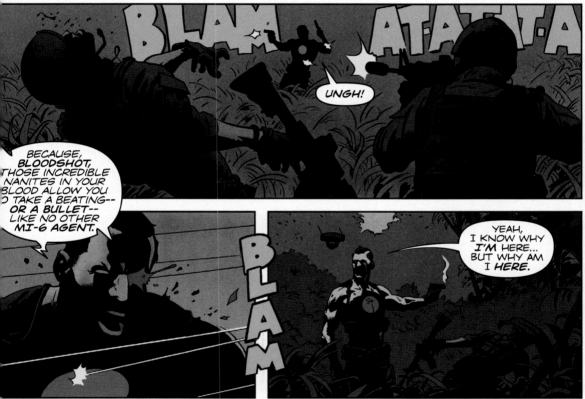

BLAM ATATTA

UNGH!

BECAUSE, BLOODSHOT, THOSE INCREDIBLE NANITES IN YOUR BLOOD ALLOW YOU TO TAKE A BEATING-- OR A BULLET-- LIKE NO OTHER MI-6 AGENT.

BLAM

YEAH, I KNOW WHY I'M HERE... BUT WHY AM I HERE.

THESE MERCENARIES WORK FOR PROJECT RISING SPIRIT... YOUR OLD PUPPET MASTERS.

YOU KNOW, THE SAME LOVELIES WHO ROBBED YOUR MEMORIES AND EXPLOITED YOU TO KILL FOR THEM ALL THOSE YEARS.

I THOUGHT YOU'D RELISH THE CHANCE TO EXACT YOUR PARTICULARLY BLOODY FLAVOR OF REVENGE ON A FEW OF THEM, WHILE STILL SECURING THE PACKAGE FOR MI-6.

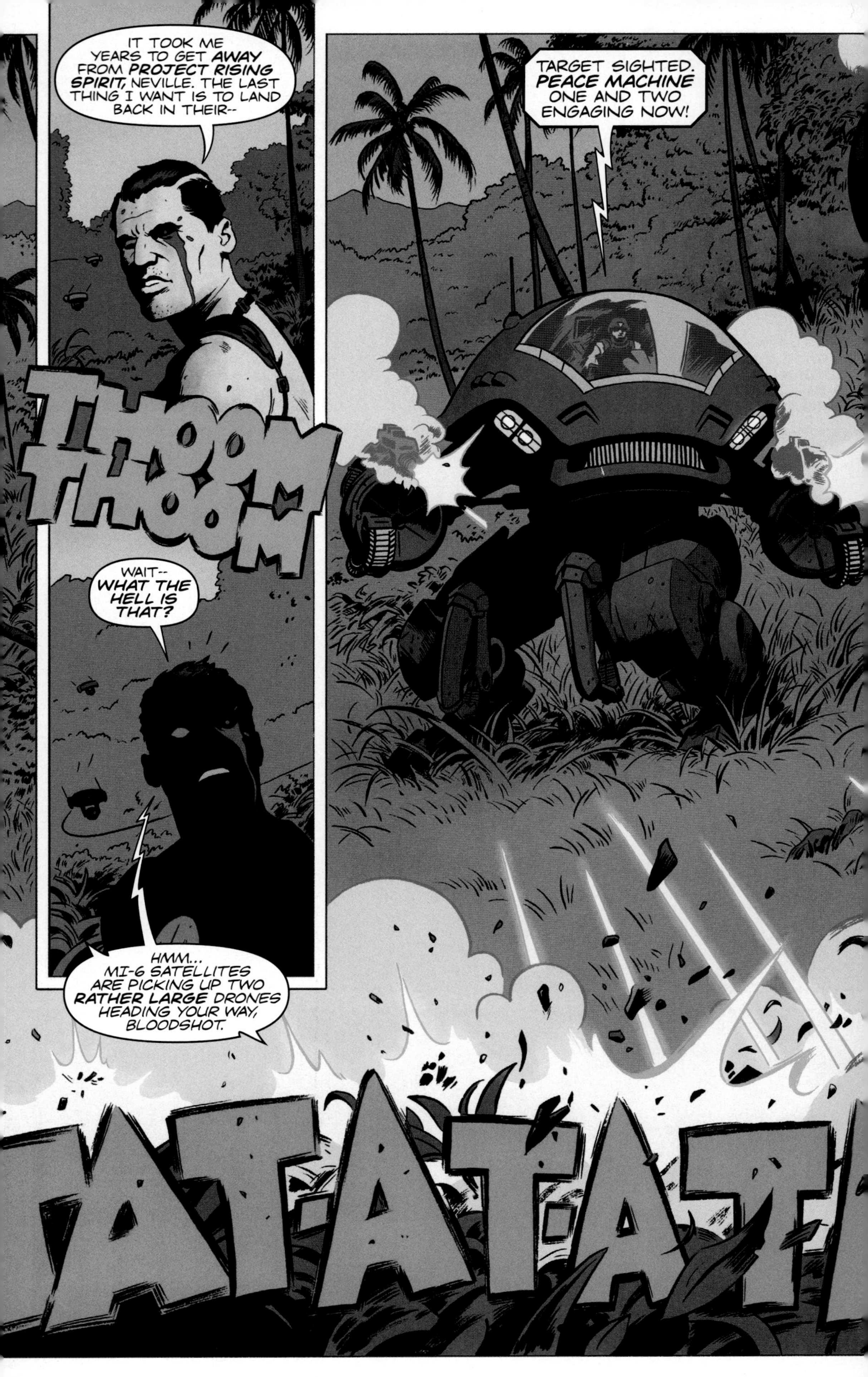
IT TOOK ME YEARS TO GET AWAY FROM PROJECT RISING SPIRIT, NEVILLE. THE LAST THING I WANT IS TO LAND BACK IN THEIR--
TARGET SIGHTED. PEACE MACHINE ONE AND TWO ENGAGING NOW!
THOOM THOOM
WAIT-- WHAT THE HELL IS THAT?
HMM... MI-6 SATELLITES ARE PICKING UP TWO RATHER LARGE DRONES HEADING YOUR WAY, BLOODSHOT.

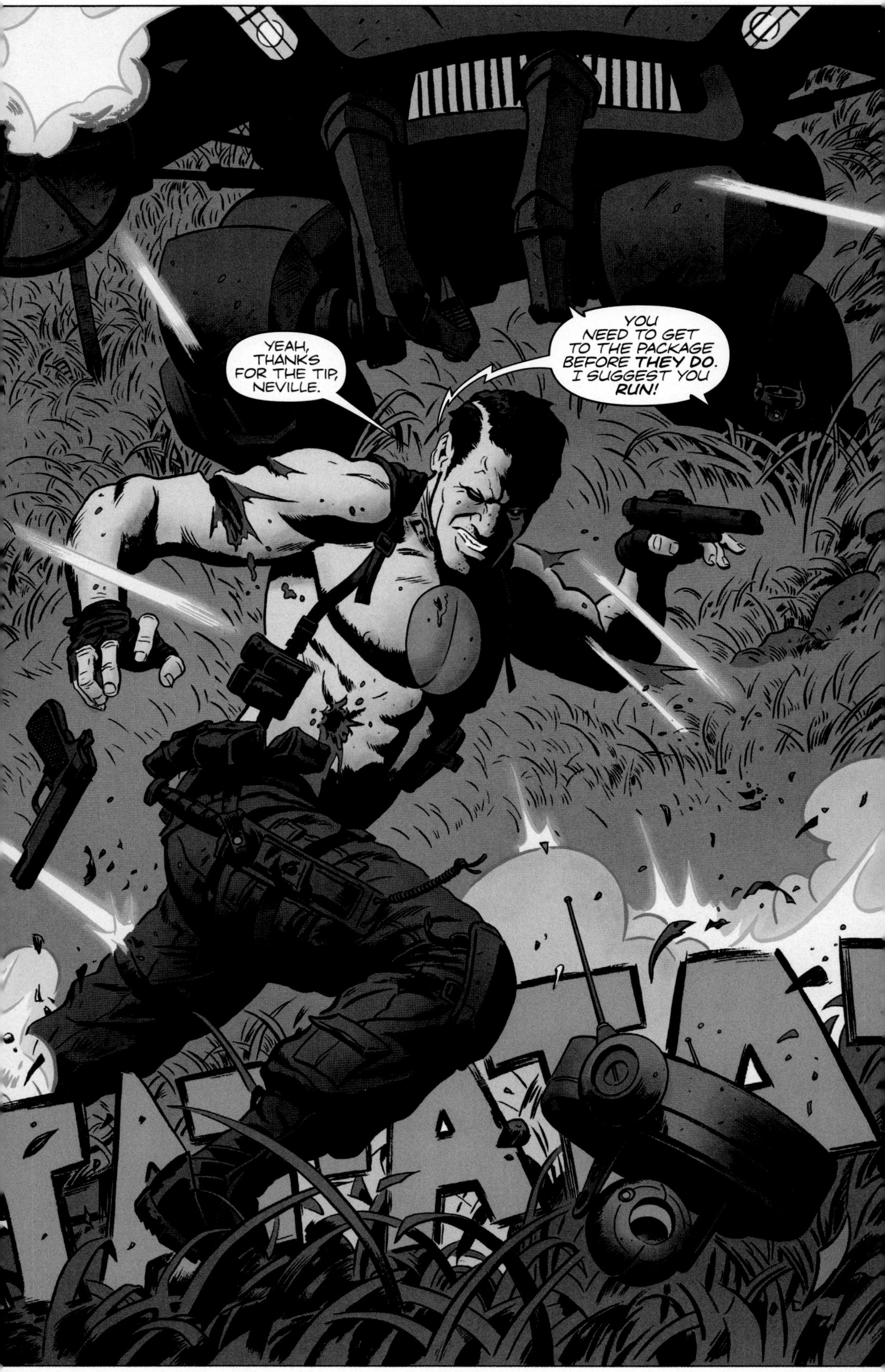
YEAH, THANKS FOR THE TIP, NEVILLE.
YOU NEED TO GET TO THE PACKAGE BEFORE THEY DO. I SUGGEST YOU RUN!

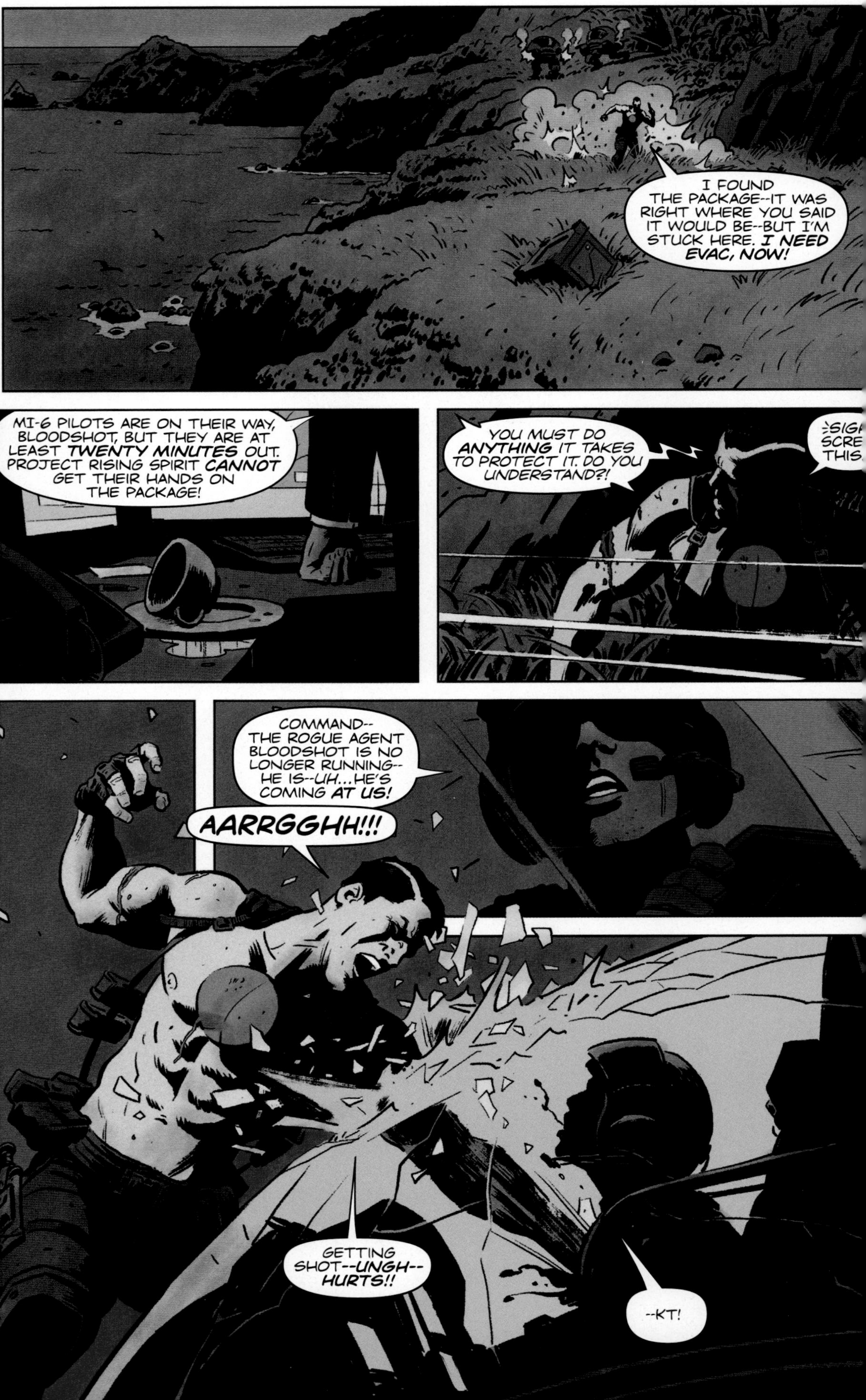
I FOUND THE PACKAGE--IT WAS RIGHT WHERE YOU SAID IT WOULD BE--BUT I'M STUCK HERE. I NEED EVAC, NOW!
MI-6 PILOTS ARE ON THEIR WAY, BLOODSHOT, BUT THEY ARE AT LEAST TWENTY MINUTES OUT. PROJECT RISING SPIRIT CANNOT GET THEIR HANDS ON THE PACKAGE!
YOU MUST DO ANYTHING IT TAKES TO PROTECT IT. DO YOU UNDERSTAND?!
COMMAND-- THE ROGUE AGENT BLOODSHOT IS NO LONGER RUNNING-- HE IS--UH...HE'S COMING AT US!
AARRGGHH!!!
GETTING SHOT--UNGH-- HURTS!!
--KT!

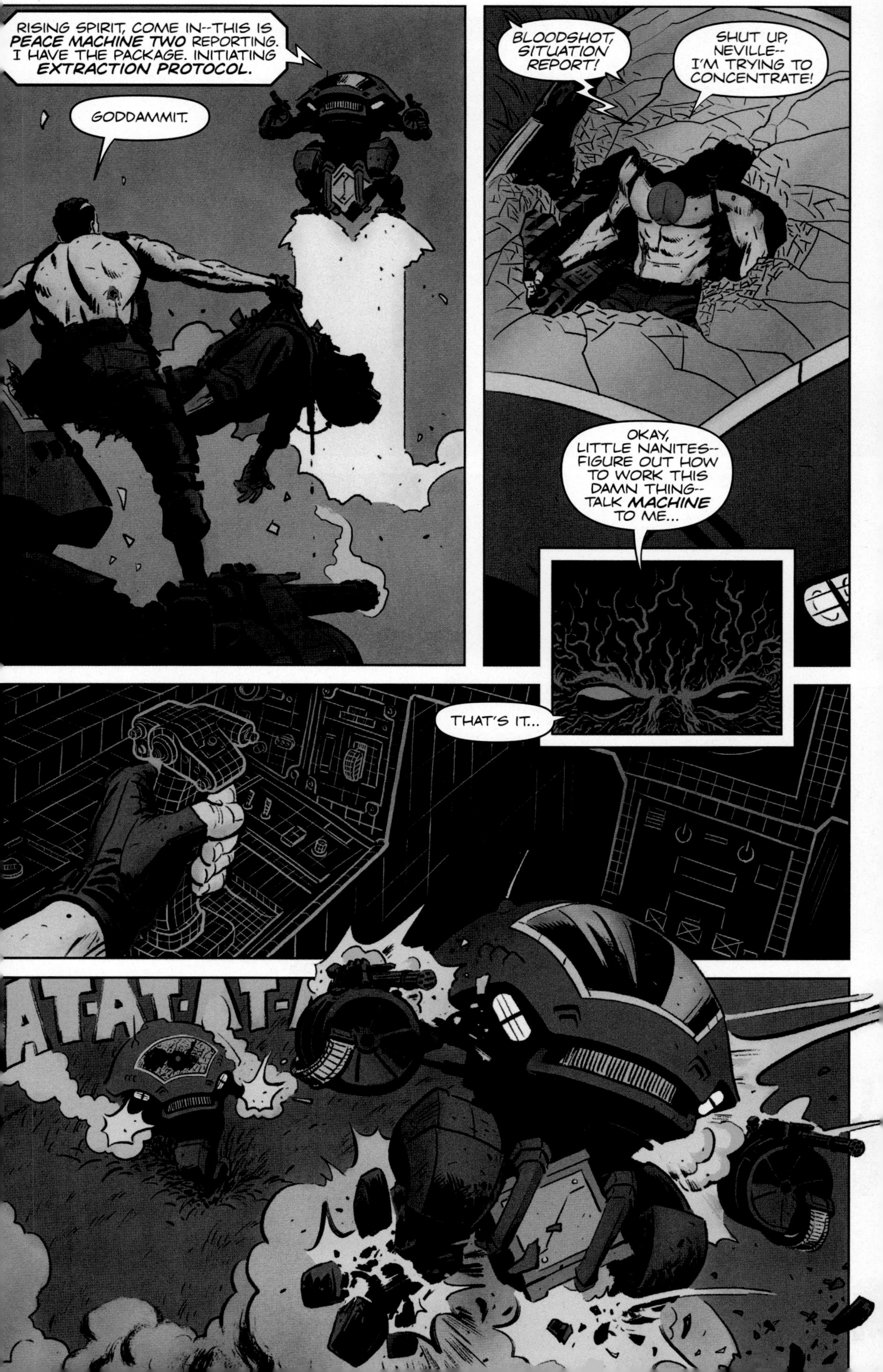
RISING SPIRIT, COME IN--THIS IS PEACE MACHINE TWO REPORTING. I HAVE THE PACKAGE. INITIATING EXTRACTION PROTOCOL.
GODDAMMIT.
BLOODSHOT, SITUATION REPORT!
SHUT UP, NEVILLE-- I'M TRYING TO CONCENTRATE!
OKAY, LITTLE NANITES-- FIGURE OUT HOW TO WORK THIS DAMN THING-- TALK MACHINE TO ME...
THAT'S IT...
AT-AT-AT-AT-A

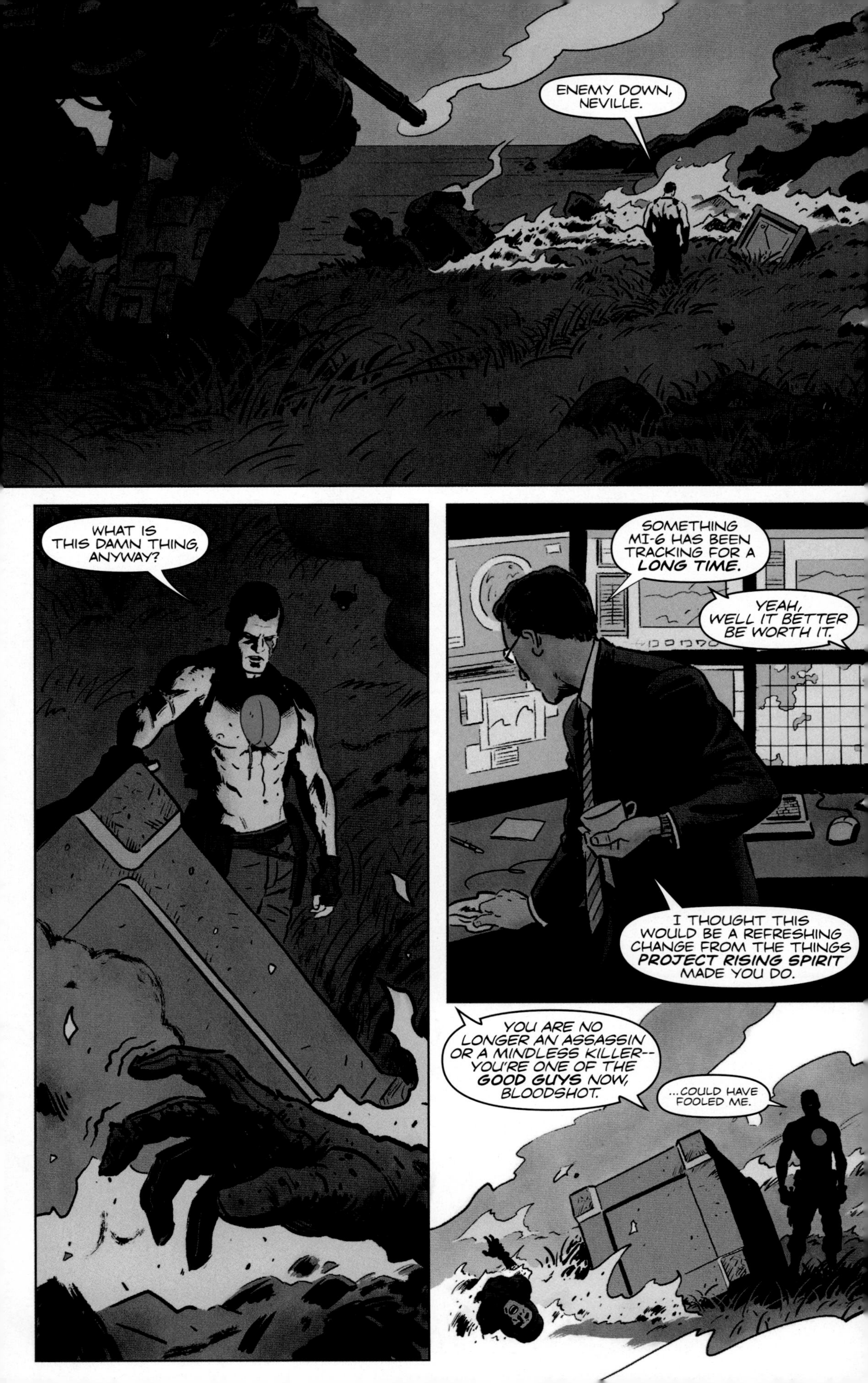
ENEMY DOWN, NEVILLE.
WHAT IS THIS DAMN THING, ANYWAY?
SOMETHING MI-6 HAS BEEN TRACKING FOR A **LONG TIME.**
YEAH, WELL IT BETTER BE WORTH IT.
I THOUGHT THIS WOULD BE A REFRESHING CHANGE FROM THE THINGS ***PROJECT RISING SPIRIT*** MADE YOU DO.
YOU ARE NO LONGER AN ASSASSIN OR A MINDLESS KILLER-- YOU'RE ONE OF THE ***GOOD GUYS*** NOW, BLOODSHOT.
...COULD HAVE FOOLED ME.

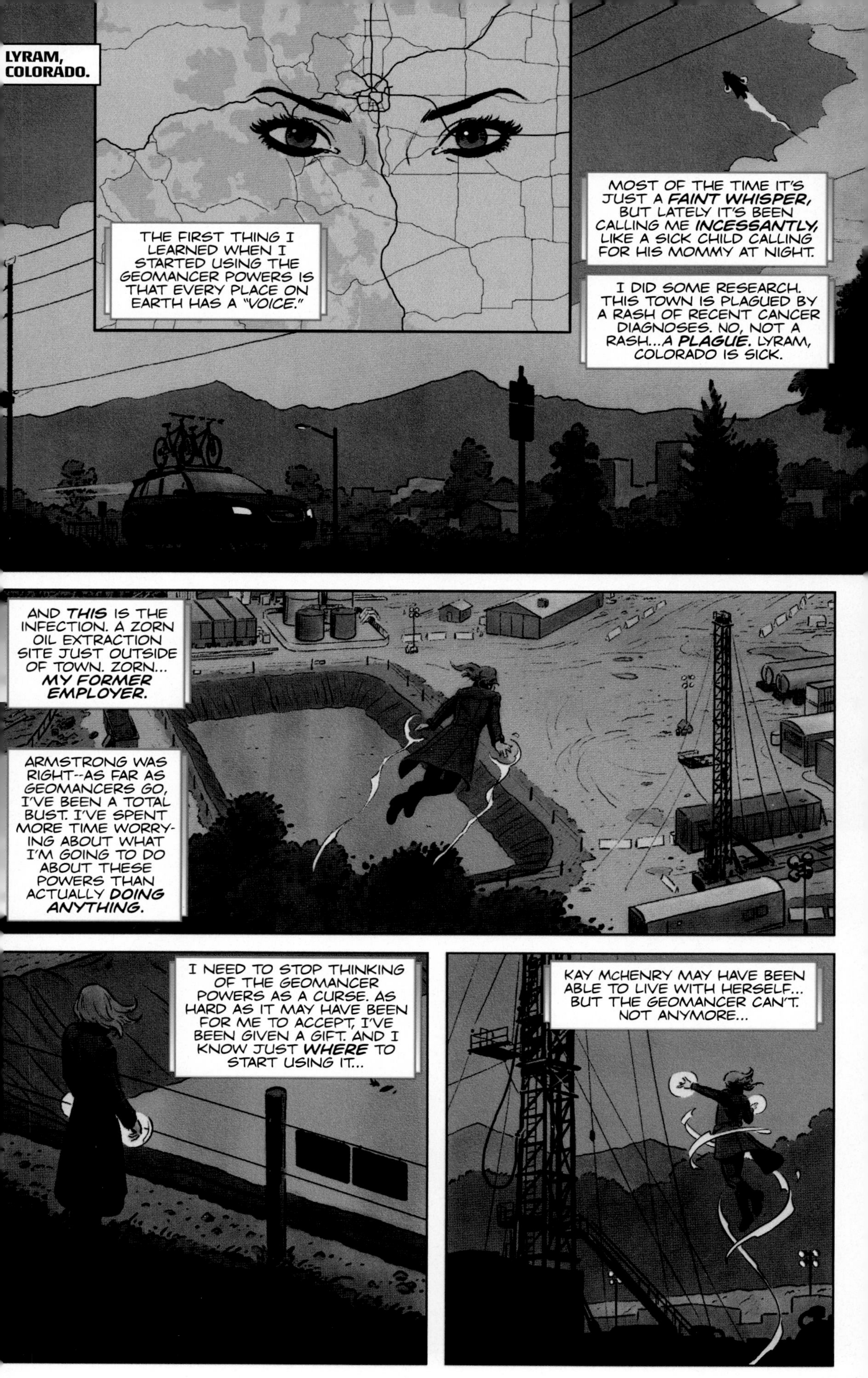
LYRAM, COLORADO.
THE FIRST THING I LEARNED WHEN I STARTED USING THE GEOMANCER POWERS IS THAT EVERY PLACE ON EARTH HAS A "VOICE."
MOST OF THE TIME IT'S JUST A FAINT WHISPER, BUT LATELY IT'S BEEN CALLING ME INCESSANTLY, LIKE A SICK CHILD CALLING FOR HIS MOMMY AT NIGHT.
I DID SOME RESEARCH. THIS TOWN IS PLAGUED BY A RASH OF RECENT CANCER DIAGNOSES. NO, NOT A RASH...A PLAGUE. LYRAM, COLORADO IS SICK.
AND THIS IS THE INFECTION. A ZORN OIL EXTRACTION SITE JUST OUTSIDE OF TOWN. ZORN... MY FORMER EMPLOYER.
ARMSTRONG WAS RIGHT--AS FAR AS GEOMANCERS GO, I'VE BEEN A TOTAL BUST. I'VE SPENT MORE TIME WORRYING ABOUT WHAT I'M GOING TO DO ABOUT THESE POWERS THAN ACTUALLY DOING ANYTHING.
I NEED TO STOP THINKING OF THE GEOMANCER POWERS AS A CURSE. AS HARD AS IT MAY HAVE BEEN FOR ME TO ACCEPT, I'VE BEEN GIVEN A GIFT. AND I KNOW JUST WHERE TO START USING IT...
KAY MCHENRY MAY HAVE BEEN ABLE TO LIVE WITH HERSELF... BUT THE GEOMANCER CAN'T. NOT ANYMORE...

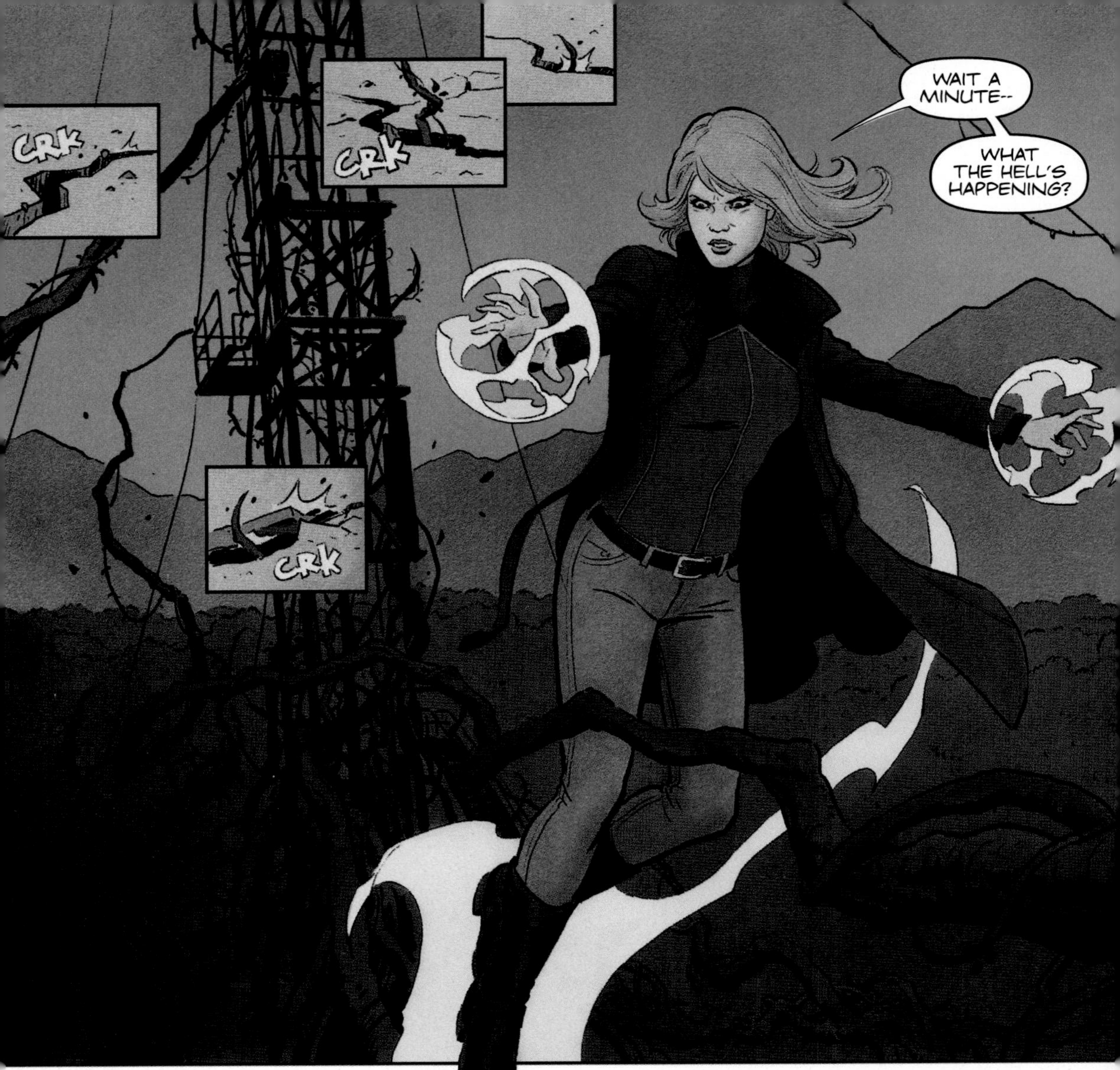
CRK
CRK
CRK
WAIT A MINUTE--
WHAT THE HELL'S HAPPENING?
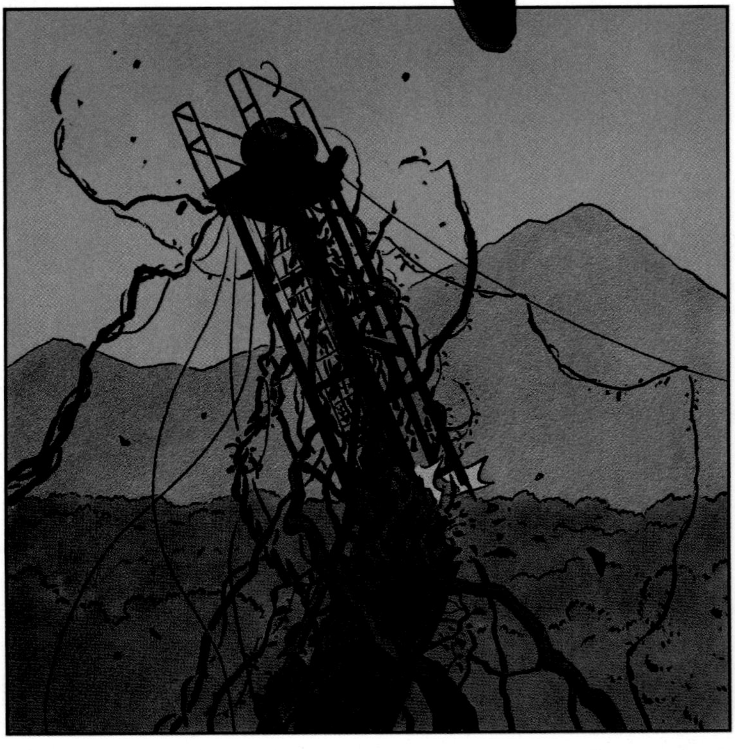
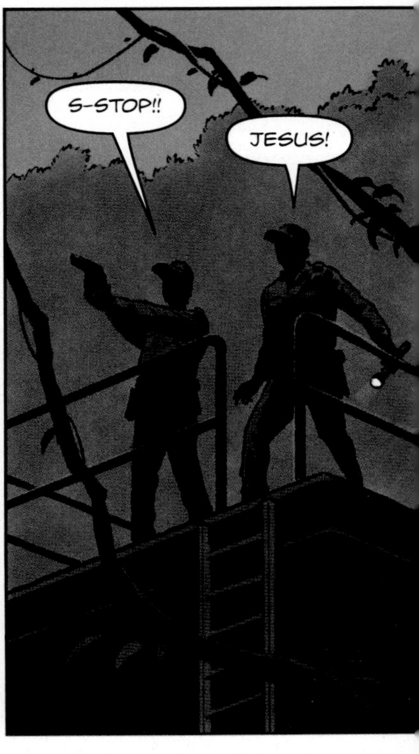
S-STOP!!
JESUS!

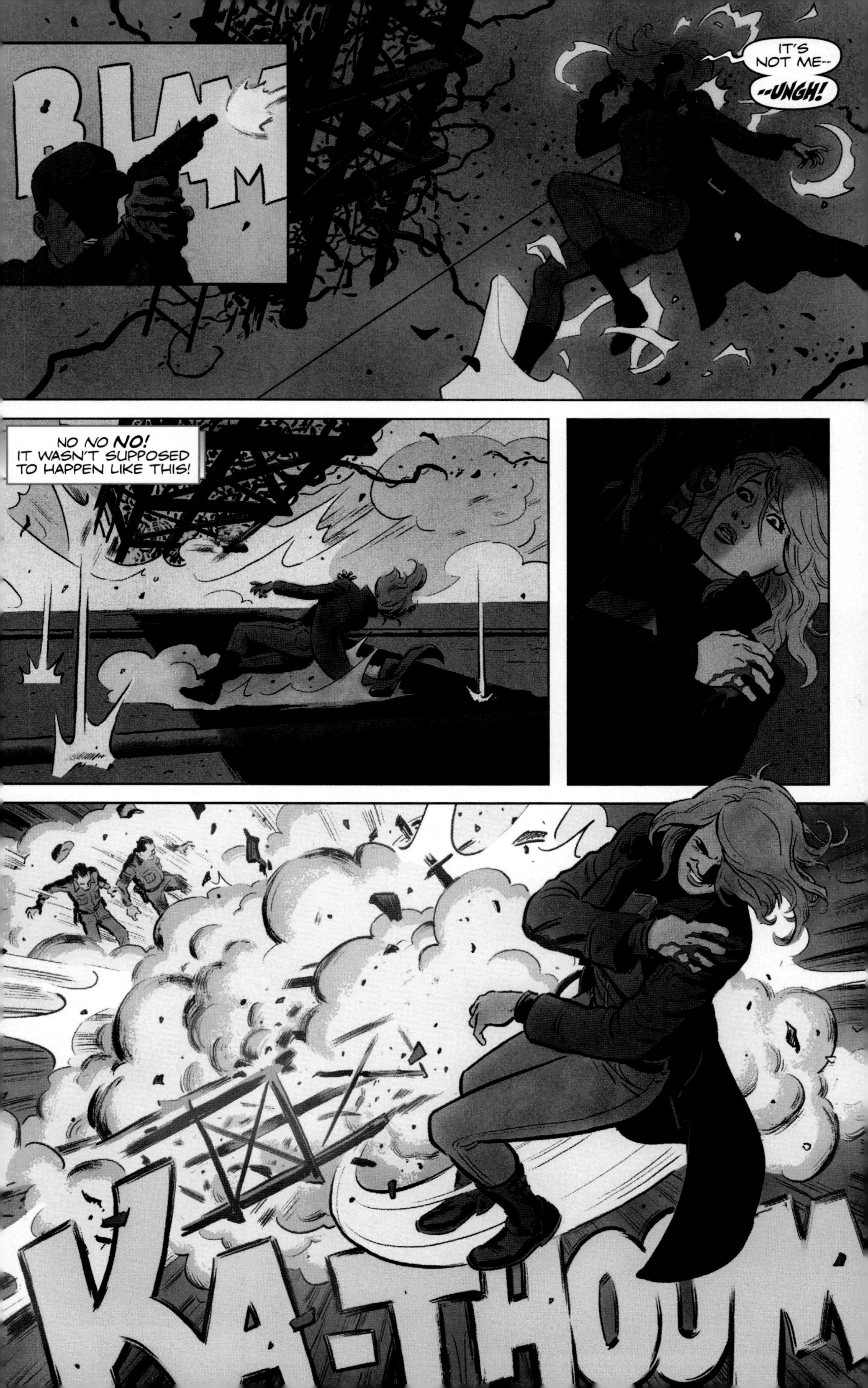
BLAM
IT'S NOT ME--
--UNGH!
NO NO NO! IT WASN'T SUPPOSED TO HAPPEN LIKE THIS!
KA-THOOM

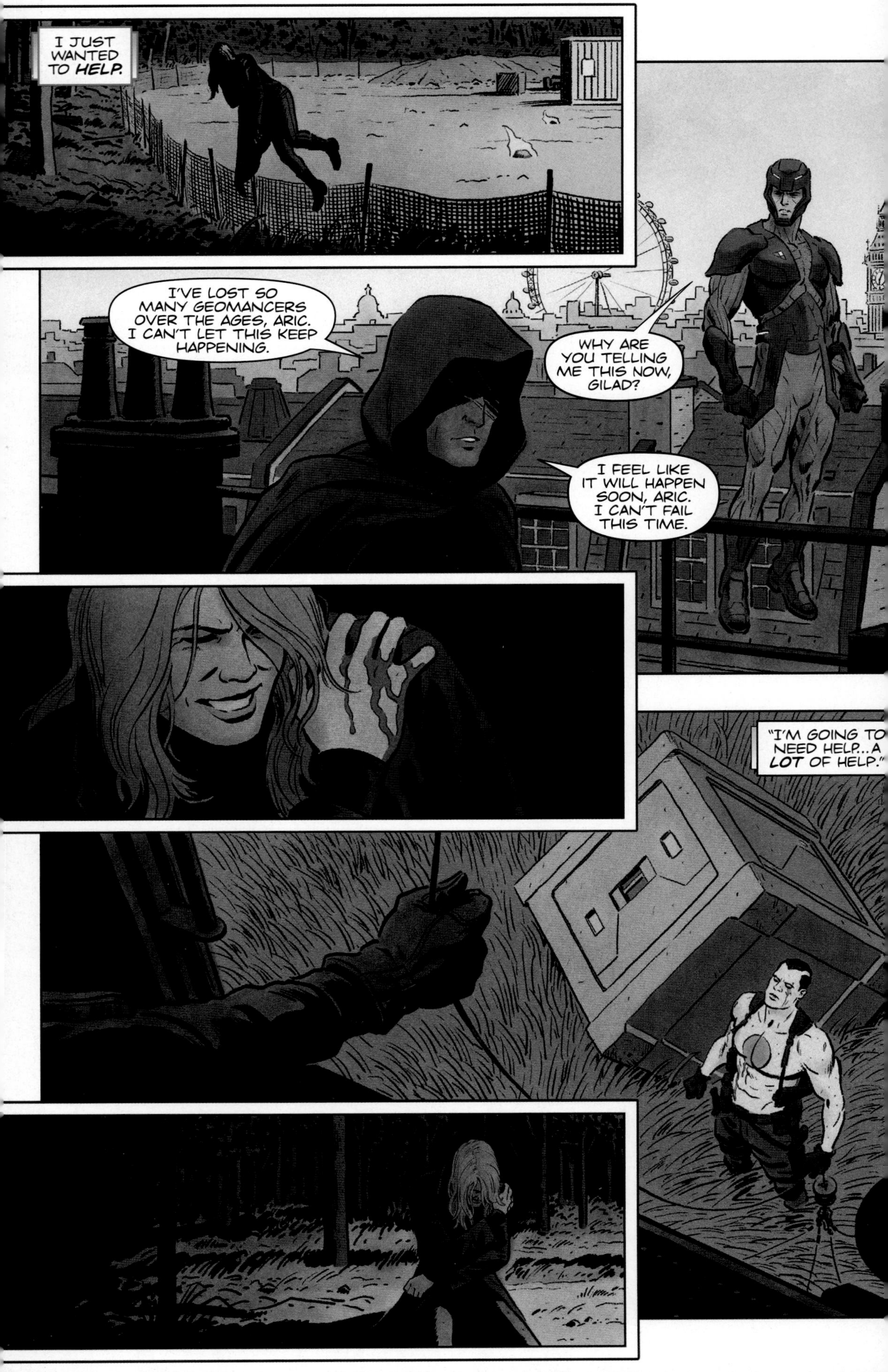
I JUST WANTED TO HELP.
I'VE LOST SO MANY GEOMANCERS OVER THE AGES, ARIC. I CAN'T LET THIS KEEP HAPPENING.
WHY ARE YOU TELLING ME THIS NOW, GILAD?
I FEEL LIKE IT WILL HAPPEN SOON, ARIC. I CAN'T FAIL THIS TIME.
"I'M GOING TO NEED HELP... A LOT OF HELP."

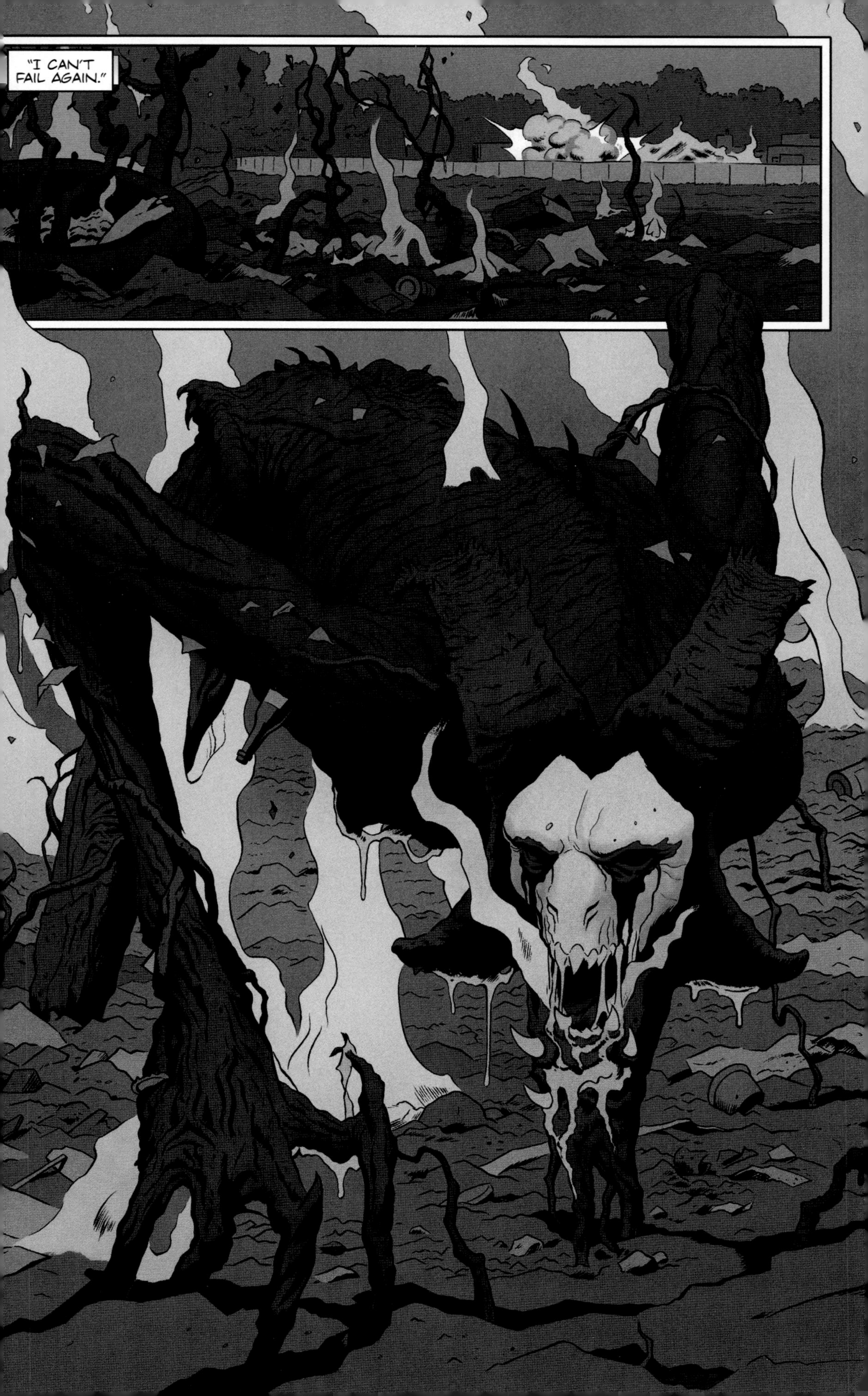
"I CAN'T FAIL AGAIN."

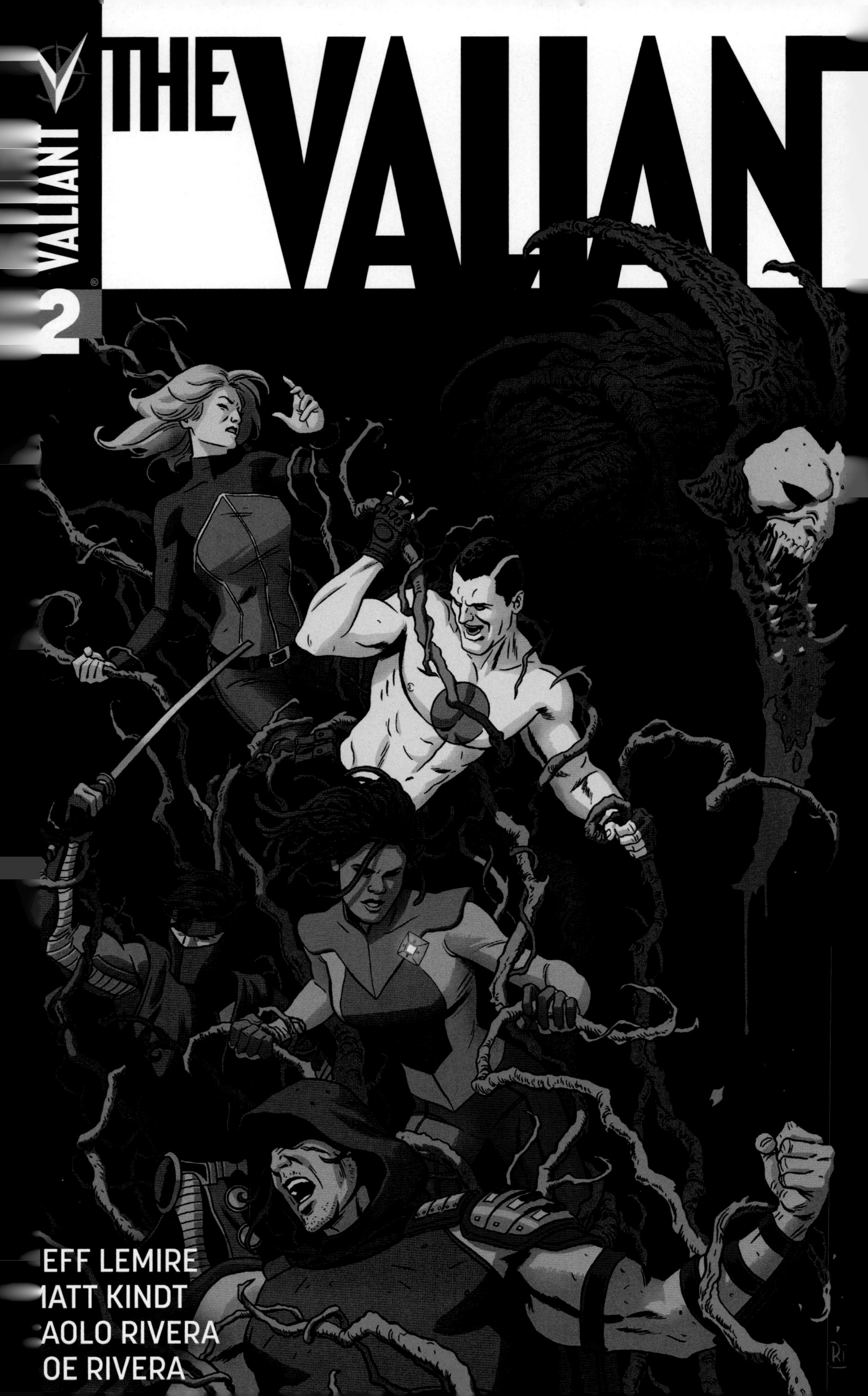

THE VALIANT
VALIANT
2
EFF LEMIRE
IATT KINDT
AOLO RIVERA
OE RIVERA

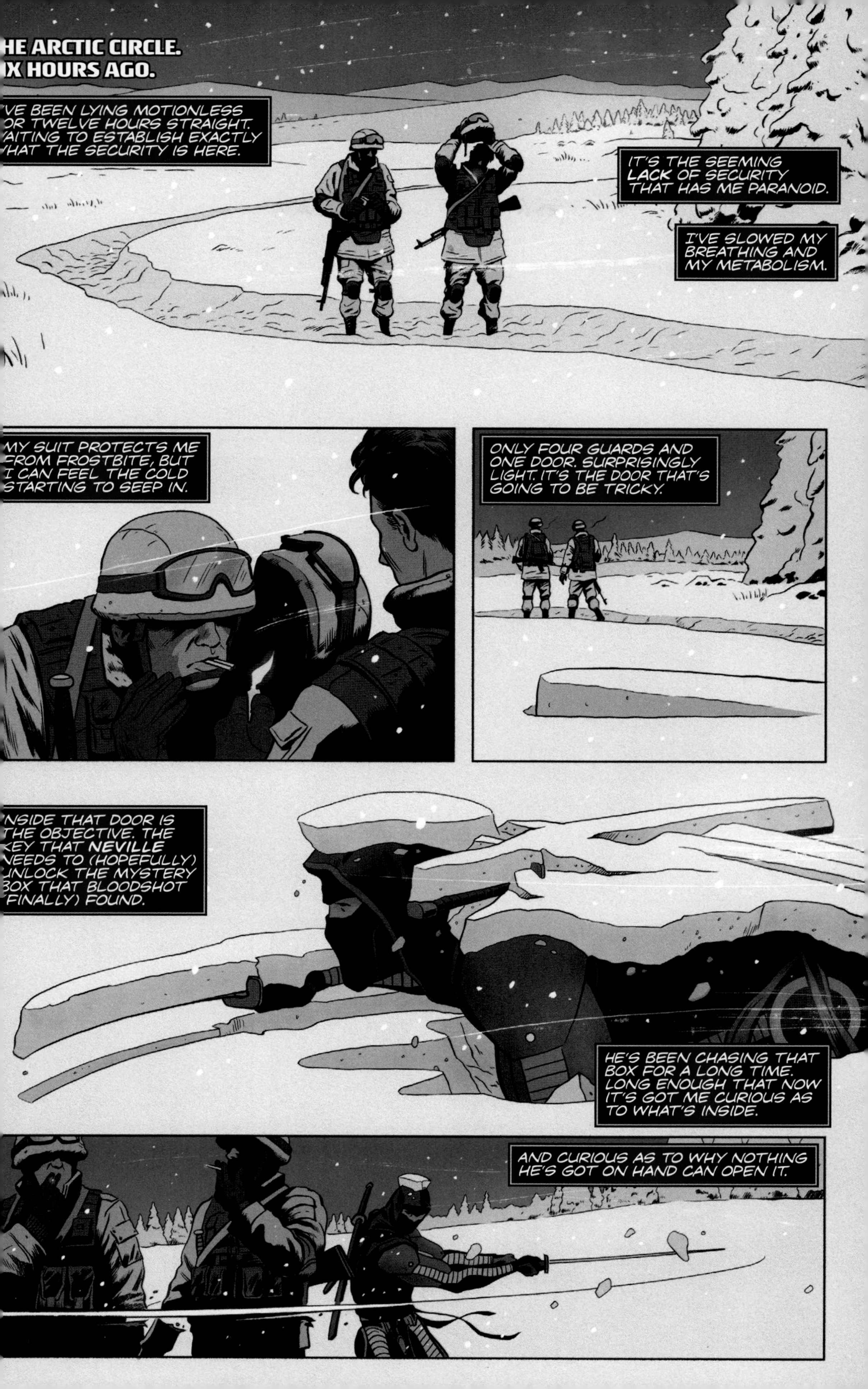

HE ARCTIC CIRCLE.
X HOURS AGO.
'VE BEEN LYING MOTIONLESS OR TWELVE HOURS STRAIGHT. VAITING TO ESTABLISH EXACTLY VHAT THE SECURITY IS HERE.
IT'S THE SEEMING LACK OF SECURITY THAT HAS ME PARANOID.
I'VE SLOWED MY BREATHING AND MY METABOLISM.
MY SUIT PROTECTS ME FROM FROSTBITE, BUT I CAN FEEL THE COLD STARTING TO SEEP IN.
ONLY FOUR GUARDS AND ONE DOOR. SURPRISINGLY LIGHT. IT'S THE DOOR THAT'S GOING TO BE TRICKY.
NSIDE THAT DOOR IS THE OBJECTIVE. THE KEY THAT NEVILLE NEEDS TO (HOPEFULLY) UNLOCK THE MYSTERY BOX THAT BLOODSHOT (FINALLY) FOUND.
HE'S BEEN CHASING THAT BOX FOR A LONG TIME. LONG ENOUGH THAT NOW IT'S GOT ME CURIOUS AS TO WHAT'S INSIDE.
AND CURIOUS AS TO WHY NOTHING HE'S GOT ON HAND CAN OPEN IT.

‹HMM.›

‹ANTON AND VADIM HAVE NOT MOVED FOR A WHILE.›

‹I THINK SOMETHING IS WRONG.›

THE DOOR ISN'T LOCKED WITH A SECURITY CODE. IT'S BASICALLY UN-HACKABLE.

WHICH IS WHY I HAVE TO LEAVE ONE GUARD ALIVE.

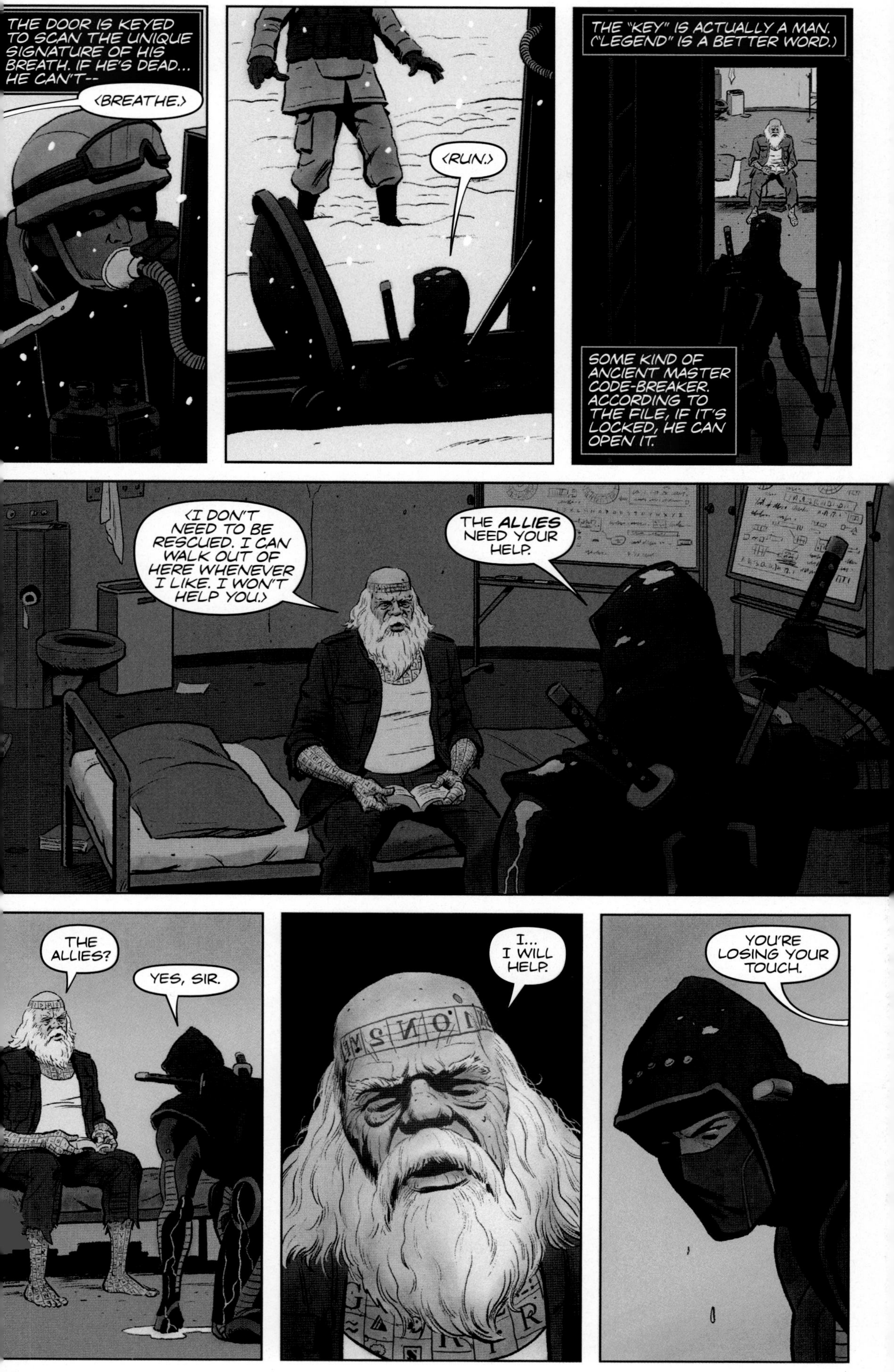
THE DOOR IS KEYED TO SCAN THE UNIQUE SIGNATURE OF HIS BREATH. IF HE'S DEAD... HE CAN'T--
<BREATHE.>
<RUN.>
THE "KEY" IS ACTUALLY A MAN. ("LEGEND" IS A BETTER WORD.)
SOME KIND OF ANCIENT MASTER CODE-BREAKER. ACCORDING TO THE FILE, IF IT'S LOCKED, HE CAN OPEN IT.
<I DON'T NEED TO BE RESCUED. I CAN WALK OUT OF HERE WHENEVER I LIKE. I WON'T HELP YOU.>
THE ALLIES NEED YOUR HELP.
THE ALLIES?
YES, SIR.
I... I WILL HELP.
YOU'RE LOSING YOUR TOUCH.

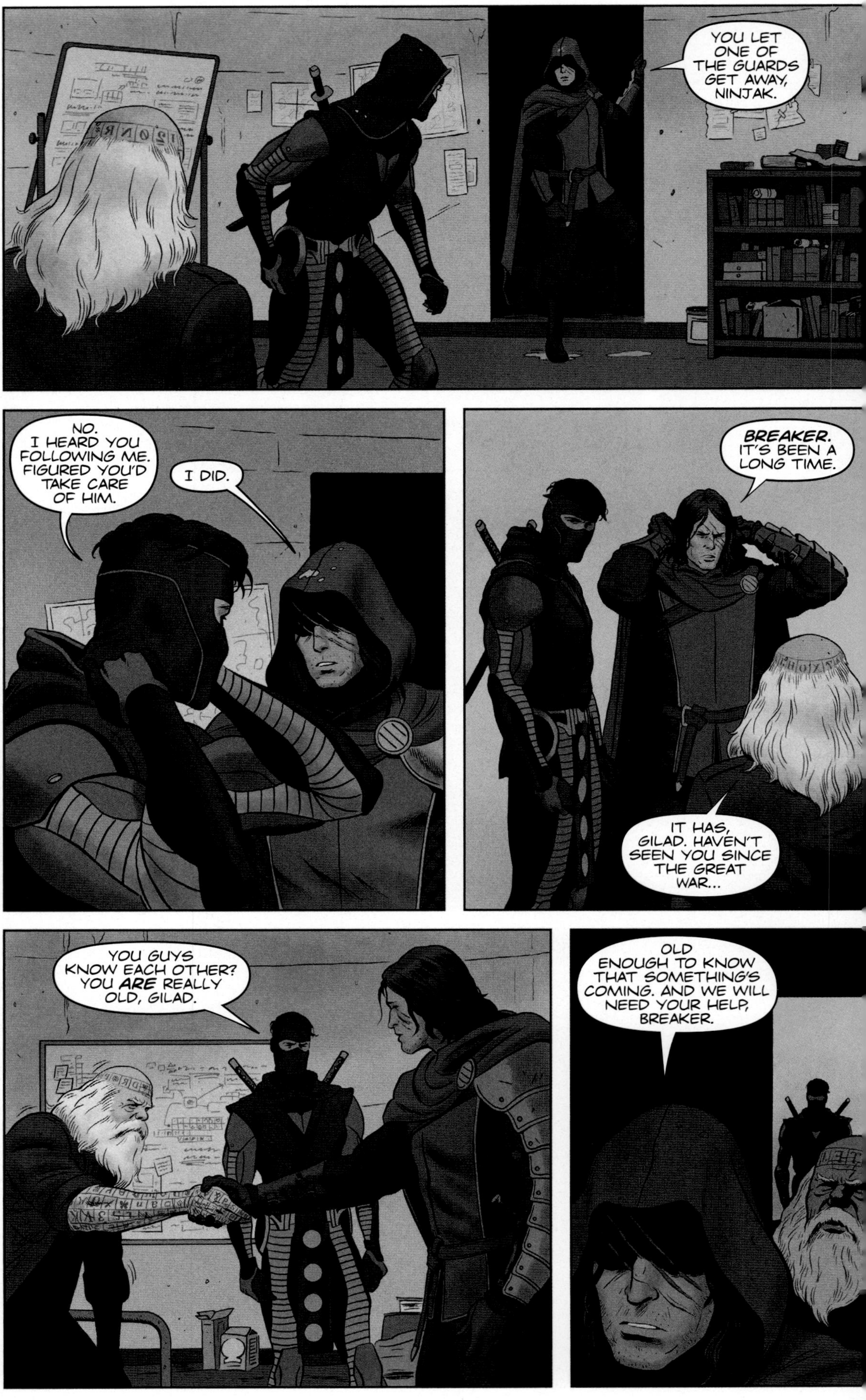
YOU LET ONE OF THE GUARDS GET AWAY, NINJAK.
NO. I HEARD YOU FOLLOWING ME. FIGURED YOU'D TAKE CARE OF HIM.
I DID.
BREAKER. IT'S BEEN A LONG TIME.
IT HAS, GILAD. HAVEN'T SEEN YOU SINCE THE GREAT WAR...
YOU GUYS KNOW EACH OTHER? YOU ARE REALLY OLD, GILAD.
OLD ENOUGH TO KNOW THAT SOMETHING'S COMING. AND WE WILL NEED YOUR HELP, BREAKER.

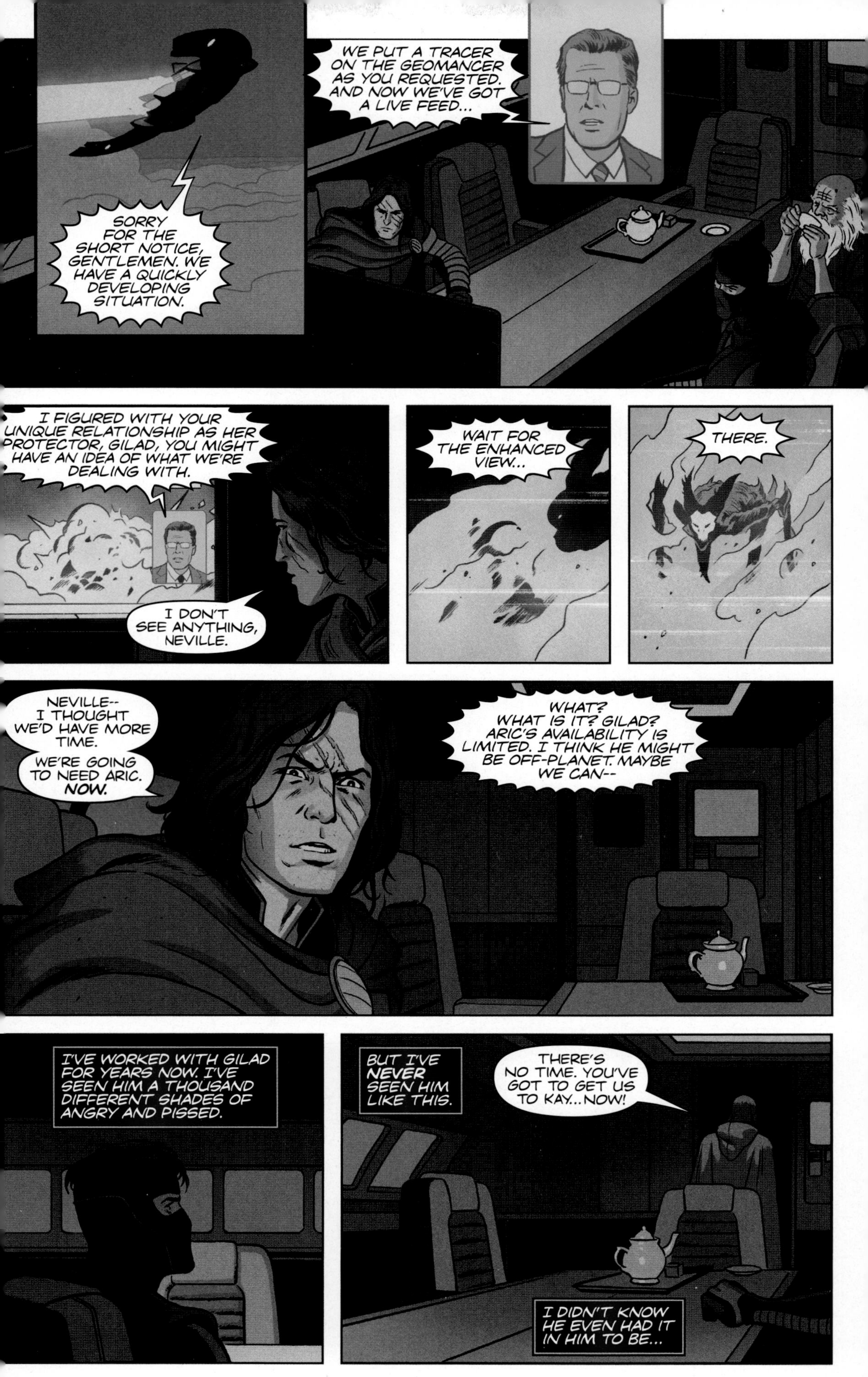
SORRY FOR THE SHORT NOTICE, GENTLEMEN. WE HAVE A QUICKLY DEVELOPING SITUATION.
WE PUT A TRACER ON THE GEOMANCER AS YOU REQUESTED. AND NOW WE'VE GOT A LIVE FEED...
I FIGURED WITH YOUR UNIQUE RELATIONSHIP AS HER PROTECTOR, GILAD, YOU MIGHT HAVE AN IDEA OF WHAT WE'RE DEALING WITH.
I DON'T SEE ANYTHING, NEVILLE.
WAIT FOR THE ENHANCED VIEW...
THERE.
NEVILLE-- I THOUGHT WE'D HAVE MORE TIME.
WE'RE GOING TO NEED ARIC. NOW.
WHAT? WHAT IS IT? GILAD? ARIC'S AVAILABILITY IS LIMITED. I THINK HE MIGHT BE OFF-PLANET. MAYBE WE CAN--
I'VE WORKED WITH GILAD FOR YEARS NOW. I'VE SEEN HIM A THOUSAND DIFFERENT SHADES OF ANGRY AND PISSED.
BUT I'VE NEVER SEEN HIM LIKE THIS.
THERE'S NO TIME. YOU'VE GOT TO GET US TO KAY...NOW!
I DIDN'T KNOW HE EVEN HAD IT IN HIM TO BE...

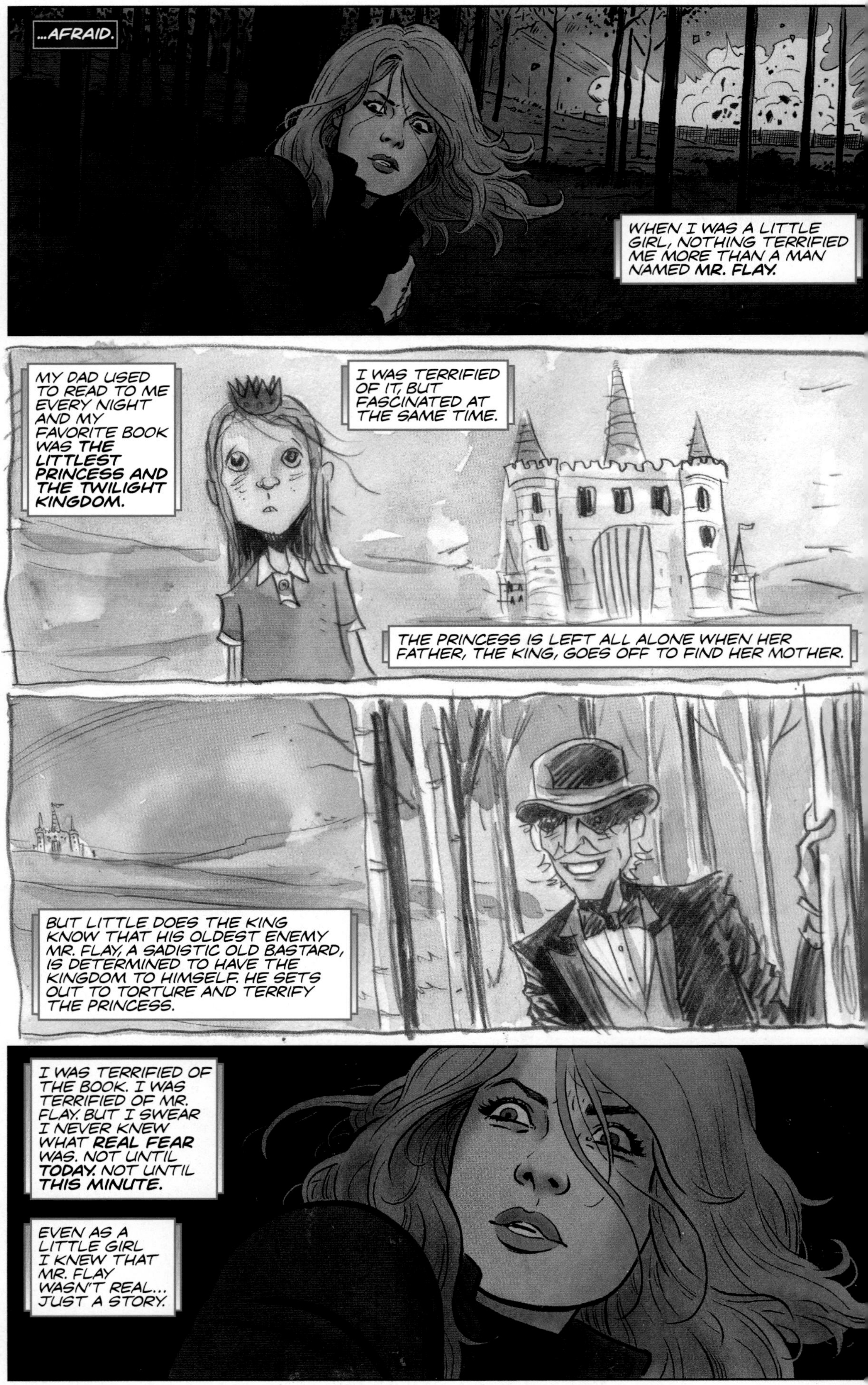

...AFRAID.
WHEN I WAS A LITTLE GIRL, NOTHING TERRIFIED ME MORE THAN A MAN NAMED MR. FLAY.
MY DAD USED TO READ TO ME EVERY NIGHT AND MY FAVORITE BOOK WAS THE LITTLEST PRINCESS AND THE TWILIGHT KINGDOM.
I WAS TERRIFIED OF IT, BUT FASCINATED AT THE SAME TIME.
THE PRINCESS IS LEFT ALL ALONE WHEN HER FATHER, THE KING, GOES OFF TO FIND HER MOTHER.
BUT LITTLE DOES THE KING KNOW THAT HIS OLDEST ENEMY MR. FLAY, A SADISTIC OLD BASTARD, IS DETERMINED TO HAVE THE KINGDOM TO HIMSELF. HE SETS OUT TO TORTURE AND TERRIFY THE PRINCESS.
I WAS TERRIFIED OF THE BOOK. I WAS TERRIFIED OF MR. FLAY. BUT I SWEAR I NEVER KNEW WHAT REAL FEAR WAS. NOT UNTIL TODAY. NOT UNTIL THIS MINUTE.
EVEN AS A LITTLE GIRL I KNEW THAT MR. FLAY WASN'T REAL... JUST A STORY.

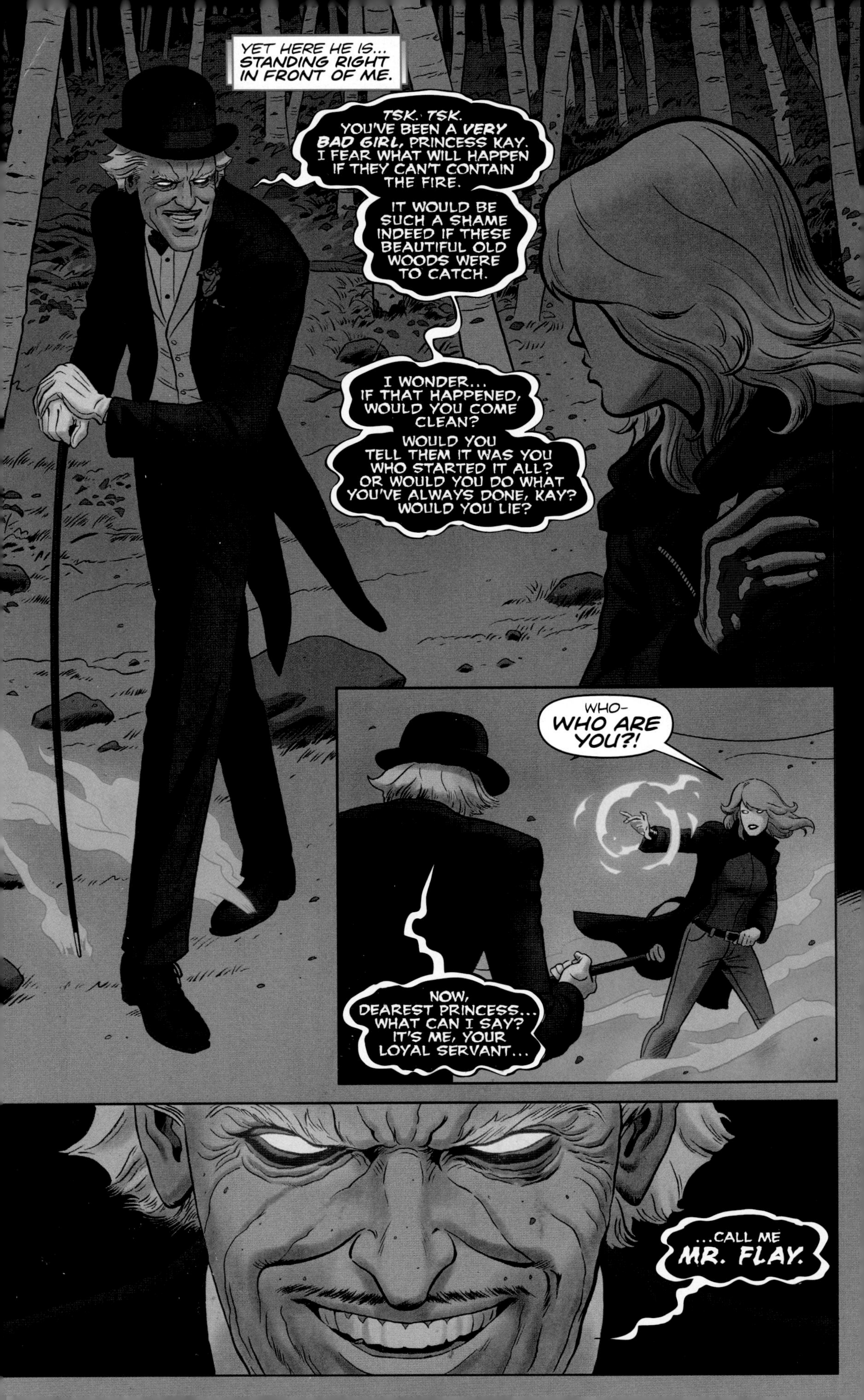
YET HERE HE IS... STANDING RIGHT IN FRONT OF ME.
TSK. TSK. YOU'VE BEEN A VERY BAD GIRL, PRINCESS KAY. I FEAR WHAT WILL HAPPEN IF THEY CAN'T CONTAIN THE FIRE.
IT WOULD BE SUCH A SHAME INDEED IF THESE BEAUTIFUL OLD WOODS WERE TO CATCH.
I WONDER... IF THAT HAPPENED, WOULD YOU COME CLEAN?
WOULD YOU TELL THEM IT WAS YOU WHO STARTED IT ALL? OR WOULD YOU DO WHAT YOU'VE ALWAYS DONE, KAY? WOULD YOU LIE?
WHO- WHO ARE YOU?!
NOW, DEAREST PRINCESS... WHAT CAN I SAY? IT'S ME, YOUR LOYAL SERVANT...
...CALL ME MR. FLAY.

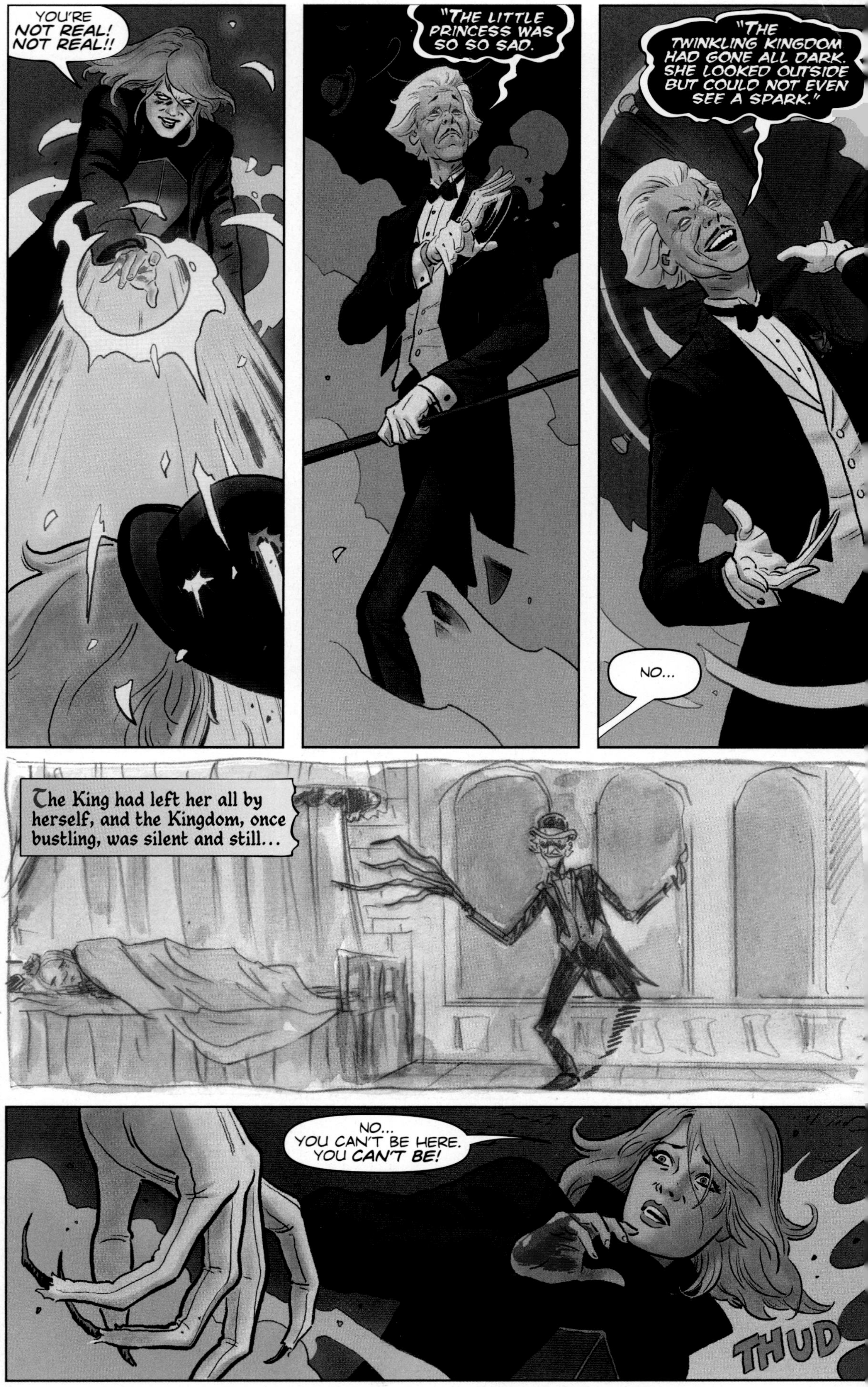
YOU'RE NOT REAL! NOT REAL!!
"THE LITTLE PRINCESS WAS SO SO SAD.
"THE TWINKLING KINGDOM HAD GONE ALL DARK. SHE LOOKED OUTSIDE BUT COULD NOT EVEN SEE A SPARK."
NO...
The King had left her all by herself, and the Kingdom, once bustling, was silent and still...
NO... YOU CAN'T BE HERE. YOU CAN'T BE!
THUD

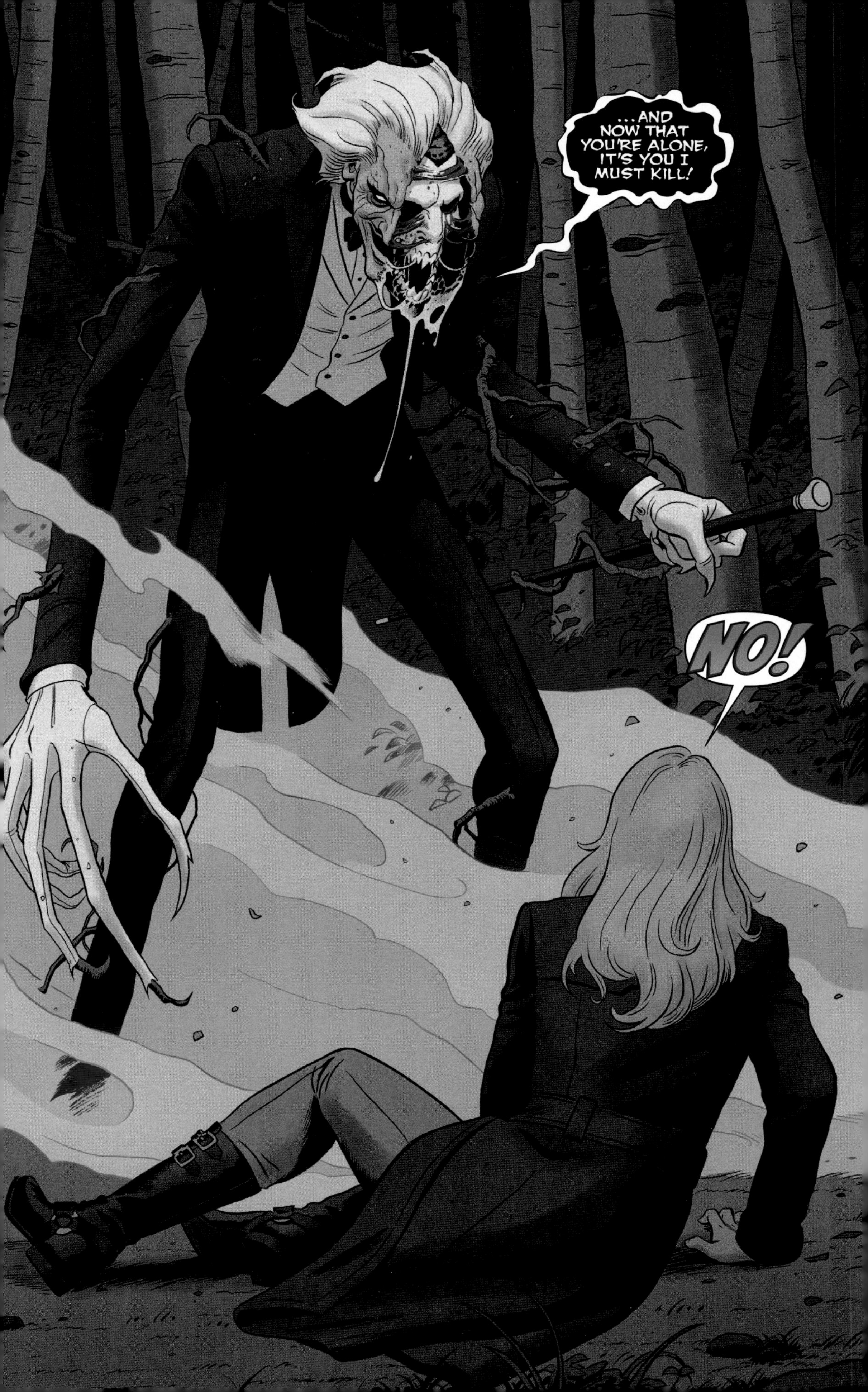
...AND NOW THAT YOU'RE ALONE, IT'S YOU I MUST KILL!
NO!

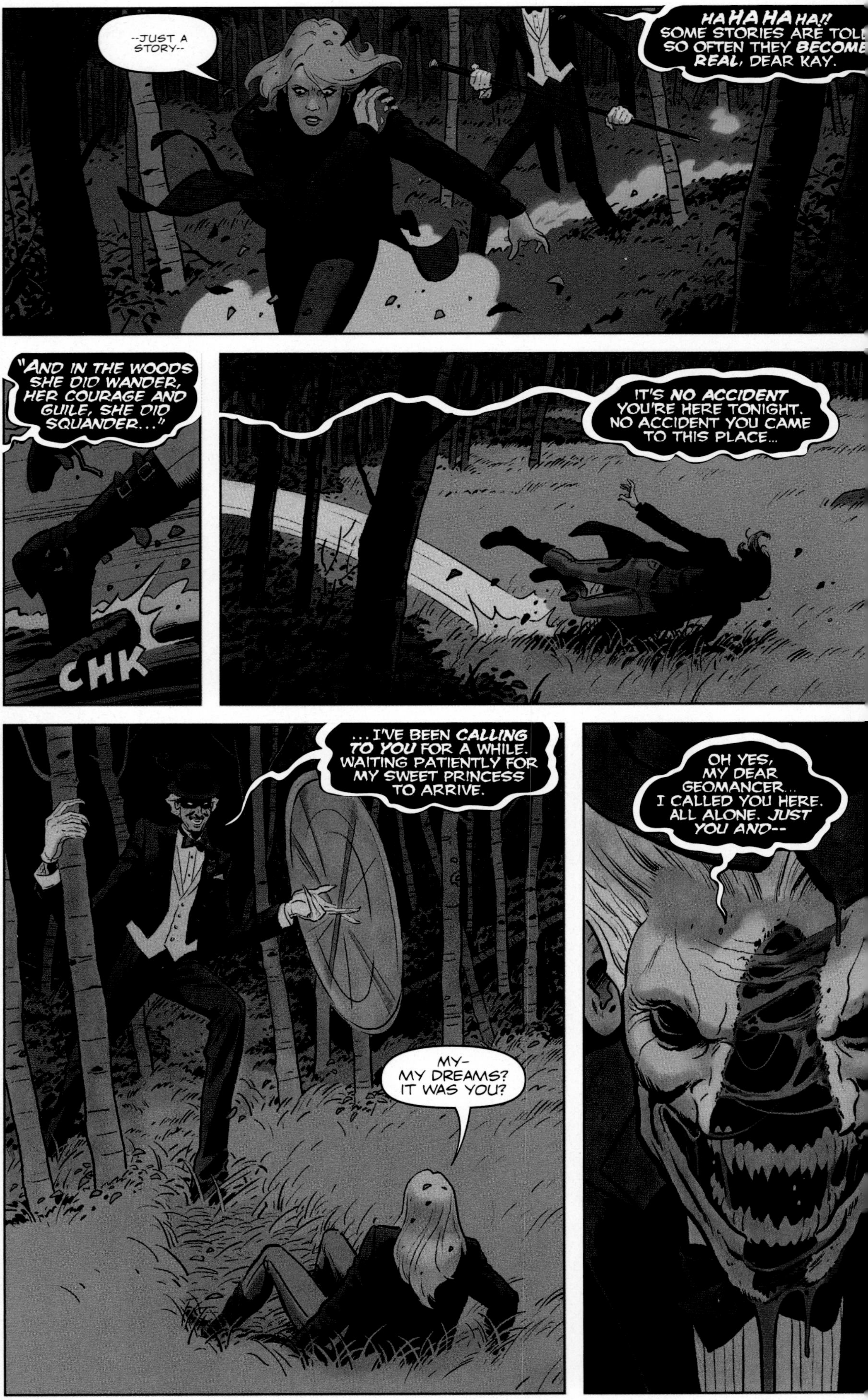
--JUST A STORY--
HA HA HA HA!! SOME STORIES ARE TOLD SO OFTEN THEY BECOME REAL, DEAR KAY.
"AND IN THE WOODS SHE DID WANDER, HER COURAGE AND GUILE, SHE DID SQUANDER..."
CHK
IT'S NO ACCIDENT YOU'RE HERE TONIGHT. NO ACCIDENT YOU CAME TO THIS PLACE...
...I'VE BEEN CALLING TO YOU FOR A WHILE. WAITING PATIENTLY FOR MY SWEET PRINCESS TO ARRIVE.
MY- MY DREAMS? IT WAS YOU?
OH YES, MY DEAR GEOMANCER... I CALLED YOU HERE. ALL ALONE. JUST YOU AND--

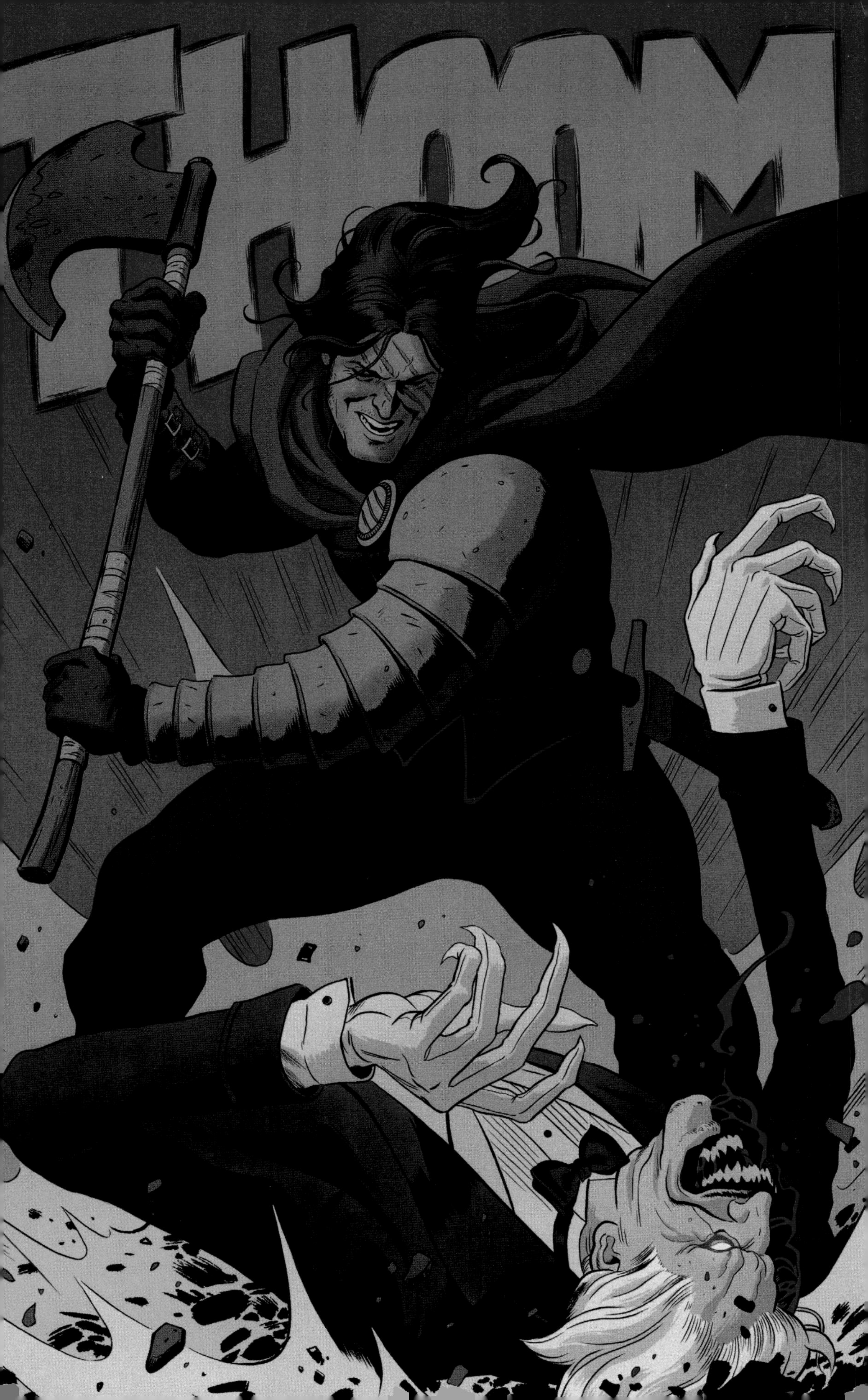

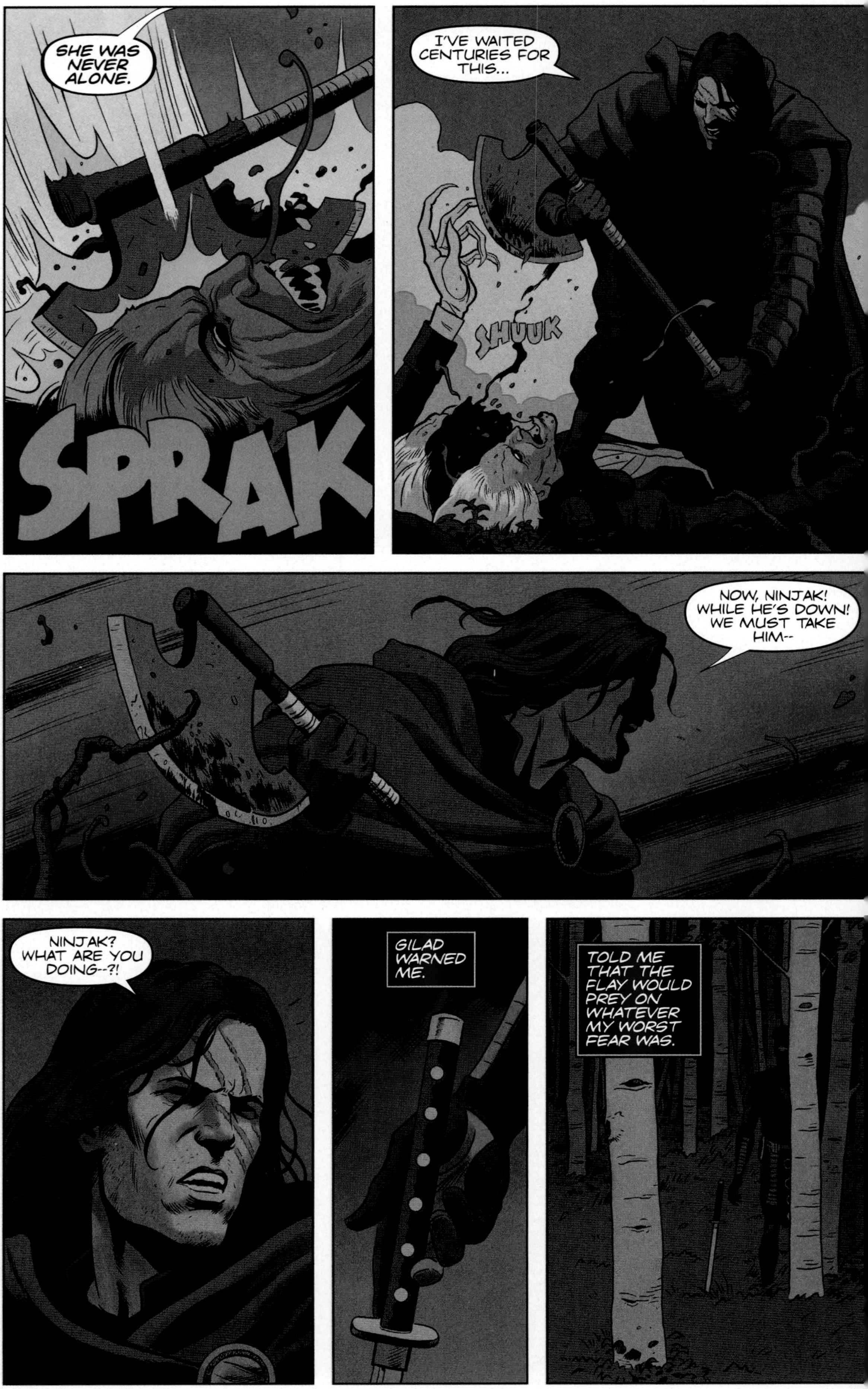
SHE WAS NEVER ALONE.
SPRAK
I'VE WAITED CENTURIES FOR THIS...
SHUUK
NOW, NINJAK! WHILE HE'S DOWN! WE MUST TAKE HIM--
NINJAK? WHAT ARE YOU DOING--?!
GILAD WARNED ME.
TOLD ME THAT THE FLAY WOULD PREY ON WHATEVER MY WORST FEAR WAS.

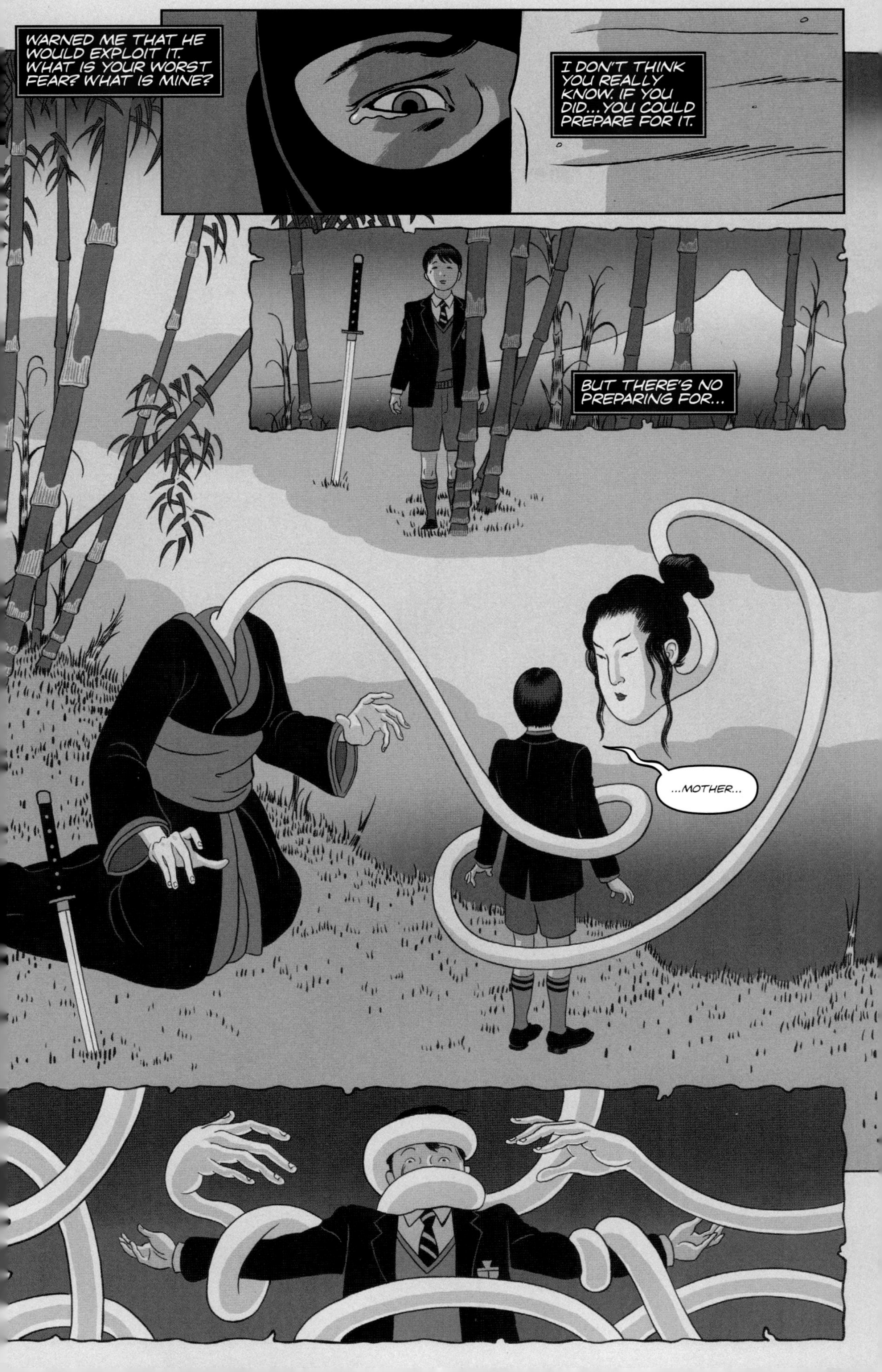
WARNED ME THAT HE WOULD EXPLOIT IT. WHAT IS YOUR WORST FEAR? WHAT IS MINE?
I DON'T THINK YOU REALLY KNOW. IF YOU DID...YOU COULD PREPARE FOR IT.
BUT THERE'S NO PREPARING FOR...
...MOTHER...

GHHHK!

OHHH! YOU'RE AN INTERESTING ONE...

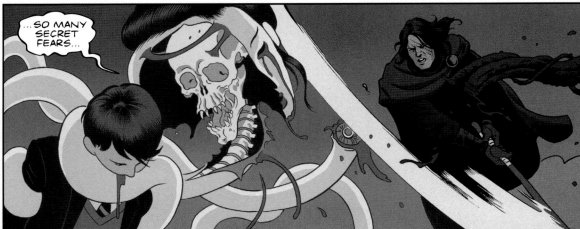

...SO MANY SECRET FEARS...

DAMMIT! SNAP OUT OF IT, NINJAK!... NGHHH!

NNNUUUHH!

YOU...

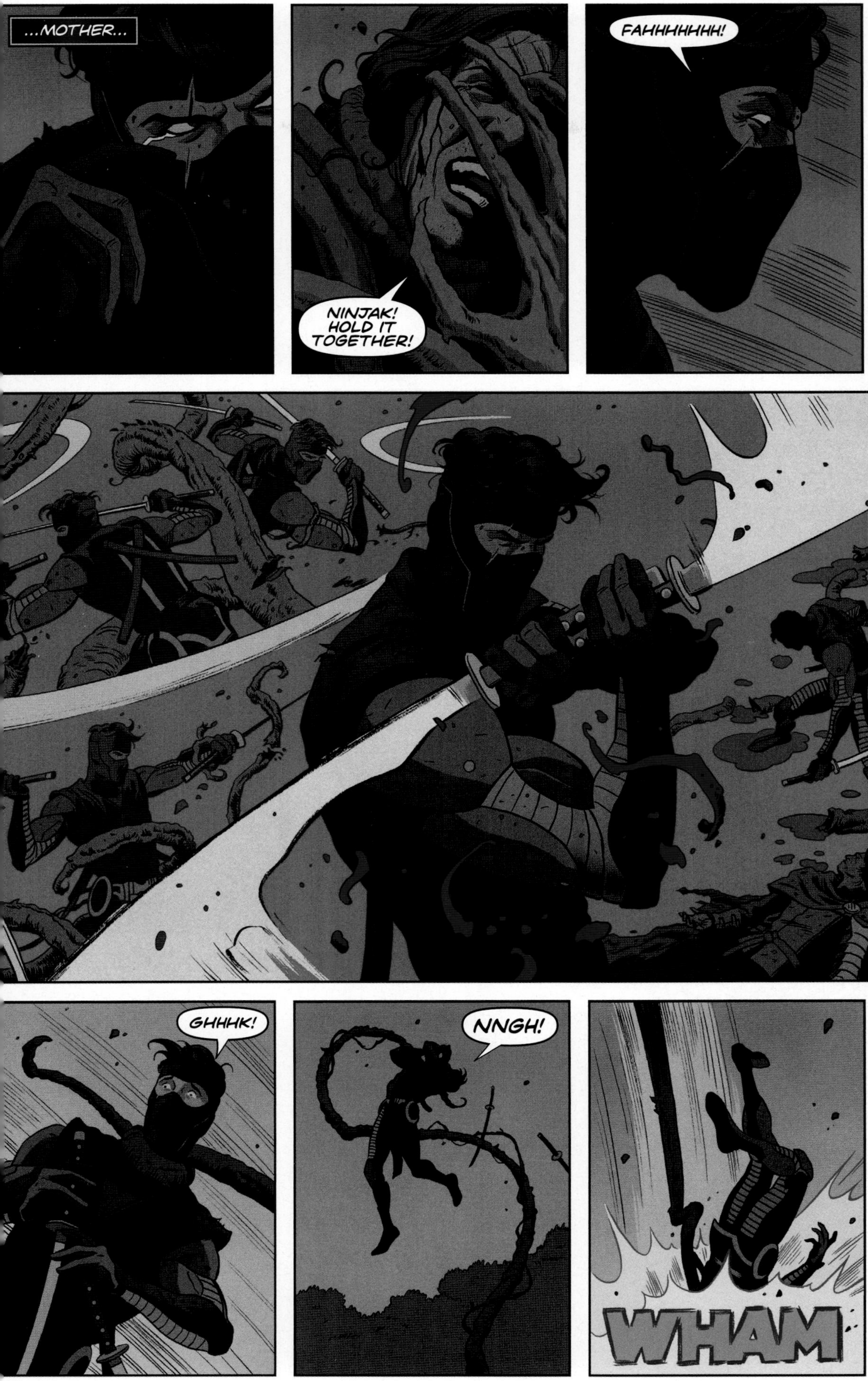
...MOTHER...
NINJAK! HOLD IT TOGETHER!
FAHHHHHHH!
GHHHK!
NNGH!
WHAM

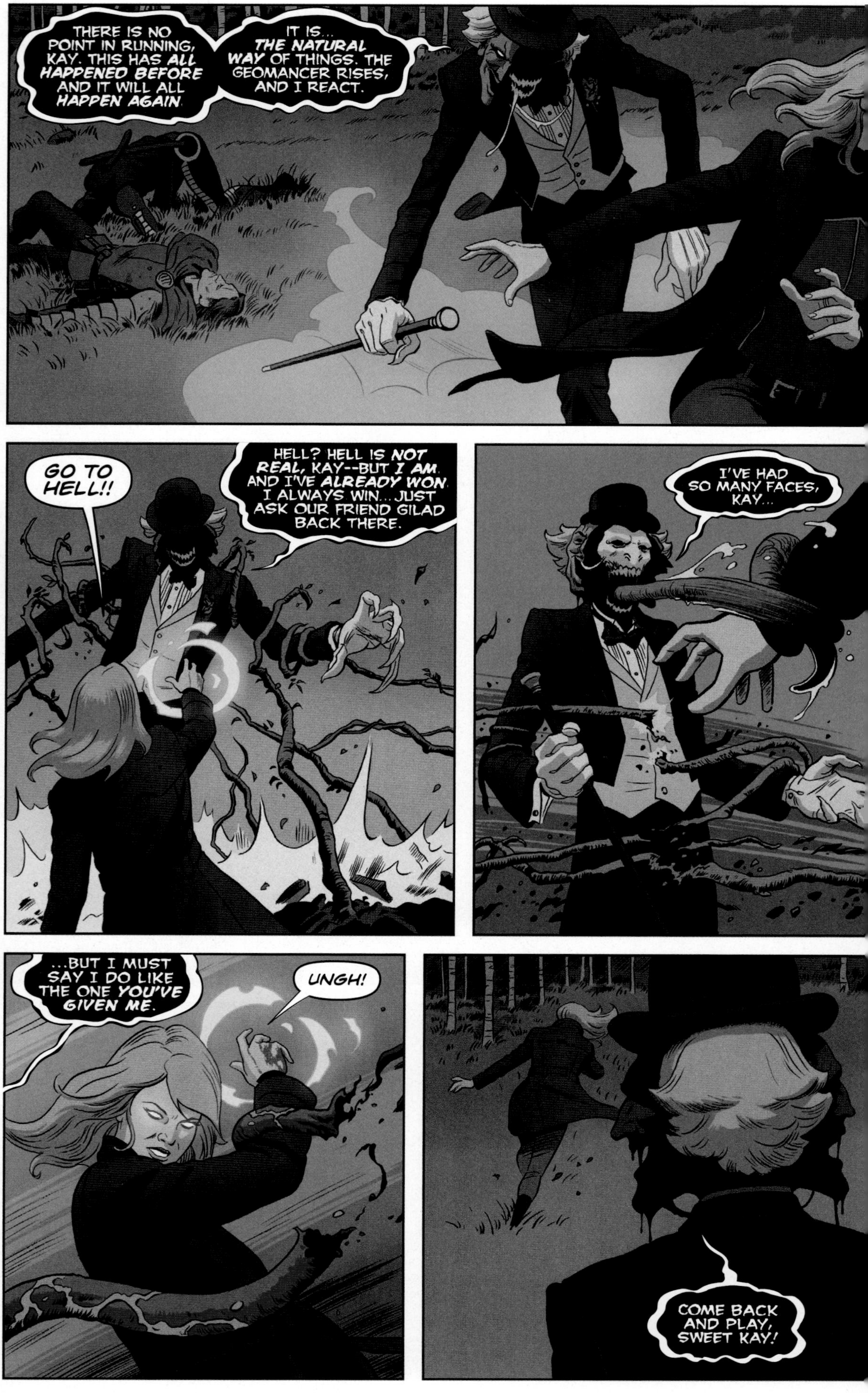
THERE IS NO POINT IN RUNNING, KAY. THIS HAS ALL HAPPENED BEFORE AND IT WILL ALL HAPPEN AGAIN.
IT IS... THE NATURAL WAY OF THINGS. THE GEOMANCER RISES, AND I REACT.
GO TO HELL!!
HELL? HELL IS NOT REAL, KAY--BUT I AM. AND I'VE ALREADY WON. I ALWAYS WIN... JUST ASK OUR FRIEND GILAD BACK THERE.
I'VE HAD SO MANY FACES, KAY...
...BUT I MUST SAY I DO LIKE THE ONE YOU'VE GIVEN ME.
UNGH!
COME BACK AND PLAY, SWEET KAY!

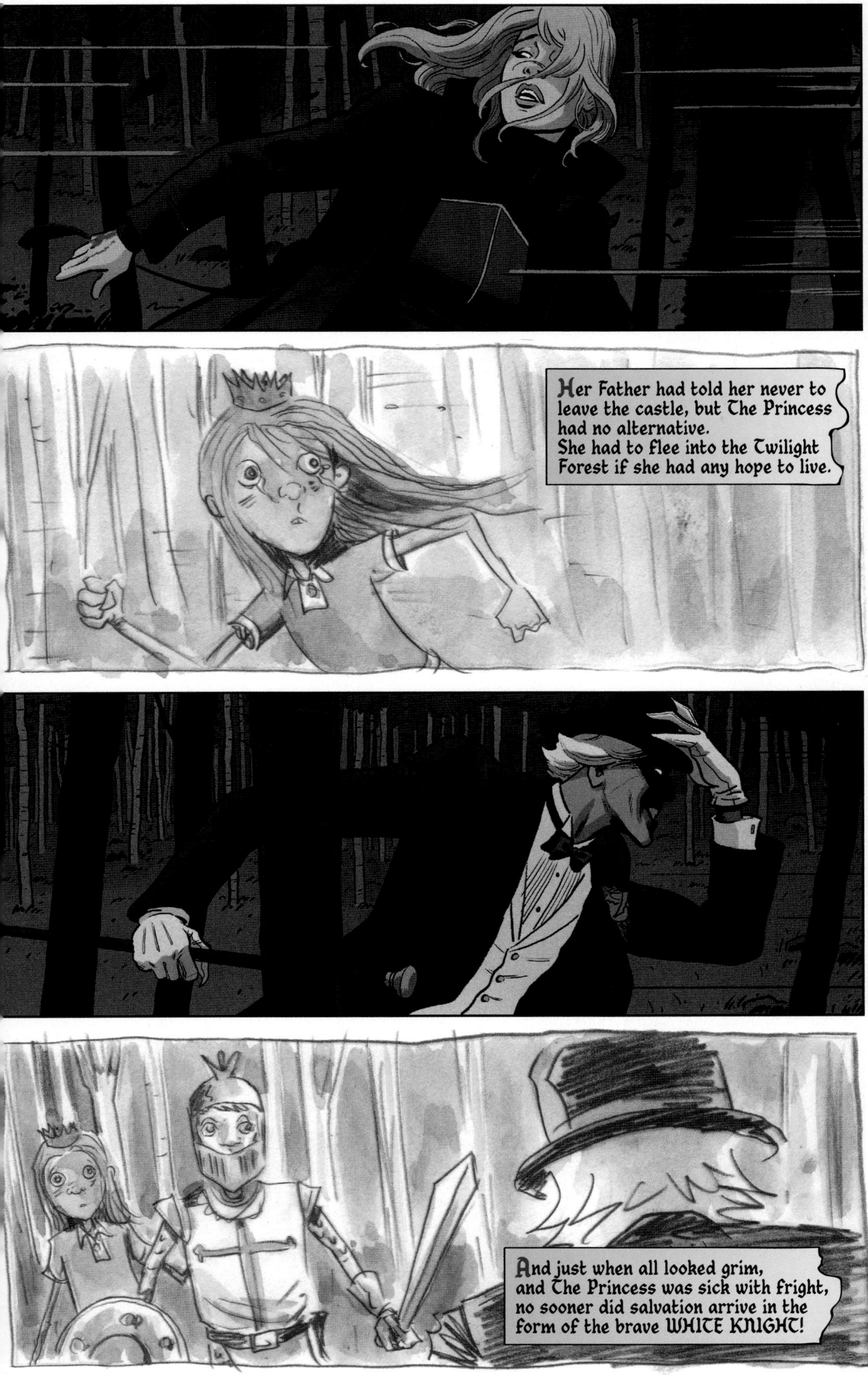
Her Father had told her never to leave the castle, but The Princess had no alternative.
She had to flee into the Twilight Forest if she had any hope to live.
And just when all looked grim, and The Princess was sick with fright, no sooner did salvation arrive in the form of the brave WHITE KNIGHT!

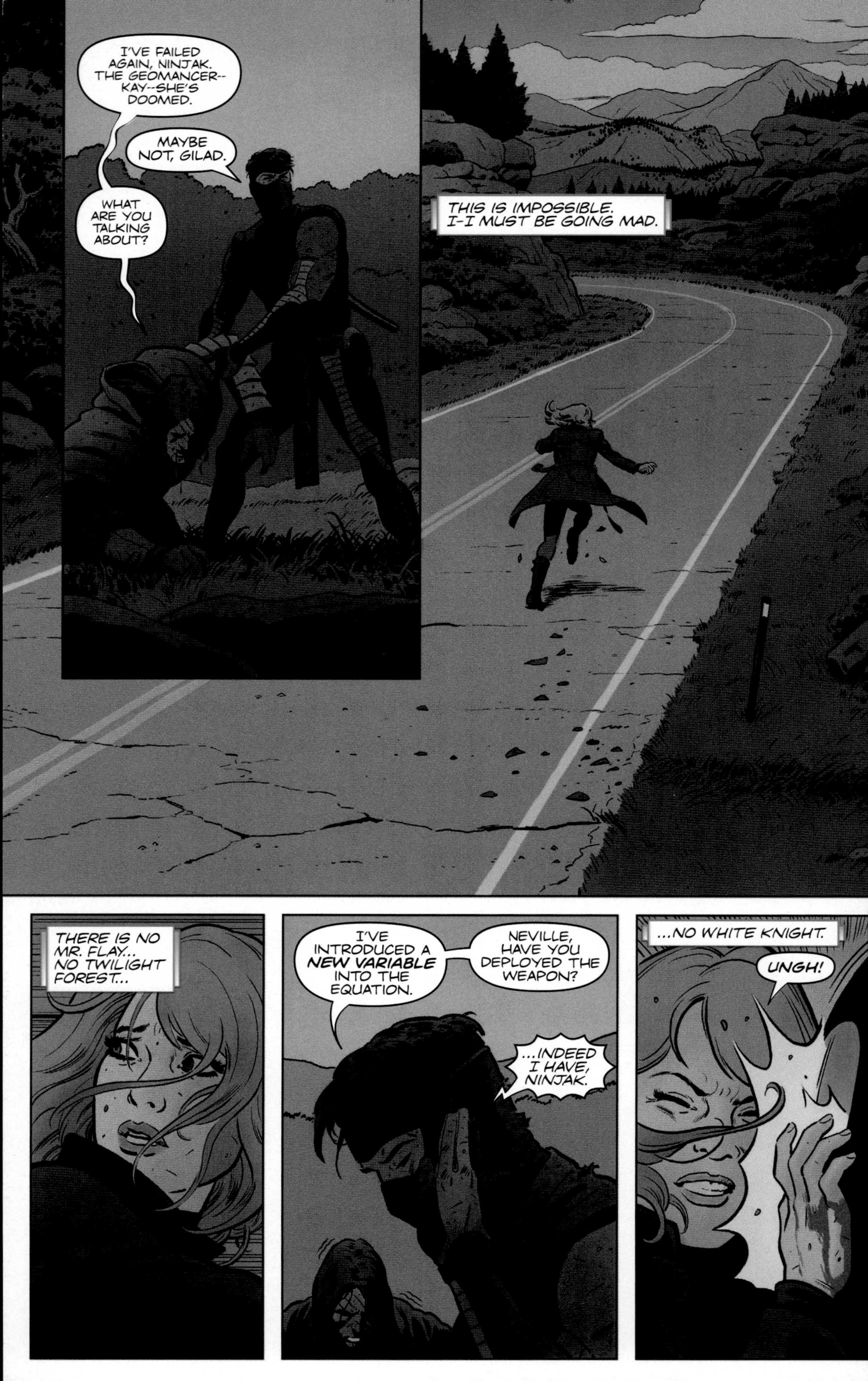
I'VE FAILED AGAIN, NINJAK. THE GEOMANCER-- KAY--SHE'S DOOMED.
MAYBE NOT, GILAD.
WHAT ARE YOU TALKING ABOUT?
THIS IS IMPOSSIBLE. I-I MUST BE GOING MAD.
THERE IS NO MR. FLAY... NO TWILIGHT FOREST...
I'VE INTRODUCED A NEW VARIABLE INTO THE EQUATION.
NEVILLE, HAVE YOU DEPLOYED THE WEAPON?
...INDEED I HAVE, NINJAK.
...NO WHITE KNIGHT.
UNGH!

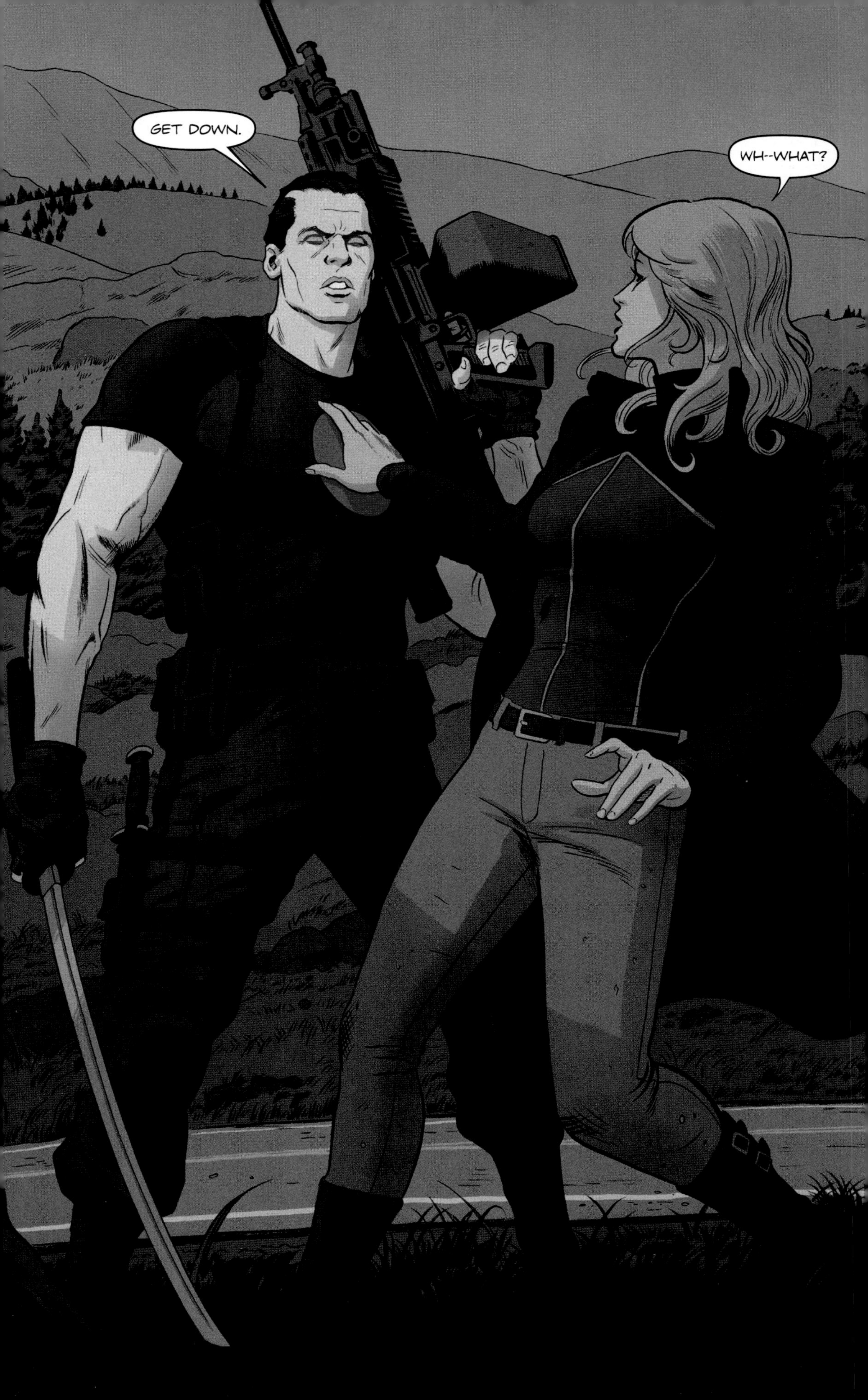
GET DOWN.
WH--WHAT?

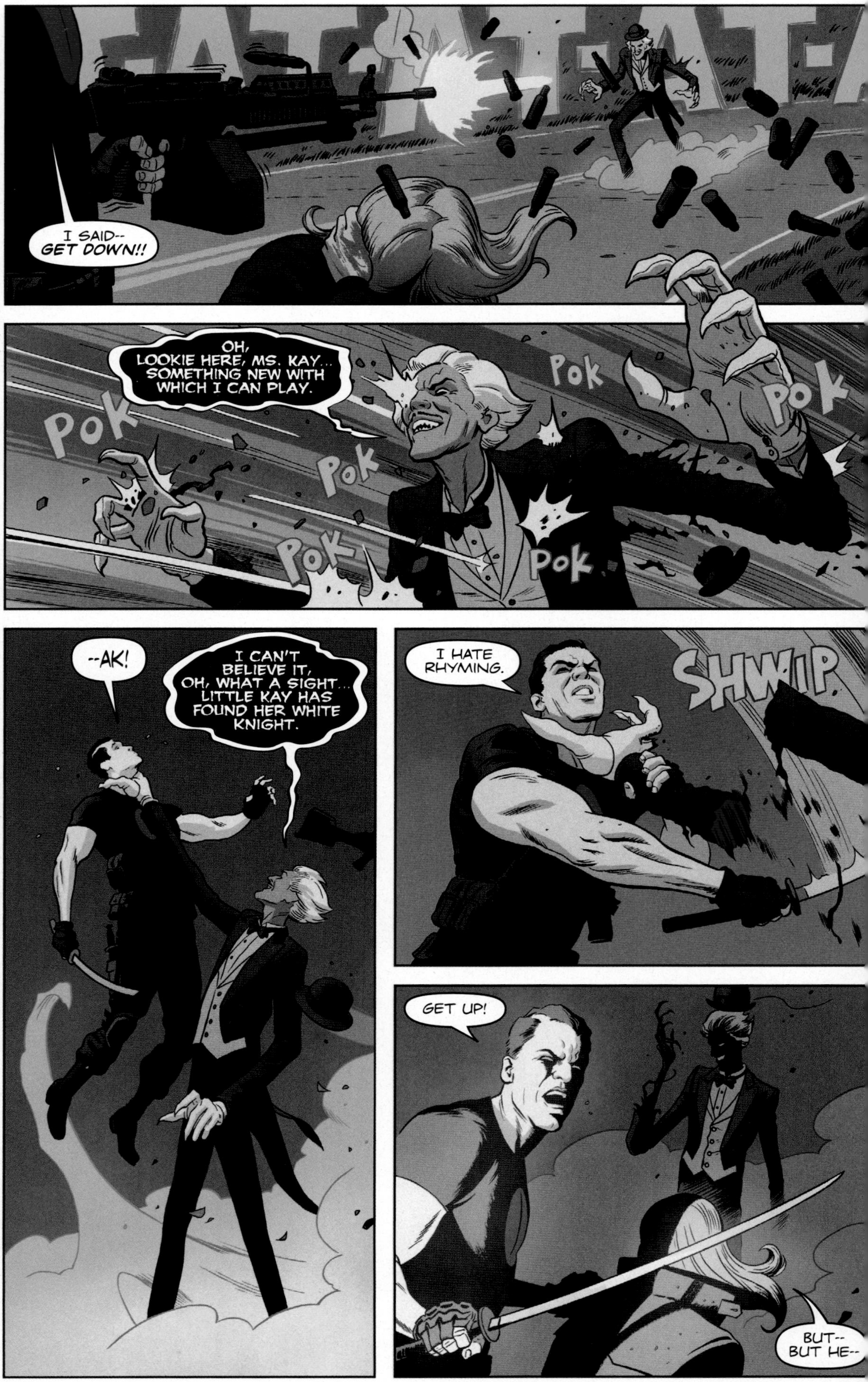
I SAID-- GET DOWN!!
OH, LOOKIE HERE, MS. KAY... SOMETHING NEW WITH WHICH I CAN PLAY.
POK
POK
POK
POK
POK
POK
--AK!
I CAN'T BELIEVE IT, OH, WHAT A SIGHT... LITTLE KAY HAS FOUND HER WHITE KNIGHT.
I HATE RHYMING.
SHWIP
GET UP!
BUT-- BUT HE--

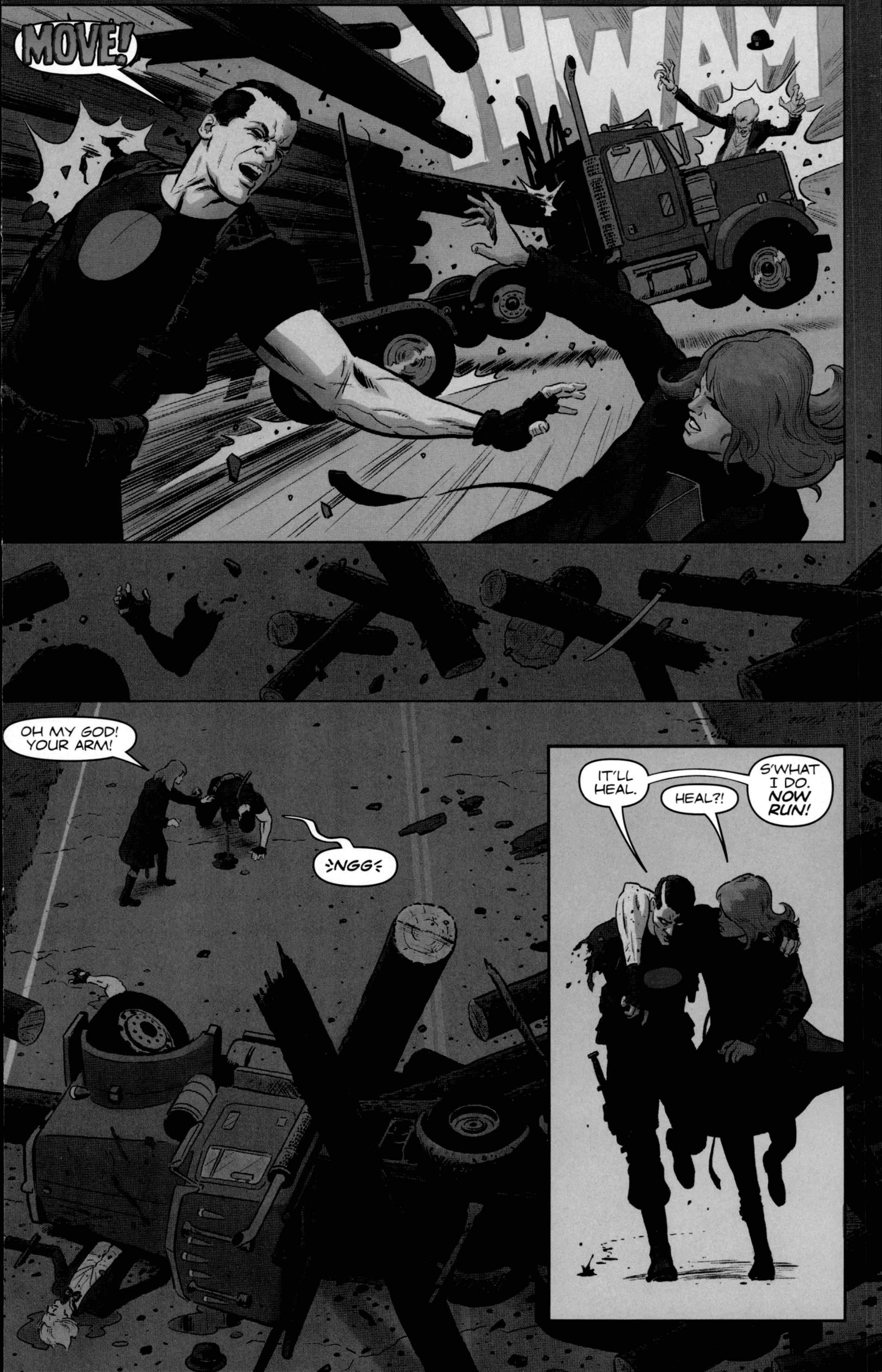
MOVE!
OH MY GOD! YOUR ARM!
NGG
IT'LL HEAL.
HEAL?!
S'WHAT I DO. NOW RUN!

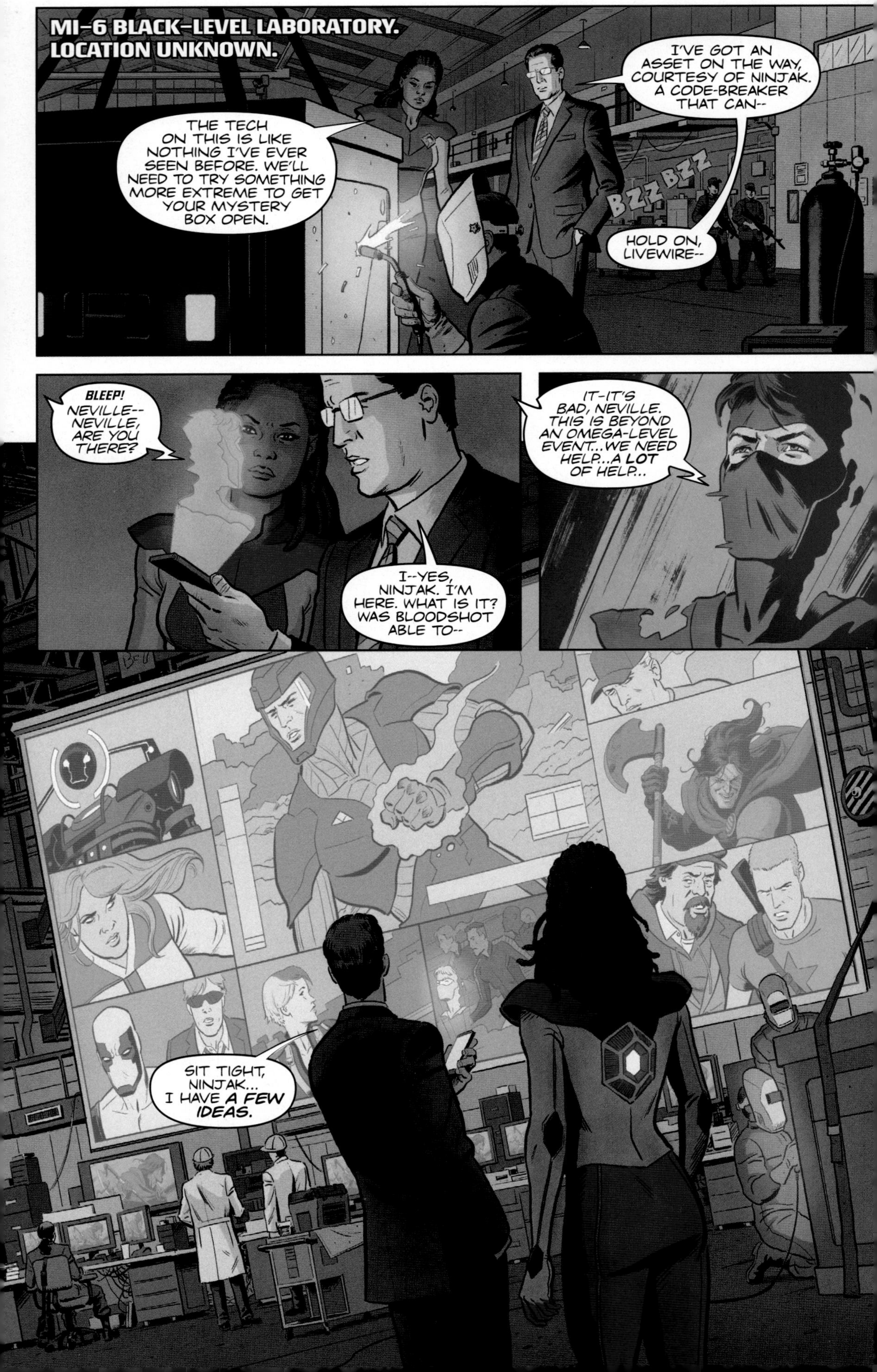
MI-6 BLACK-LEVEL LABORATORY.
LOCATION UNKNOWN.
THE TECH ON THIS IS LIKE NOTHING I'VE EVER SEEN BEFORE. WE'LL NEED TO TRY SOMETHING MORE EXTREME TO GET YOUR MYSTERY BOX OPEN.
I'VE GOT AN ASSET ON THE WAY, COURTESY OF NINJAK. A CODE-BREAKER THAT CAN--
BZZ BZZ
HOLD ON, LIVEWIRE--
BLEEP! NEVILLE-- NEVILLE, ARE YOU THERE?
I--YES, NINJAK. I'M HERE. WHAT IS IT? WAS BLOODSHOT ABLE TO--
IT-IT'S BAD, NEVILLE. THIS IS BEYOND AN OMEGA-LEVEL EVENT...WE NEED HELP...A LOT OF HELP...
SIT TIGHT, NINJAK... I HAVE A FEW IDEAS.

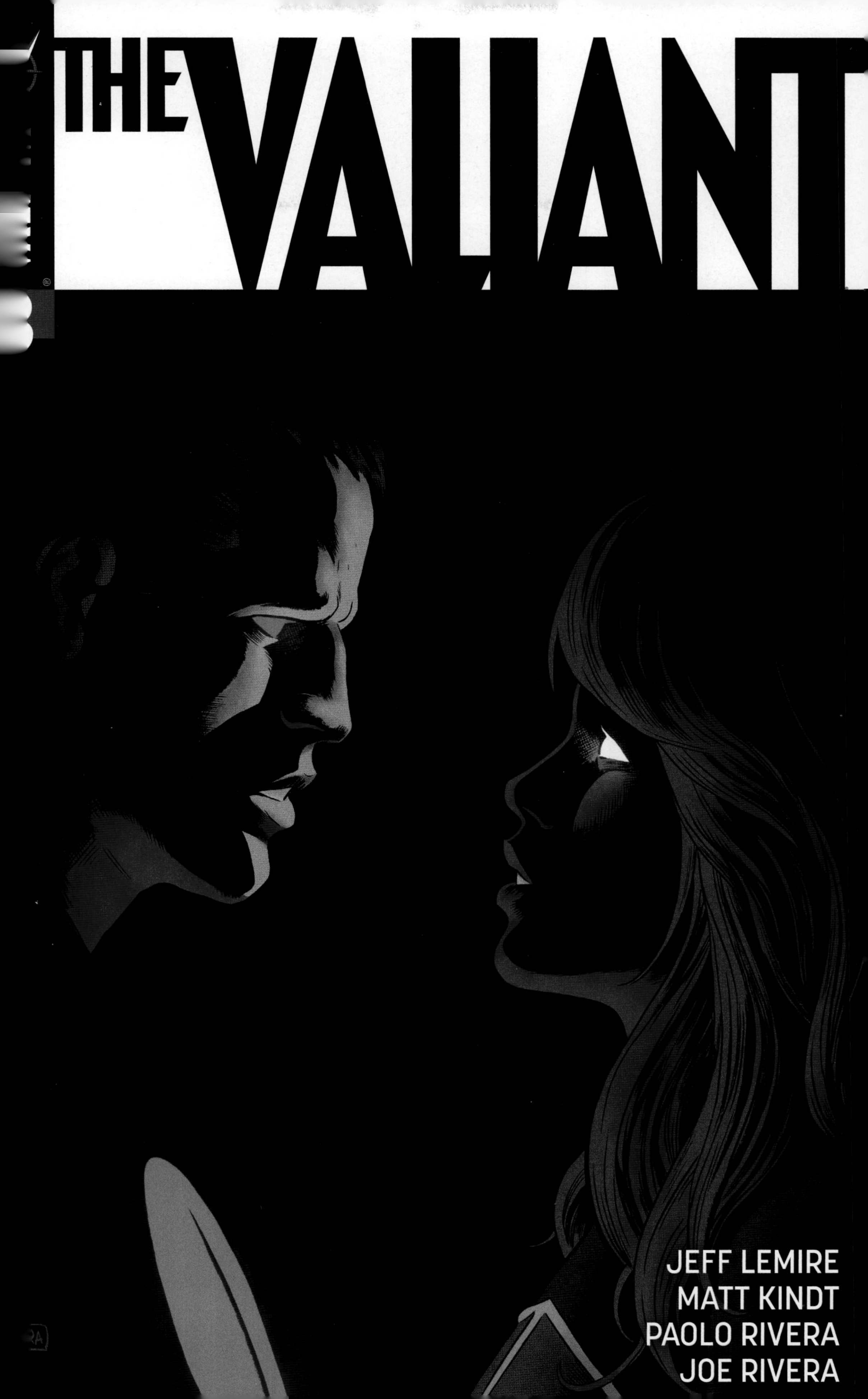
THE VALIANT
JEFF LEMIRE
MATT KINDT
PAOLO RIVERA
JOE RIVERA

MI-6 BLACK-LEVEL LABORATORY. LOCATION UNKNOWN.
NEVER MET A LOCKED BOX I COULDN'T OPEN. THERE'S SOMETHING STRANGE ABOUT THIS ONE... SOMETHING NOT RIGHT...
SO... WHAT'S IN IT, BREAKER?
HRRRR...
WE'RE TRYING TO PREVENT WORLD WAR III AND YOU'RE BUSY TRYING TO BREAK OPEN A TREASURE CHEST? WHAT'S THE URGENCY?
I FOUND A MEMO WHEN I WAS WORKING IN ARCHIVES. IT MENTIONED SOMETHING I'D SEEN REFERENCED HERE AND THERE OVER THE YEARS. AN ENIGMA BOX. HAD MY FEELERS OUT EVER SINCE, TRYING TO TRACK IT DOWN.
THAT MEMO I FOUND? IT HAD A PERSONAL MESSAGE TO ME. IT MENTIONED THE ENIGMA BOX. AND? IT HAD TODAY'S DATE ON IT.
SO?
SO. THAT MEMO WAS DATED SEPTEMBER 1993. TWELVE YEARS BEFORE I HAD EVEN THOUGHT ABOUT WORKING FOR MI-6.
YOU'RE FREAKING ME OUT A LITTLE, NEVILLE.
FORGET IT. TIME TO FOCUS ON THE PROBLEM AT HAND, CAPSHAW.
WE JUST SPENT THREE BILLION DOLLARS OF OUR GOVERNMENT'S MONEY TO GET THE MOST POWERFUL HUMAN BEINGS TOGETHER. IN ONE PLACE. AT THE SAME TIME. TO STOP THIS...THING.
YOU SURE WE'RE NOT OVERREACTING TO THIS THREAT?
I'VE NEVER SEEN GILAD... SCARED BEFORE. IF HALF OF WHAT HE SAID ENDS UP BEING TRUE, EVEN THE COMBINED RESOURCES OF EVERYONE ON THIS PLANET MIGHT NOT BE ENOUGH.
OKAY, TEAM. WE'VE GOT EYES AND EARS.

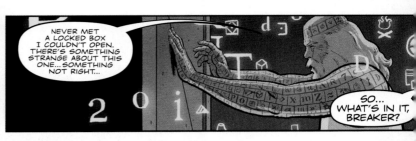

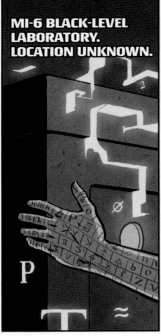

"LET'S TEAR THIS GUY APART!"
SPLURRRCHHH
WELL, WELL, GILAD... YOU'VE FINALLY MADE SOME FRIENDS...

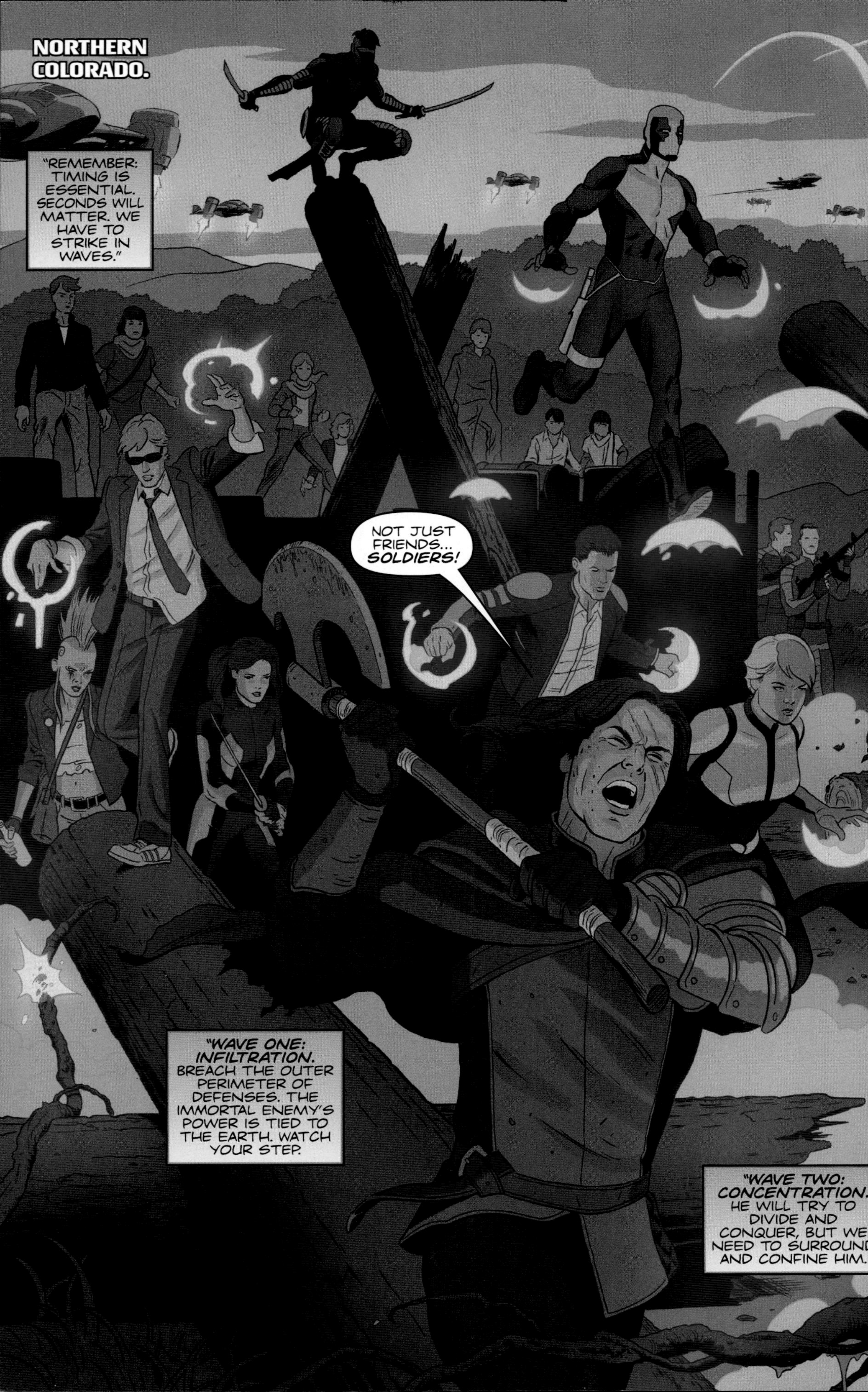
NORTHERN COLORADO.
"REMEMBER: TIMING IS ESSENTIAL. SECONDS WILL MATTER. WE HAVE TO STRIKE IN WAVES."
NOT JUST FRIENDS... SOLDIERS!
"WAVE ONE: INFILTRATION. BREACH THE OUTER PERIMETER OF DEFENSES. THE IMMORTAL ENEMY'S POWER IS TIED TO THE EARTH. WATCH YOUR STEP.
"WAVE TWO: CONCENTRATION. HE WILL TRY TO DIVIDE AND CONQUER, BUT WE NEED TO SURROUND AND CONFINE HIM.

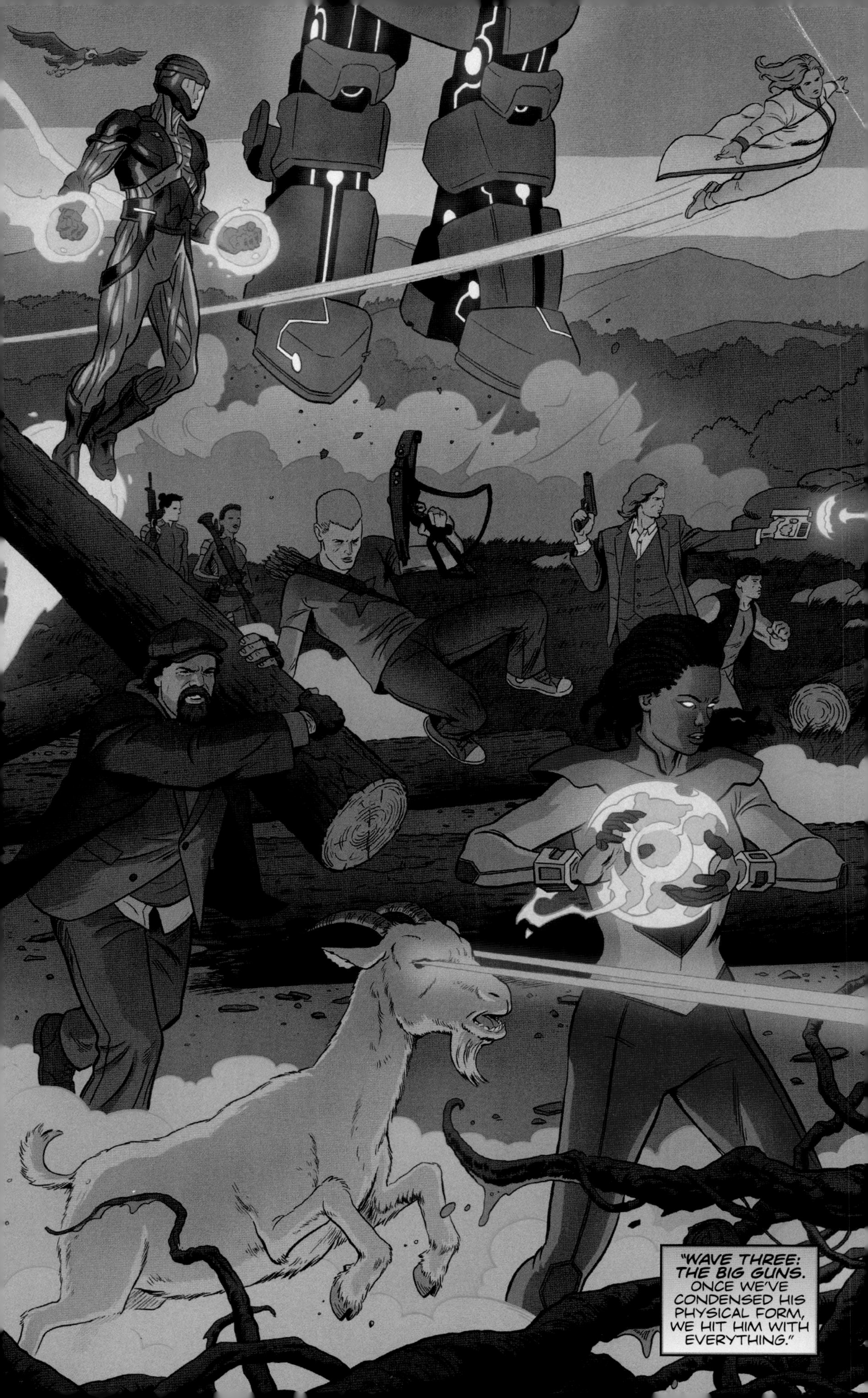
"WAVE THREE: THE BIG GUNS. ONCE WE'VE CONDENSED HIS PHYSICAL FORM, WE HIT HIM WITH EVERYTHING."

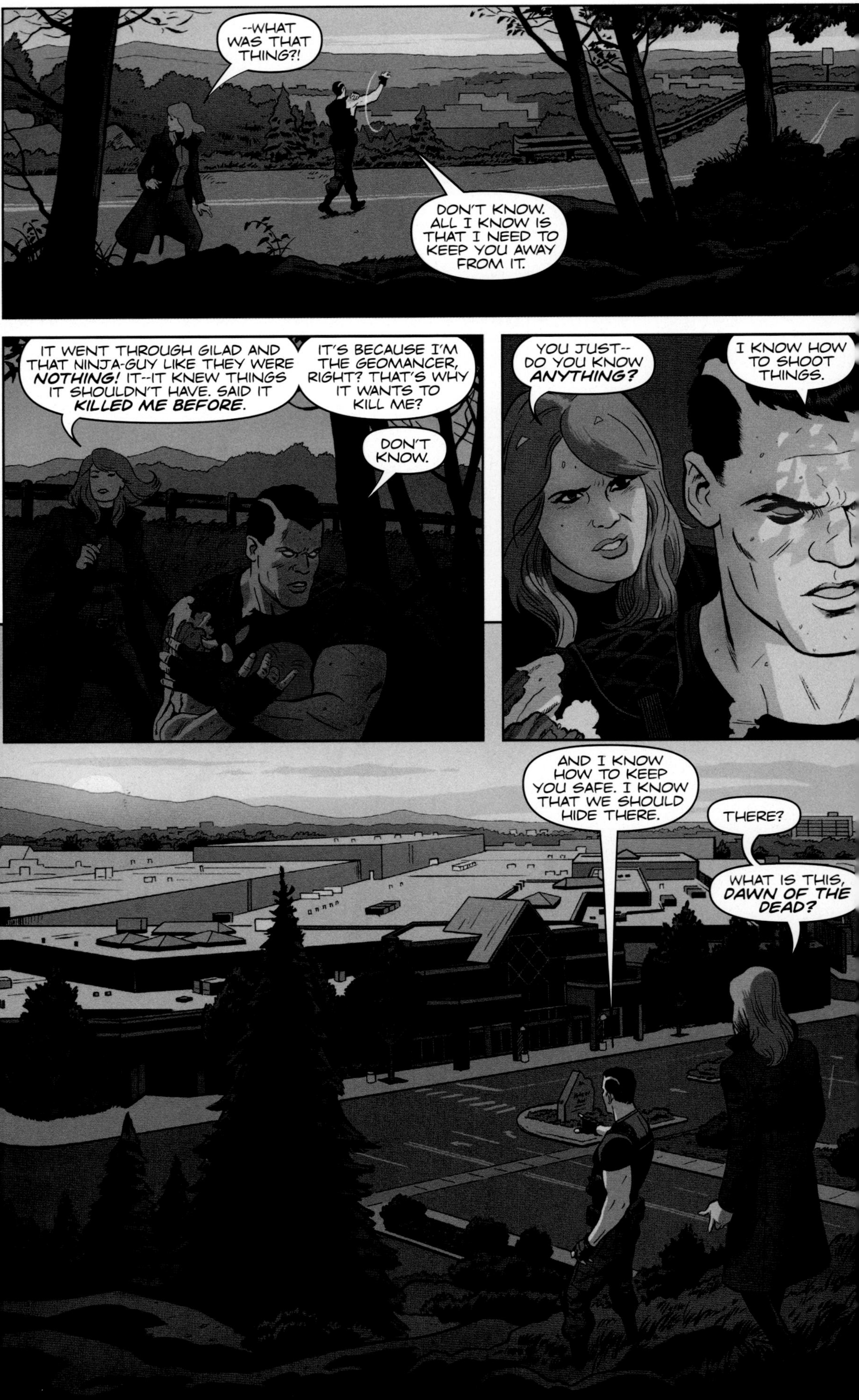
--WHAT WAS THAT THING?!
DON'T KNOW. ALL I KNOW IS THAT I NEED TO KEEP YOU AWAY FROM IT.
IT WENT THROUGH GILAD AND THAT NINJA-GUY LIKE THEY WERE *NOTHING!* IT--IT KNEW THINGS IT SHOULDN'T HAVE. SAID IT *KILLED ME BEFORE*.
IT'S BECAUSE I'M THE GEOMANCER, RIGHT? THAT'S WHY IT WANTS TO KILL ME?
DON'T KNOW.
YOU JUST-- DO YOU KNOW *ANYTHING?*
I KNOW HOW TO SHOOT THINGS.
AND I KNOW HOW TO KEEP YOU SAFE. I KNOW THAT WE SHOULD HIDE THERE.
THERE?
WHAT IS THIS, *DAWN OF THE DEAD?*

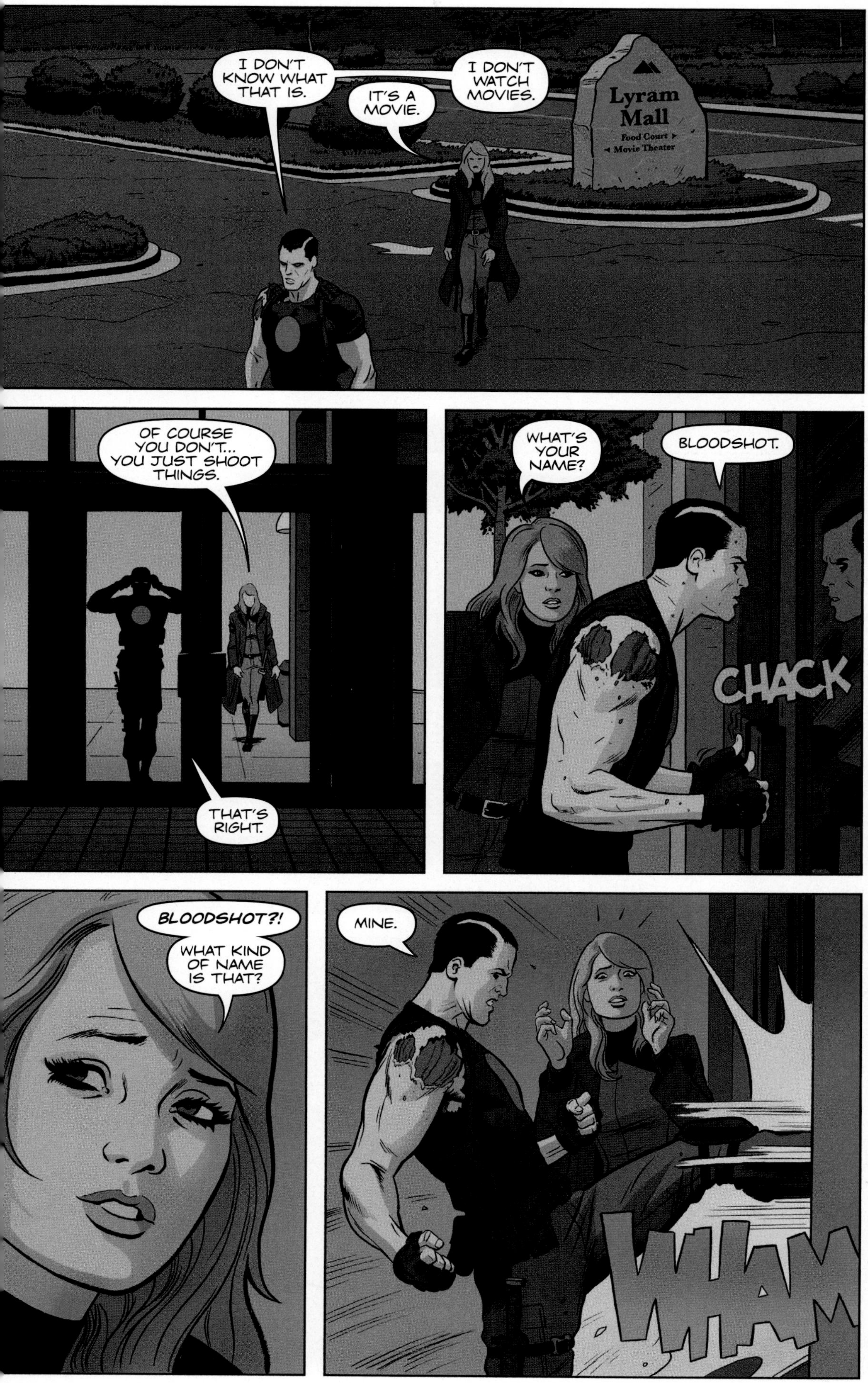
I DON'T KNOW WHAT THAT IS.
IT'S A MOVIE.
I DON'T WATCH MOVIES.
Lyram Mall
Food Court
Movie Theater
OF COURSE YOU DON'T... YOU JUST SHOOT THINGS.
THAT'S RIGHT.
WHAT'S YOUR NAME?
BLOODSHOT.
CHACK
BLOODSHOT?!
WHAT KIND OF NAME IS THAT?
MINE.
WHAM

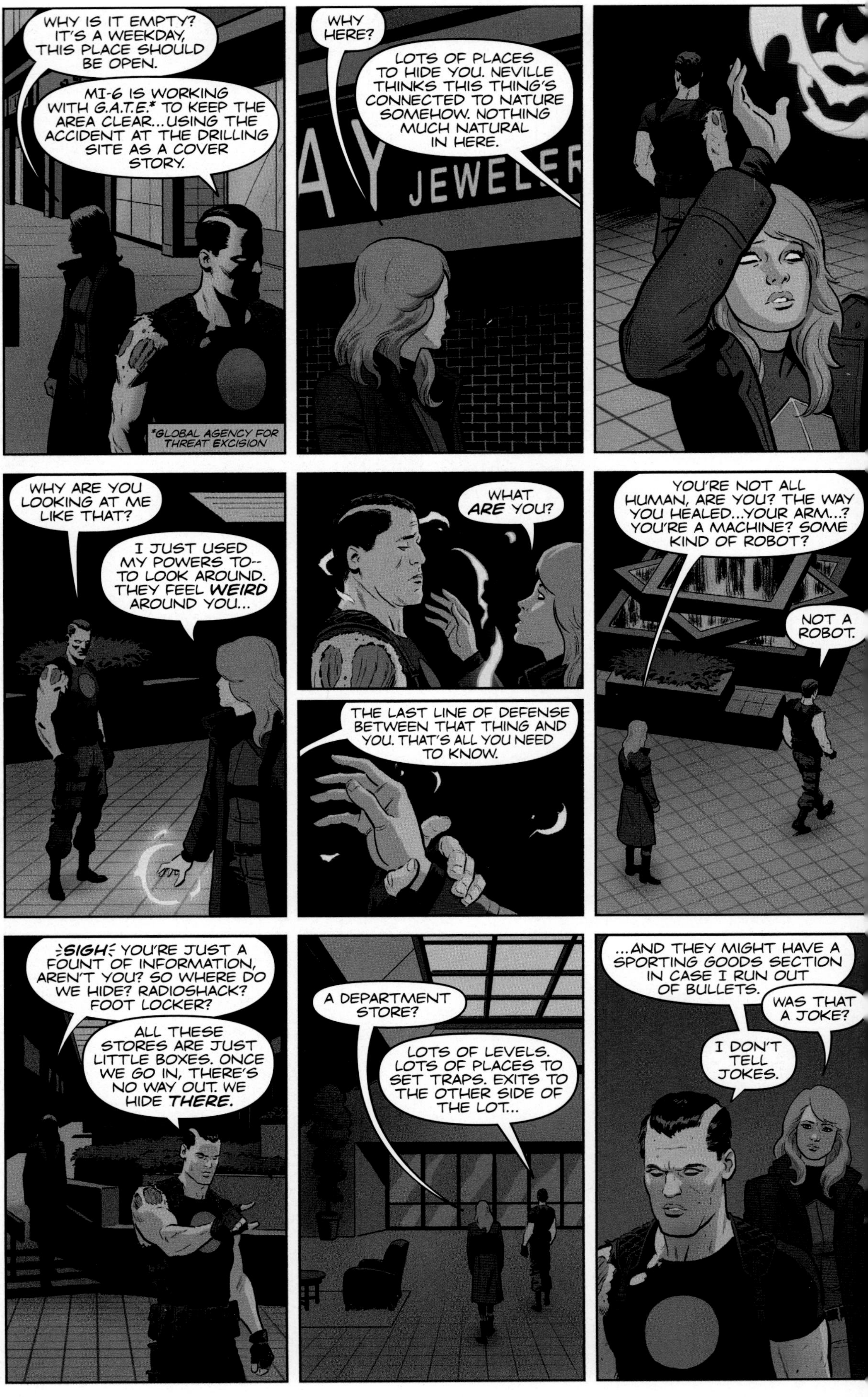
WHY IS IT EMPTY? IT'S A WEEKDAY, THIS PLACE SHOULD BE OPEN.
MI-6 IS WORKING WITH G.A.T.E.* TO KEEP THE AREA CLEAR...USING THE ACCIDENT AT THE DRILLING SITE AS A COVER STORY.
*GLOBAL AGENCY FOR THREAT EXCISION
WHY HERE?
LOTS OF PLACES TO HIDE YOU. NEVILLE THINKS THIS THING'S CONNECTED TO NATURE SOMEHOW. NOTHING MUCH NATURAL IN HERE.
AY JEWELER
WHY ARE YOU LOOKING AT ME LIKE THAT?
I JUST USED MY POWERS TO-- TO LOOK AROUND. THEY FEEL WEIRD AROUND YOU...
WHAT ARE YOU?
THE LAST LINE OF DEFENSE BETWEEN THAT THING AND YOU. THAT'S ALL YOU NEED TO KNOW.
YOU'RE NOT ALL HUMAN, ARE YOU? THE WAY YOU HEALED...YOUR ARM...? YOU'RE A MACHINE? SOME KIND OF ROBOT?
NOT A ROBOT.
SIGH YOU'RE JUST A FOUNT OF INFORMATION, AREN'T YOU? SO WHERE DO WE HIDE? RADIOSHACK? FOOT LOCKER?
ALL THESE STORES ARE JUST LITTLE BOXES. ONCE WE GO IN, THERE'S NO WAY OUT. WE HIDE THERE.
A DEPARTMENT STORE?
LOTS OF LEVELS. LOTS OF PLACES TO SET TRAPS. EXITS TO THE OTHER SIDE OF THE LOT...
...AND THEY MIGHT HAVE A SPORTING GOODS SECTION IN CASE I RUN OUT OF BULLETS.
WAS THAT A JOKE?
I DON'T TELL JOKES.

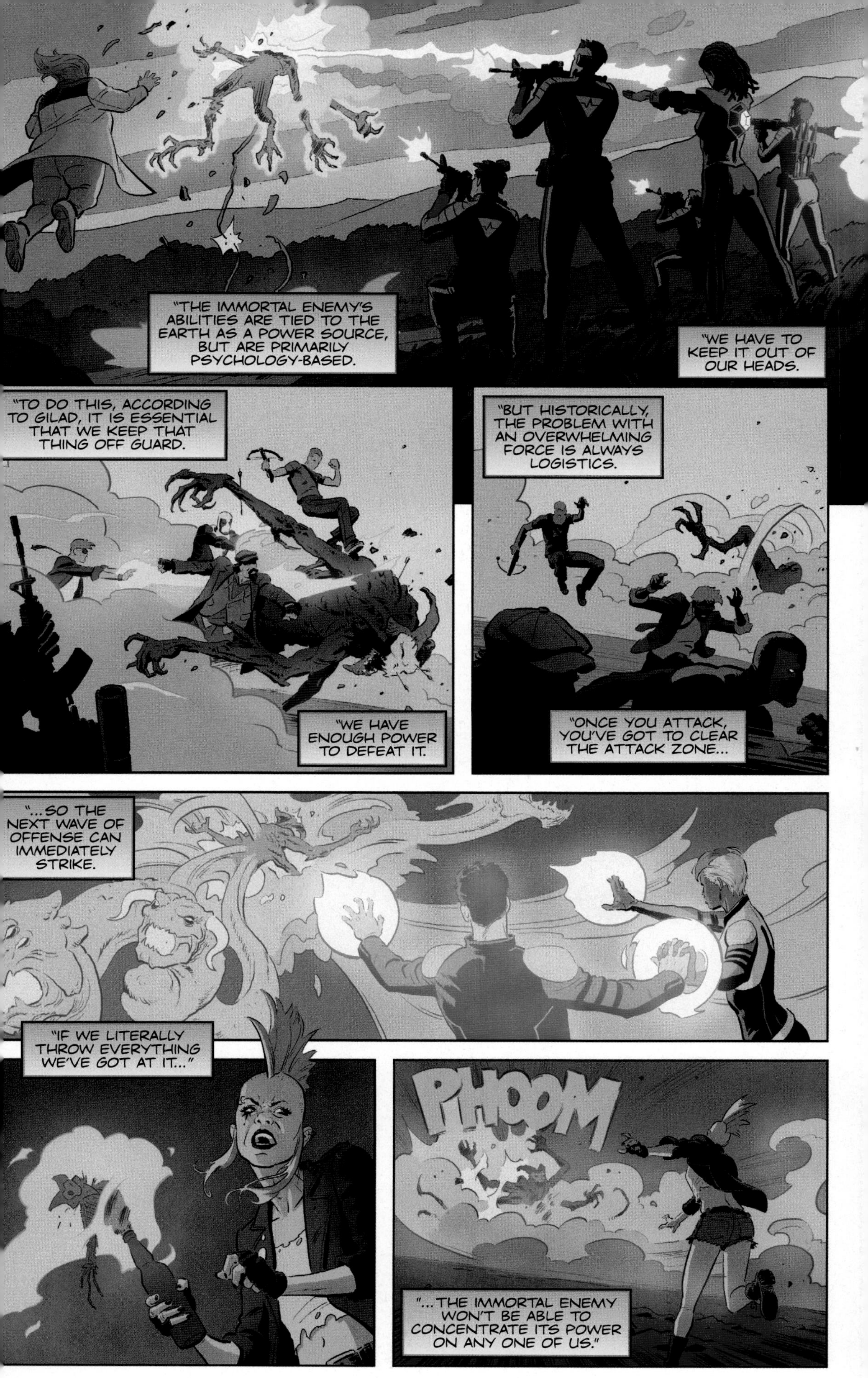
"THE IMMORTAL ENEMY'S ABILITIES ARE TIED TO THE EARTH AS A POWER SOURCE, BUT ARE PRIMARILY PSYCHOLOGY-BASED.
"WE HAVE TO KEEP IT OUT OF OUR HEADS.
"TO DO THIS, ACCORDING TO GILAD, IT IS ESSENTIAL THAT WE KEEP THAT THING OFF GUARD.
"WE HAVE ENOUGH POWER TO DEFEAT IT.
"BUT HISTORICALLY, THE PROBLEM WITH AN OVERWHELMING FORCE IS ALWAYS LOGISTICS.
"ONCE YOU ATTACK, YOU'VE GOT TO CLEAR THE ATTACK ZONE...
"...SO THE NEXT WAVE OF OFFENSE CAN IMMEDIATELY STRIKE.
"IF WE LITERALLY THROW EVERYTHING WE'VE GOT AT IT..."
PHOOM
"...THE IMMORTAL ENEMY WON'T BE ABLE TO CONCENTRATE ITS POWER ON ANY ONE OF US."

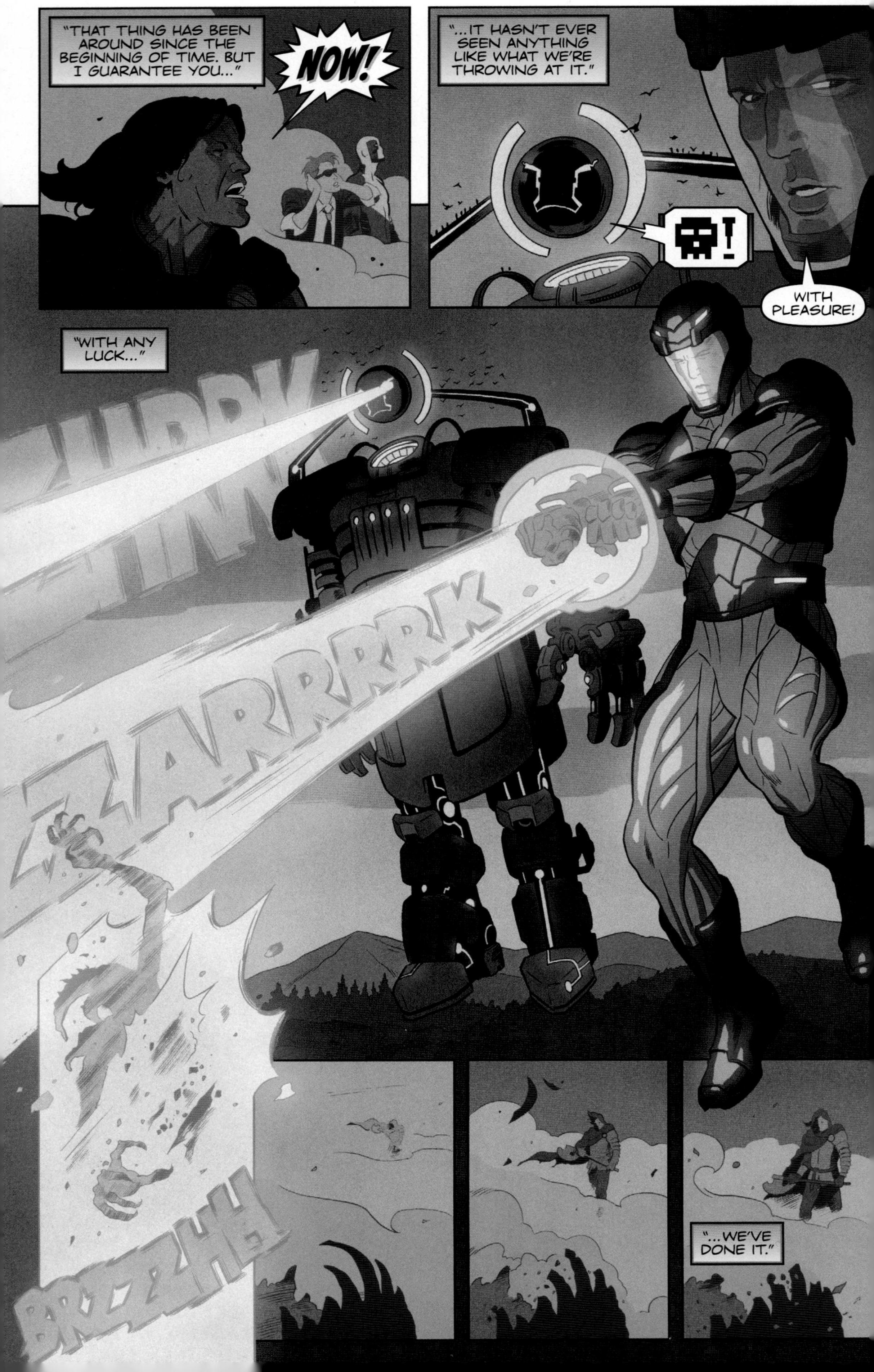
"THAT THING HAS BEEN AROUND SINCE THE BEGINNING OF TIME. BUT I GUARANTEE YOU..."
NOW!
"...IT HASN'T EVER SEEN ANYTHING LIKE WHAT WE'RE THROWING AT IT."
!
WITH PLEASURE!
"WITH ANY LUCK..."
ZARRRRK
BRZZHE
"...WE'VE DONE IT."

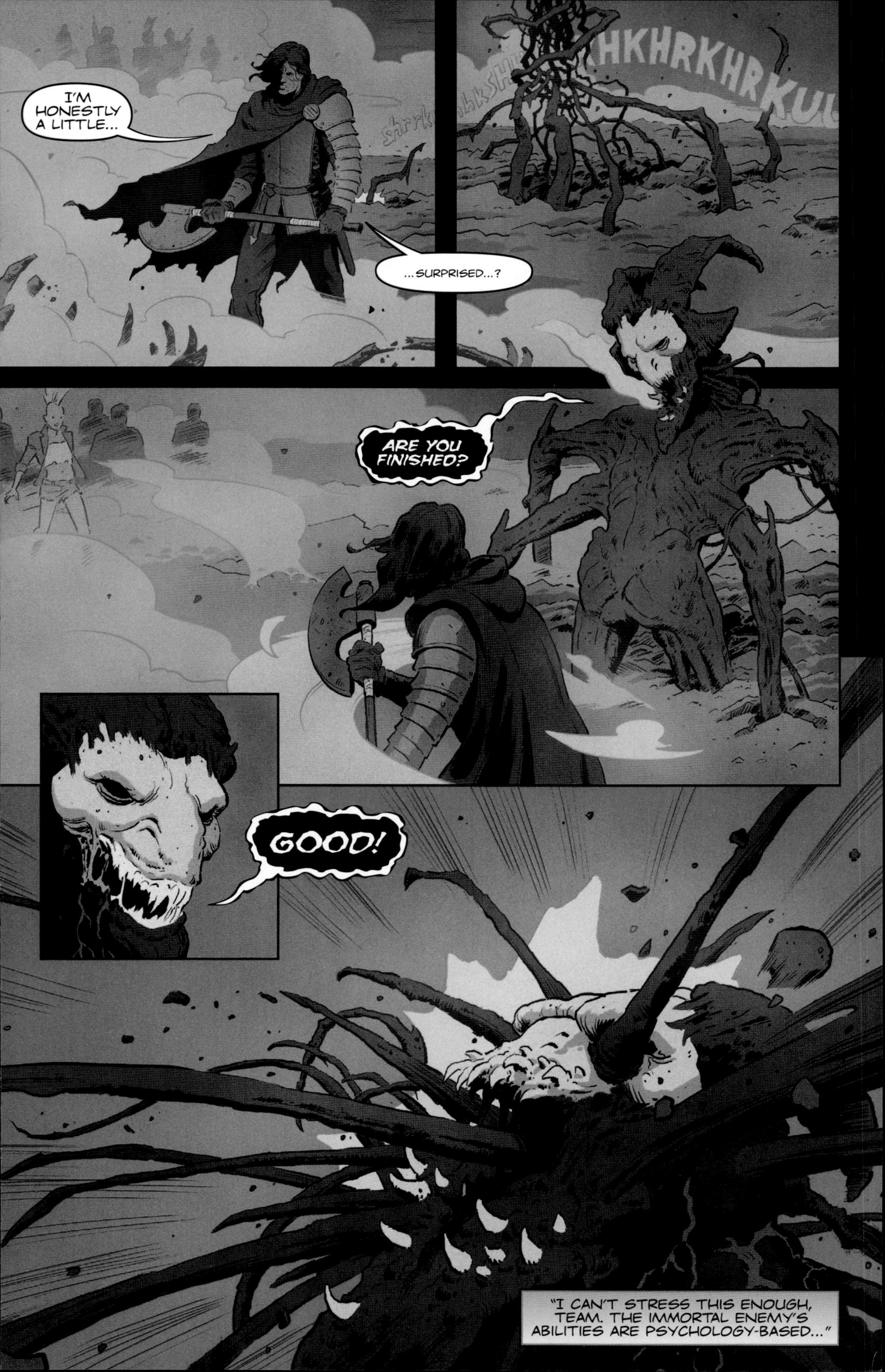

I'M HONESTLY A LITTLE...
...SURPRISED...?
HKHRKHRKUU
ARE YOU FINISHED?
GOOD!
"I CAN'T STRESS THIS ENOUGH, TEAM. THE IMMORTAL ENEMY'S ABILITIES ARE PSYCHOLOGY-BASED..."

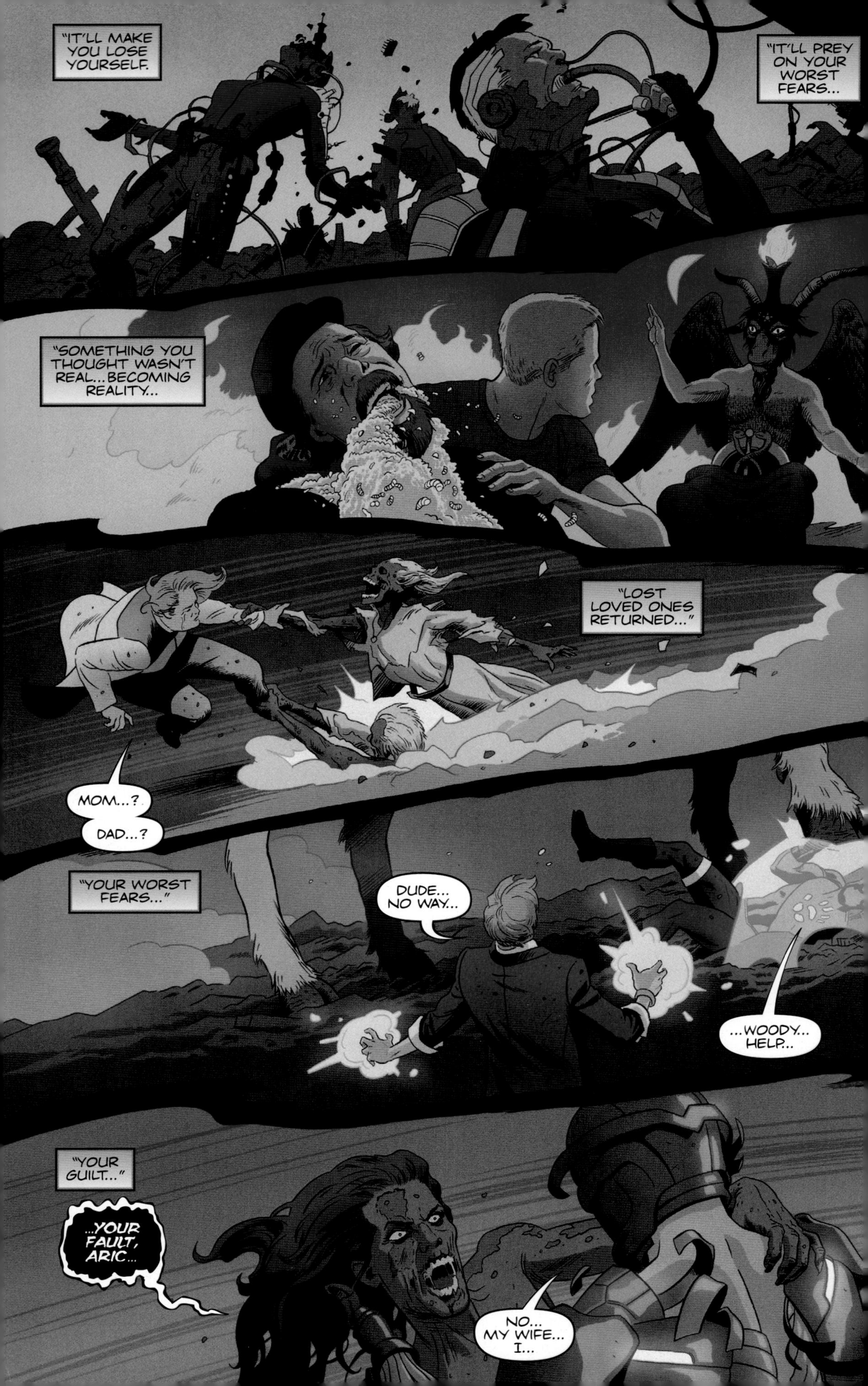
"IT'LL MAKE YOU LOSE YOURSELF.
"IT'LL PREY ON YOUR WORST FEARS...
"SOMETHING YOU THOUGHT WASN'T REAL...BECOMING REALITY...
"LOST LOVED ONES RETURNED..."
MOM...?
DAD...?
"YOUR WORST FEARS..."
DUDE... NO WAY...
...WOODY... HELP...
"YOUR GUILT..."
...YOUR FAULT, ARIC...
NO... MY WIFE... I...

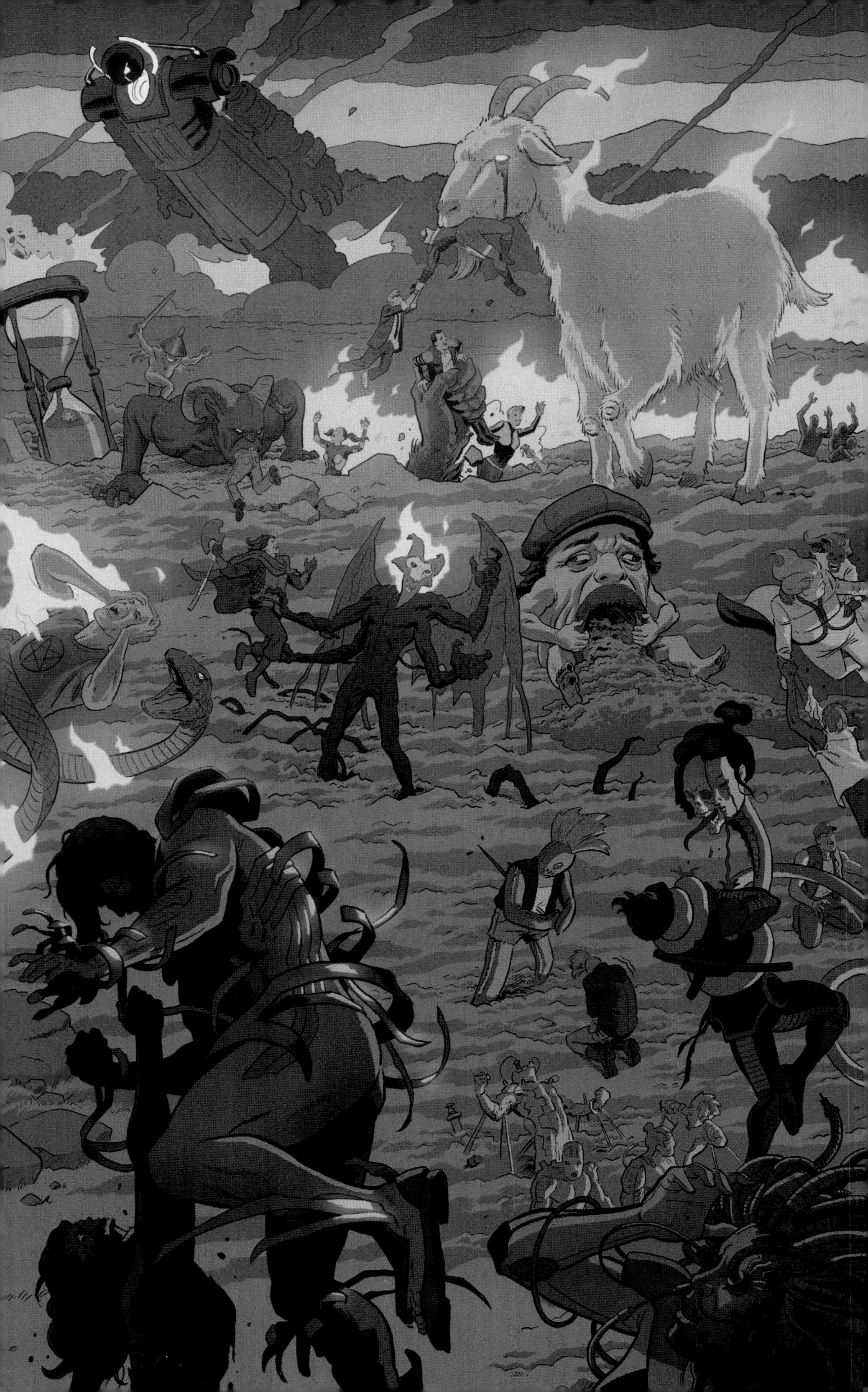

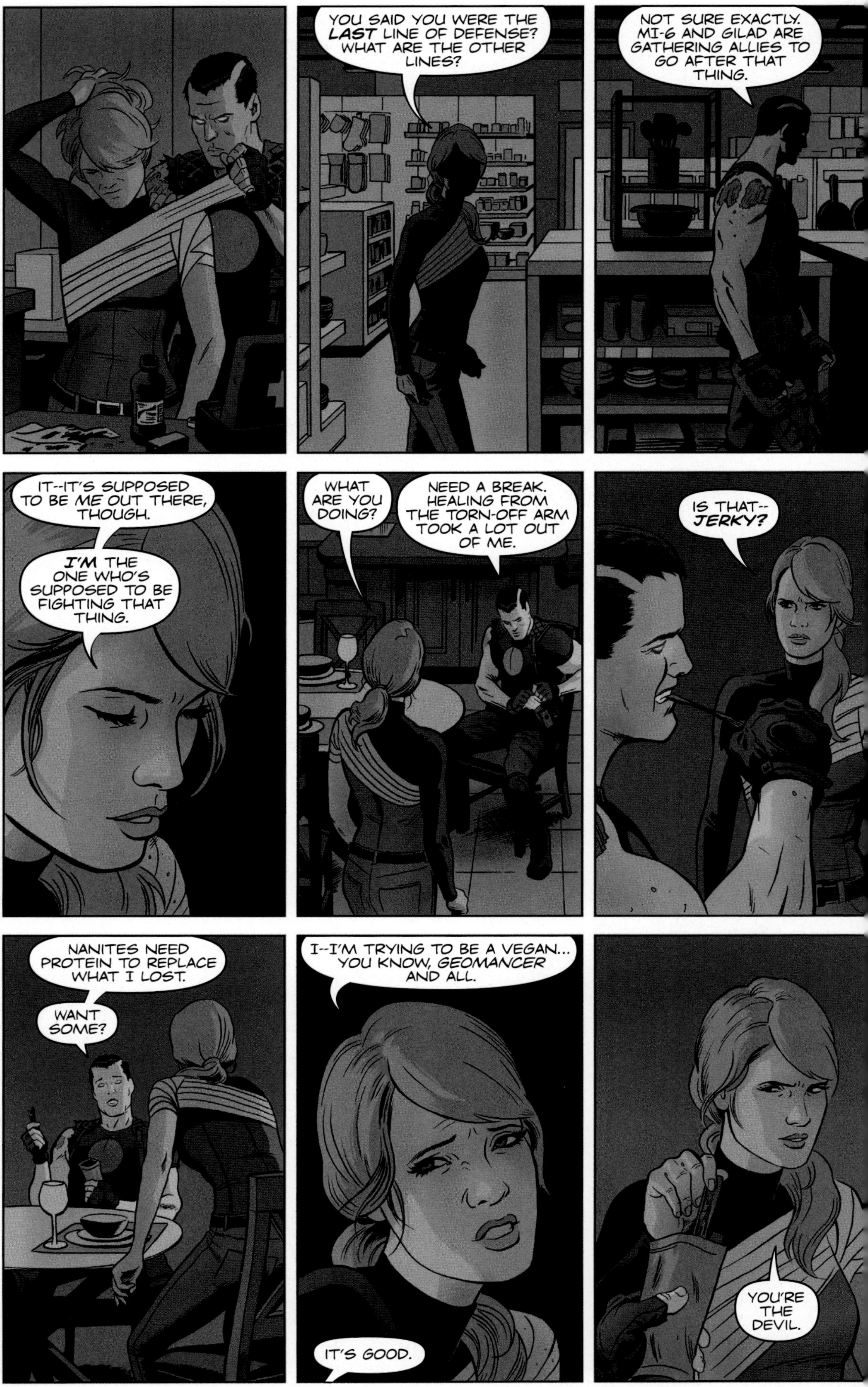
YOU SAID YOU WERE THE LAST LINE OF DEFENSE? WHAT ARE THE OTHER LINES?
NOT SURE EXACTLY. MI-6 AND GILAD ARE GATHERING ALLIES TO GO AFTER THAT THING.
IT--IT'S SUPPOSED TO BE ME OUT THERE, THOUGH.
I'M THE ONE WHO'S SUPPOSED TO BE FIGHTING THAT THING.
WHAT ARE YOU DOING?
NEED A BREAK. HEALING FROM THE TORN-OFF ARM TOOK A LOT OUT OF ME.
IS THAT-- JERKY?
NANITES NEED PROTEIN TO REPLACE WHAT I LOST.
WANT SOME?
I--I'M TRYING TO BE A VEGAN... YOU KNOW, GEOMANCER AND ALL.
IT'S GOOD.
YOU'RE THE DEVIL.

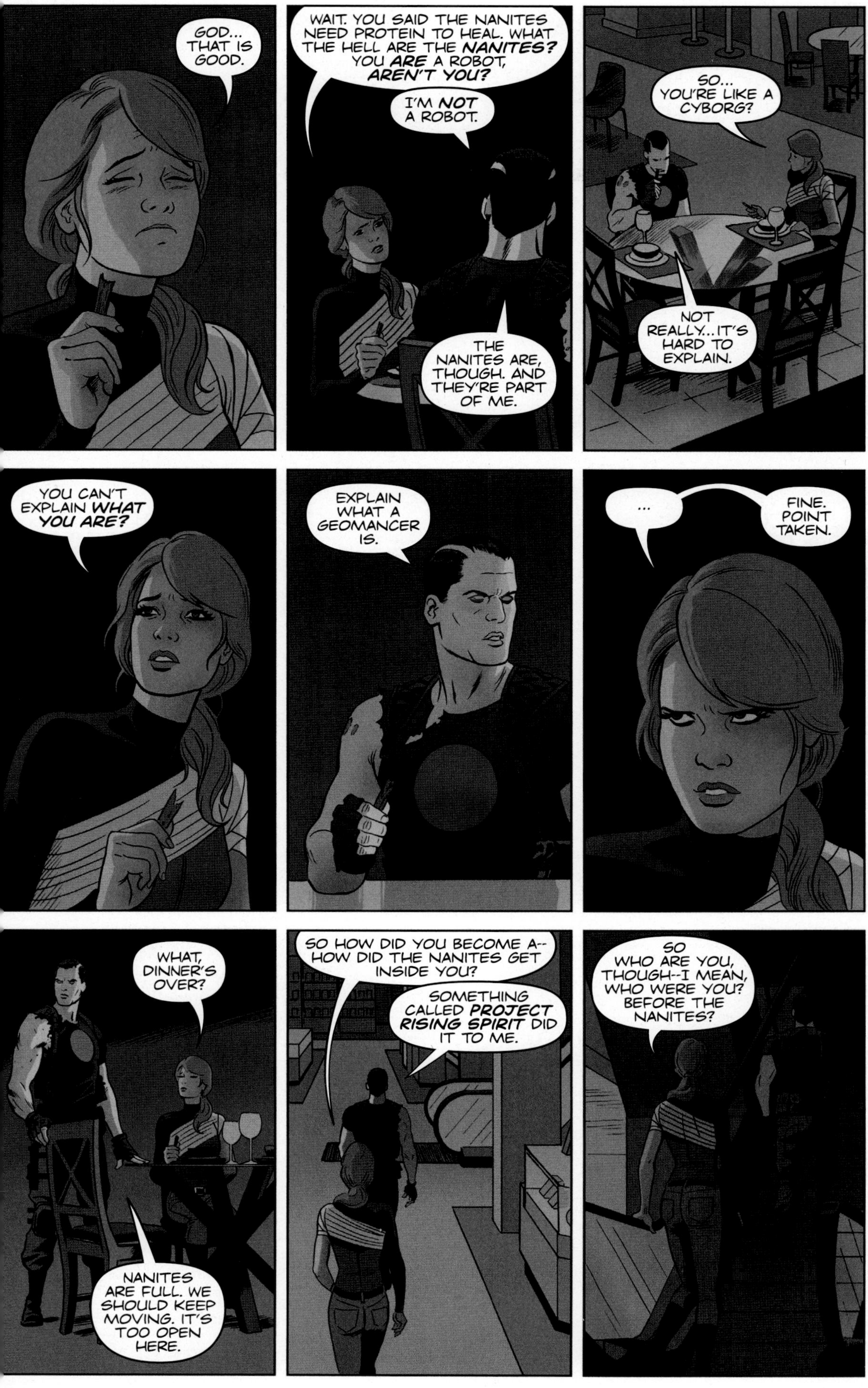
GOD... THAT IS GOOD.
WAIT. YOU SAID THE NANITES NEED PROTEIN TO HEAL. WHAT THE HELL ARE THE NANITES? YOU ARE A ROBOT, AREN'T YOU?
I'M NOT A ROBOT.
THE NANITES ARE, THOUGH. AND THEY'RE PART OF ME.
SO... YOU'RE LIKE A CYBORG?
NOT REALLY...IT'S HARD TO EXPLAIN.
YOU CAN'T EXPLAIN WHAT YOU ARE?
EXPLAIN WHAT A GEOMANCER IS.
...
FINE. POINT TAKEN.
WHAT, DINNER'S OVER?
NANITES ARE FULL. WE SHOULD KEEP MOVING. IT'S TOO OPEN HERE.
SO HOW DID YOU BECOME A-- HOW DID THE NANITES GET INSIDE YOU?
SOMETHING CALLED PROJECT RISING SPIRIT DID IT TO ME.
SO WHO ARE YOU, THOUGH--I MEAN, WHO WERE YOU? BEFORE THE NANITES?

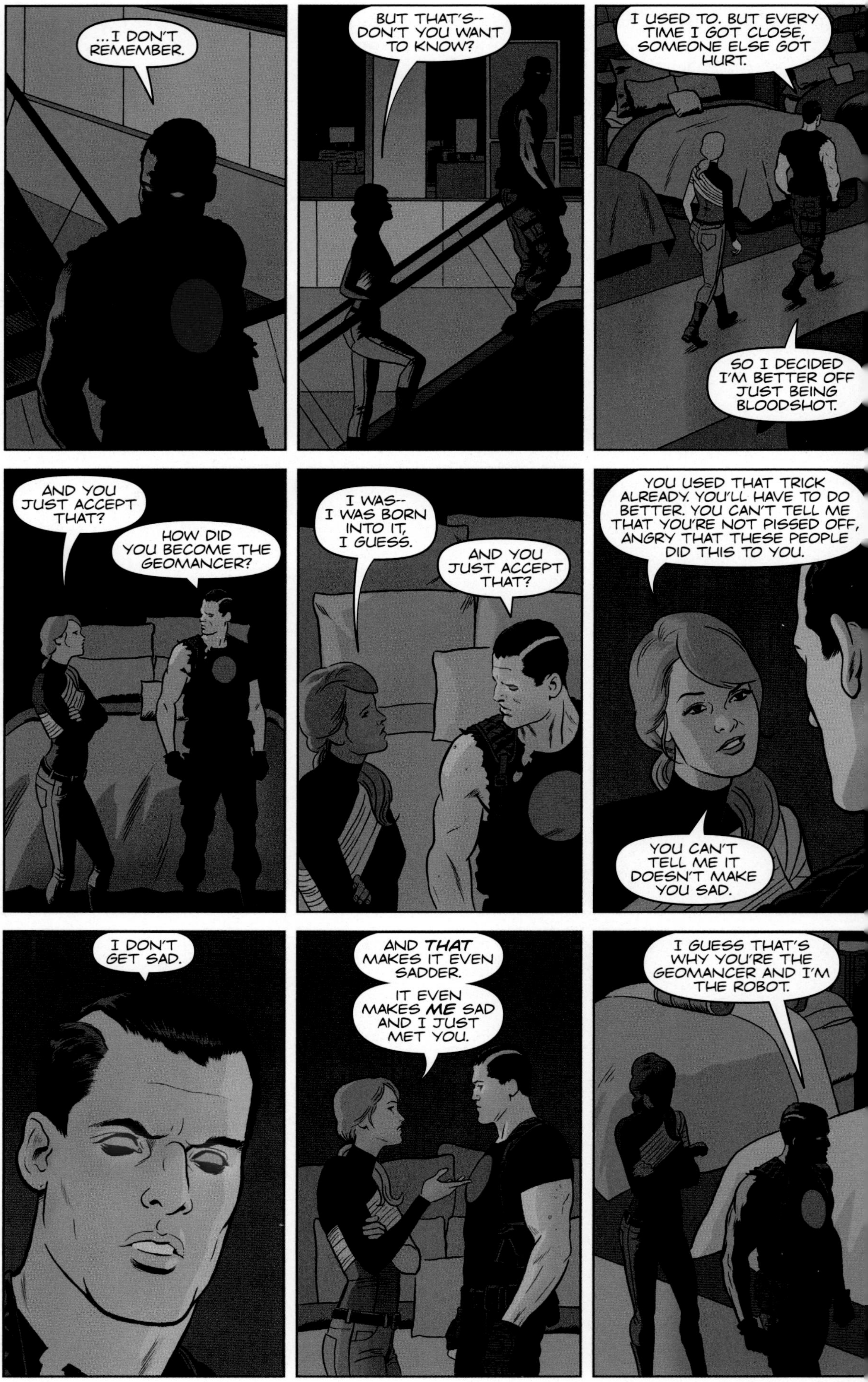
...I DON'T REMEMBER.
BUT THAT'S-- DON'T YOU WANT TO KNOW?
I USED TO. BUT EVERY TIME I GOT CLOSE, SOMEONE ELSE GOT HURT.
SO I DECIDED I'M BETTER OFF JUST BEING BLOODSHOT.
AND YOU JUST ACCEPT THAT?
HOW DID YOU BECOME THE GEOMANCER?
I WAS-- I WAS BORN INTO IT, I GUESS.
AND YOU JUST ACCEPT THAT?
YOU USED THAT TRICK ALREADY. YOU'LL HAVE TO DO BETTER. YOU CAN'T TELL ME THAT YOU'RE NOT PISSED OFF, ANGRY THAT THESE PEOPLE DID THIS TO YOU.
YOU CAN'T TELL ME IT DOESN'T MAKE YOU SAD.
I DON'T GET SAD.
AND THAT MAKES IT EVEN SADDER.
IT EVEN MAKES ME SAD AND I JUST MET YOU.
I GUESS THAT'S WHY YOU'RE THE GEOMANCER AND I'M THE ROBOT.

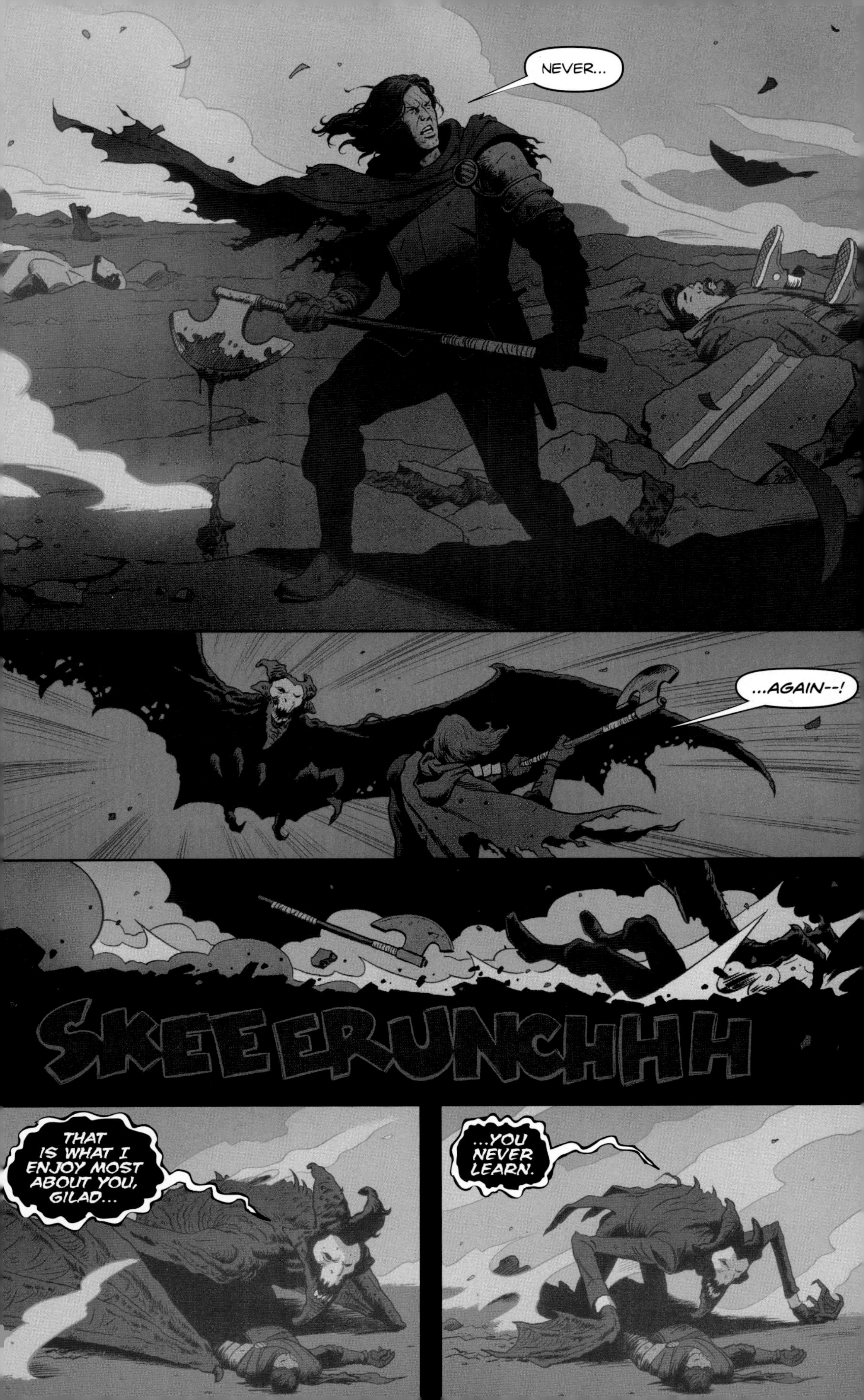
NEVER...
...AGAIN--!
SKEEERUNCHHH
THAT IS WHAT I ENJOY MOST ABOUT YOU, GILAD...
...YOU NEVER LEARN.

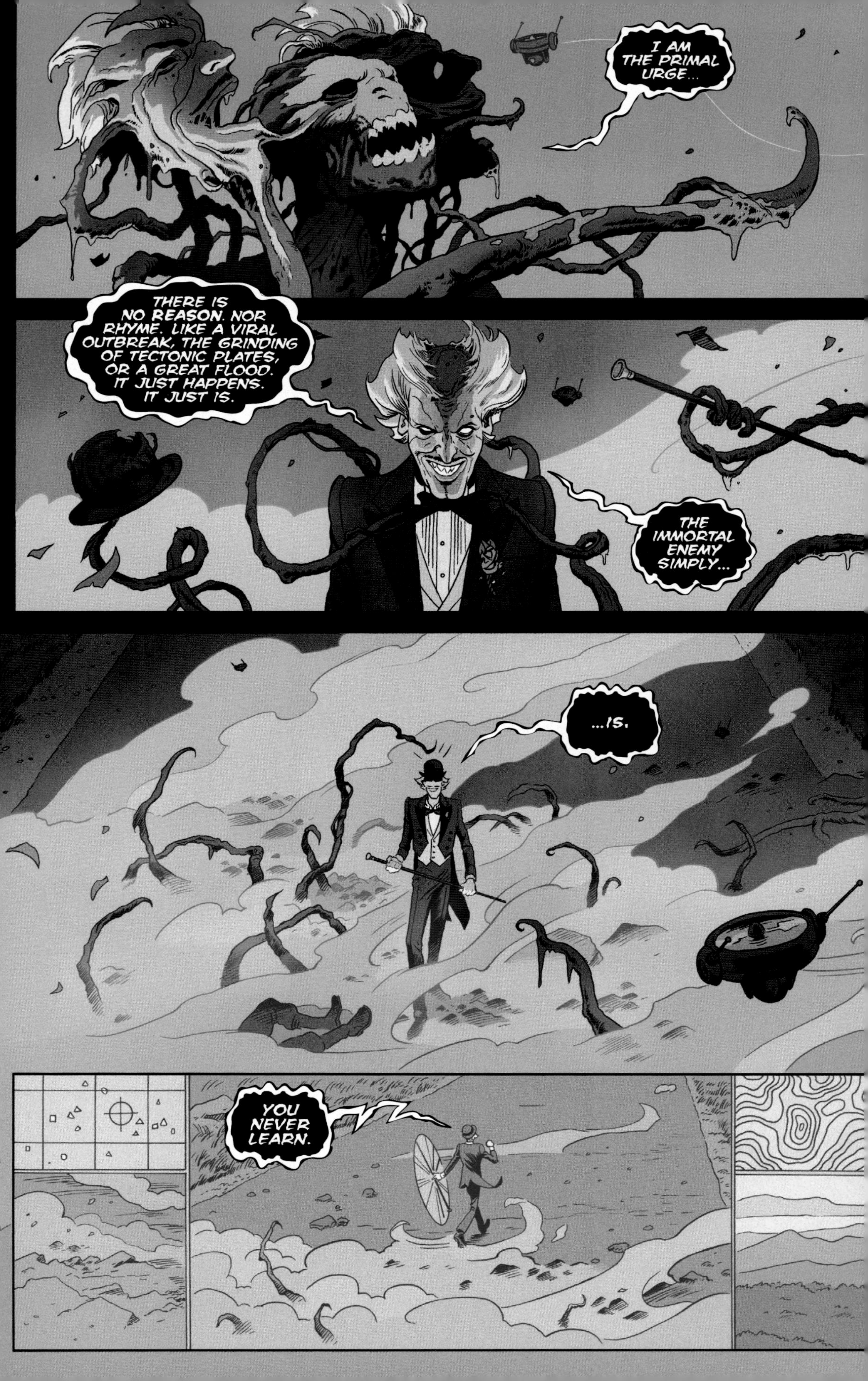
I AM THE PRIMAL URGE...
THERE IS NO REASON. NOR RHYME. LIKE A VIRAL OUTBREAK, THE GRINDING OF TECTONIC PLATES, OR A GREAT FLOOD. IT JUST HAPPENS. IT JUST IS.
THE IMMORTAL ENEMY SIMPLY...
...IS.
YOU NEVER LEARN.

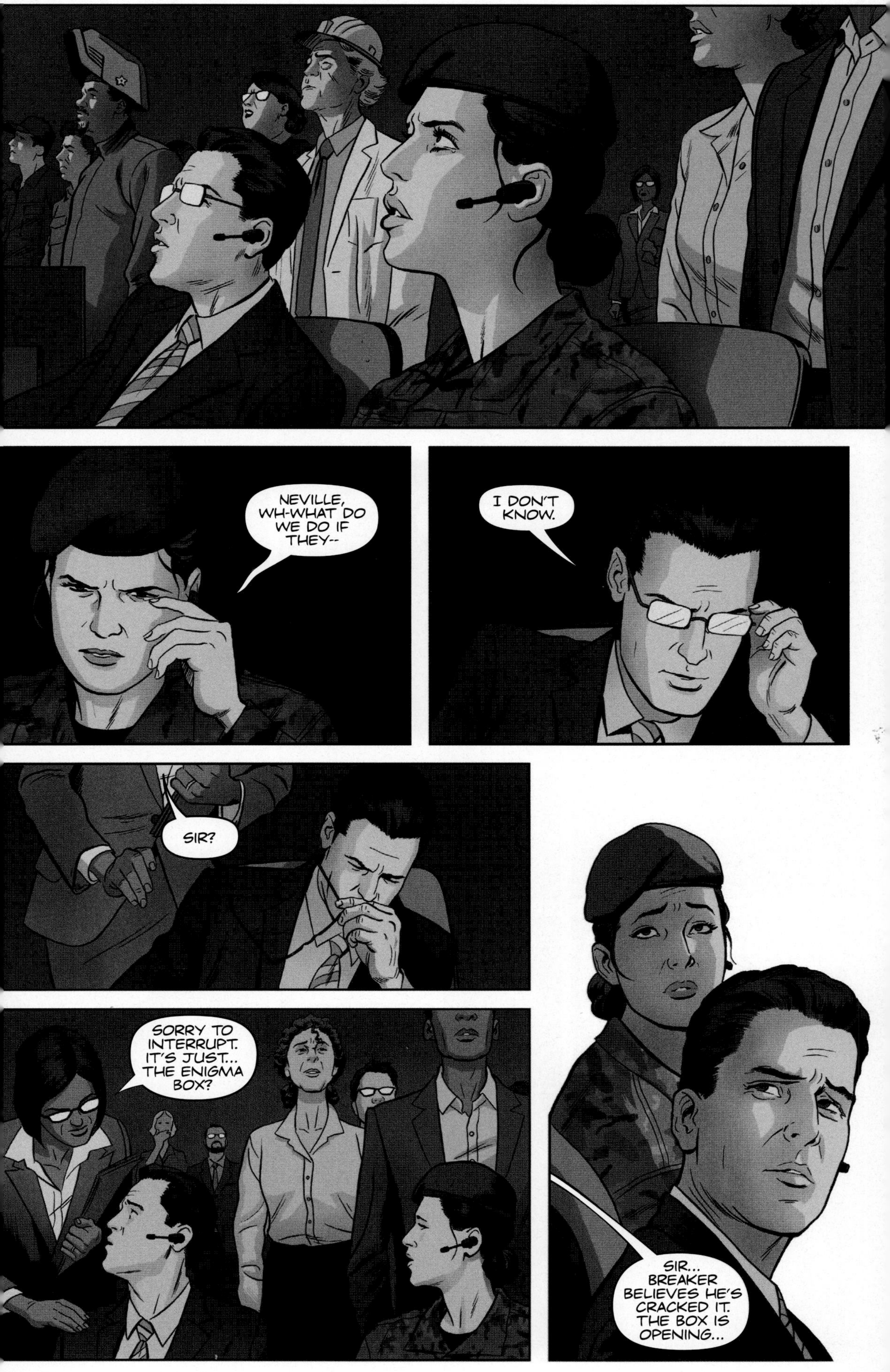
NEVILLE, WH-WHAT DO WE DO IF THEY--
I DON'T KNOW.
SIR?
SORRY TO INTERRUPT. IT'S JUST... THE ENIGMA BOX?
SIR... BREAKER BELIEVES HE'S CRACKED IT. THE BOX IS OPENING...

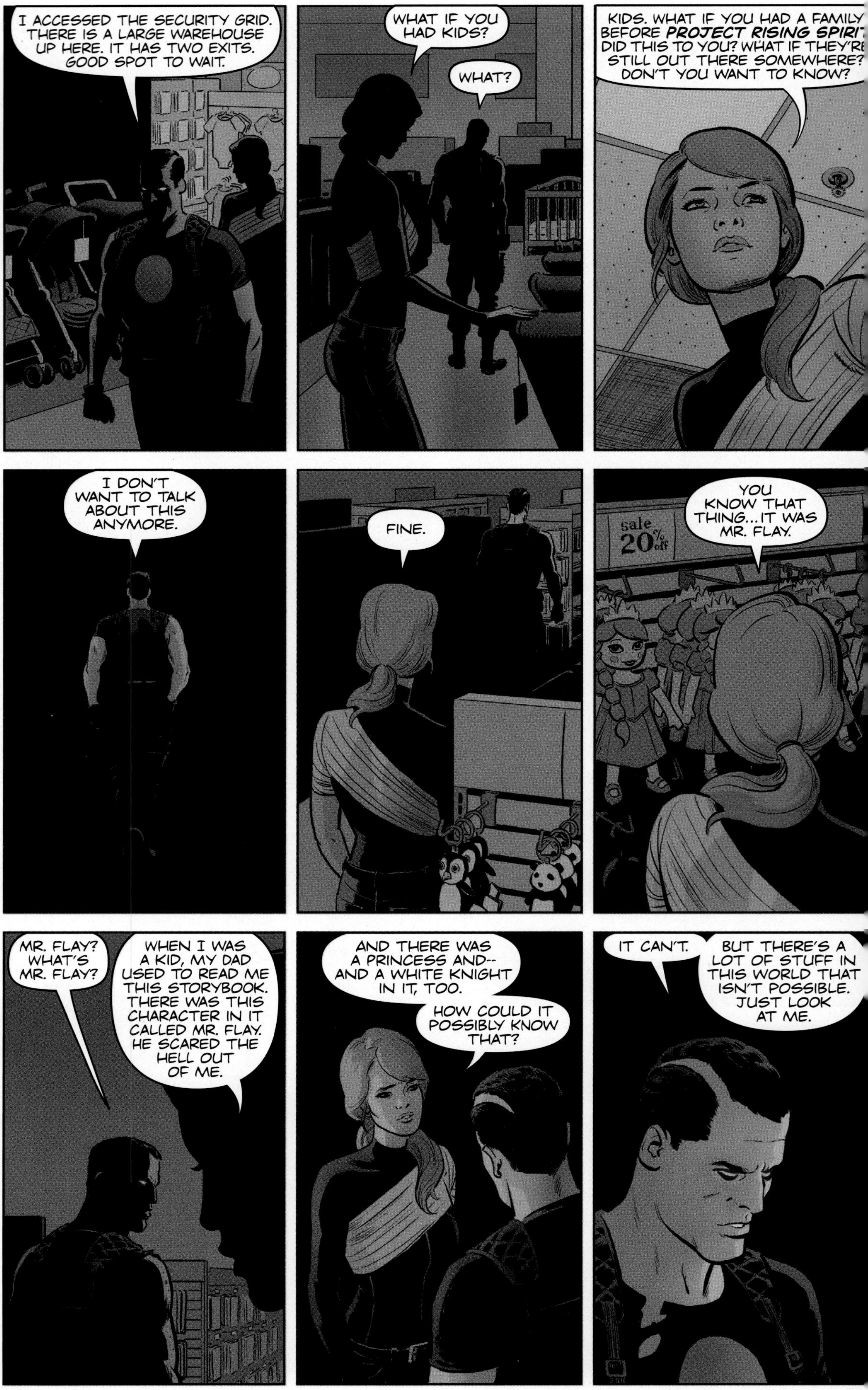

I ACCESSED THE SECURITY GRID. THERE IS A LARGE WAREHOUSE UP HERE. IT HAS TWO EXITS. GOOD SPOT TO WAIT.
WHAT IF YOU HAD KIDS?
WHAT?
KIDS. WHAT IF YOU HAD A FAMILY BEFORE PROJECT RISING SPIRIT DID THIS TO YOU? WHAT IF THEY'RE STILL OUT THERE SOMEWHERE? DON'T YOU WANT TO KNOW?
I DON'T WANT TO TALK ABOUT THIS ANYMORE.
FINE.
sale 20% off
YOU KNOW THAT THING...IT WAS MR. FLAY.
MR. FLAY? WHAT'S MR. FLAY?
WHEN I WAS A KID, MY DAD USED TO READ ME THIS STORYBOOK. THERE WAS THIS CHARACTER IN IT CALLED MR. FLAY. HE SCARED THE HELL OUT OF ME.
AND THERE WAS A PRINCESS AND-- AND A WHITE KNIGHT IN IT, TOO.
HOW COULD IT POSSIBLY KNOW THAT?
IT CAN'T.
BUT THERE'S A LOT OF STUFF IN THIS WORLD THAT ISN'T POSSIBLE. JUST LOOK AT ME.

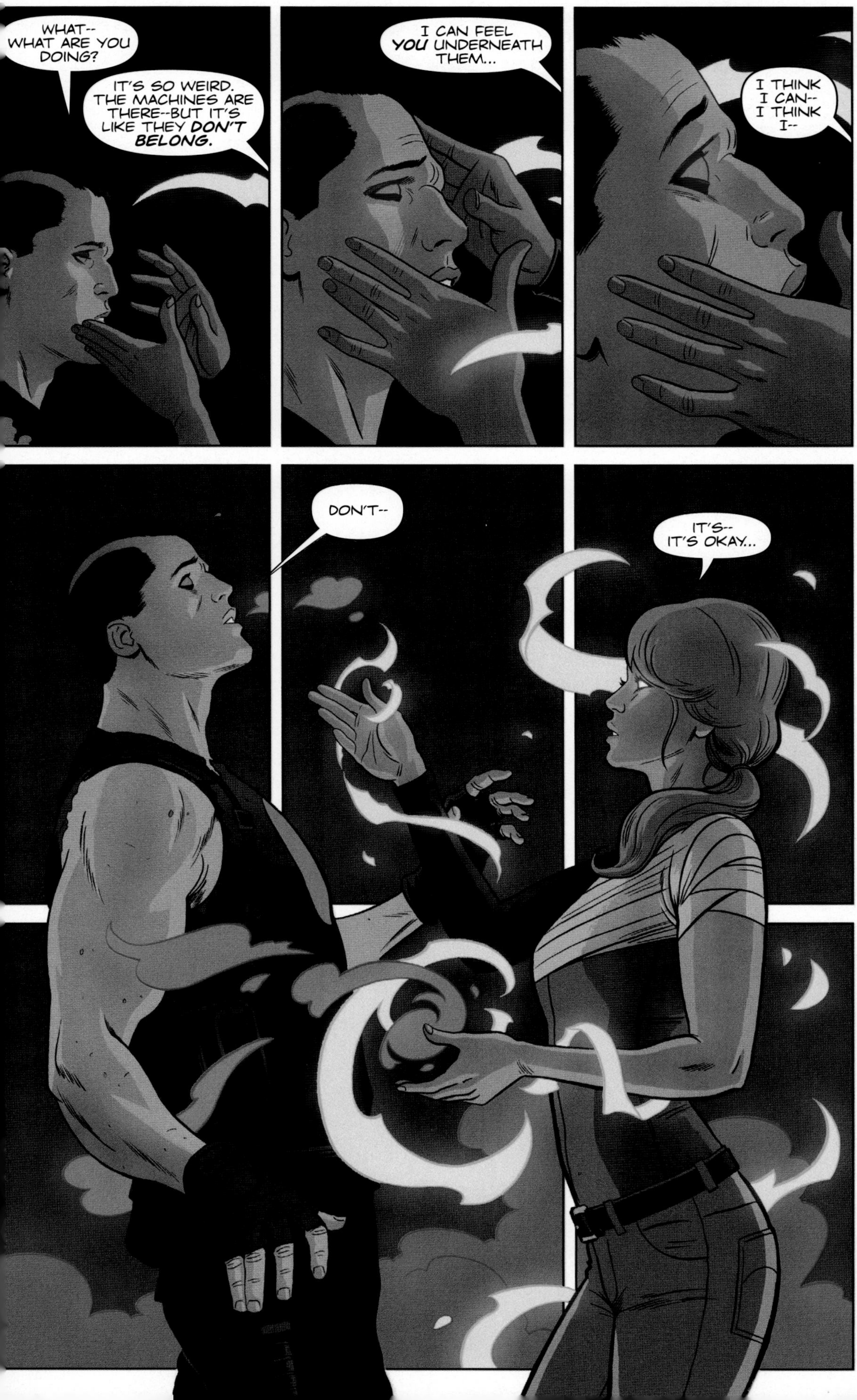
WHAT-- WHAT ARE YOU DOING?
IT'S SO WEIRD. THE MACHINES ARE THERE--BUT IT'S LIKE THEY **DON'T BELONG.**
I CAN FEEL **YOU** UNDERNEATH THEM...
I THINK I CAN-- I THINK I--
DON'T--
IT'S-- IT'S OKAY...

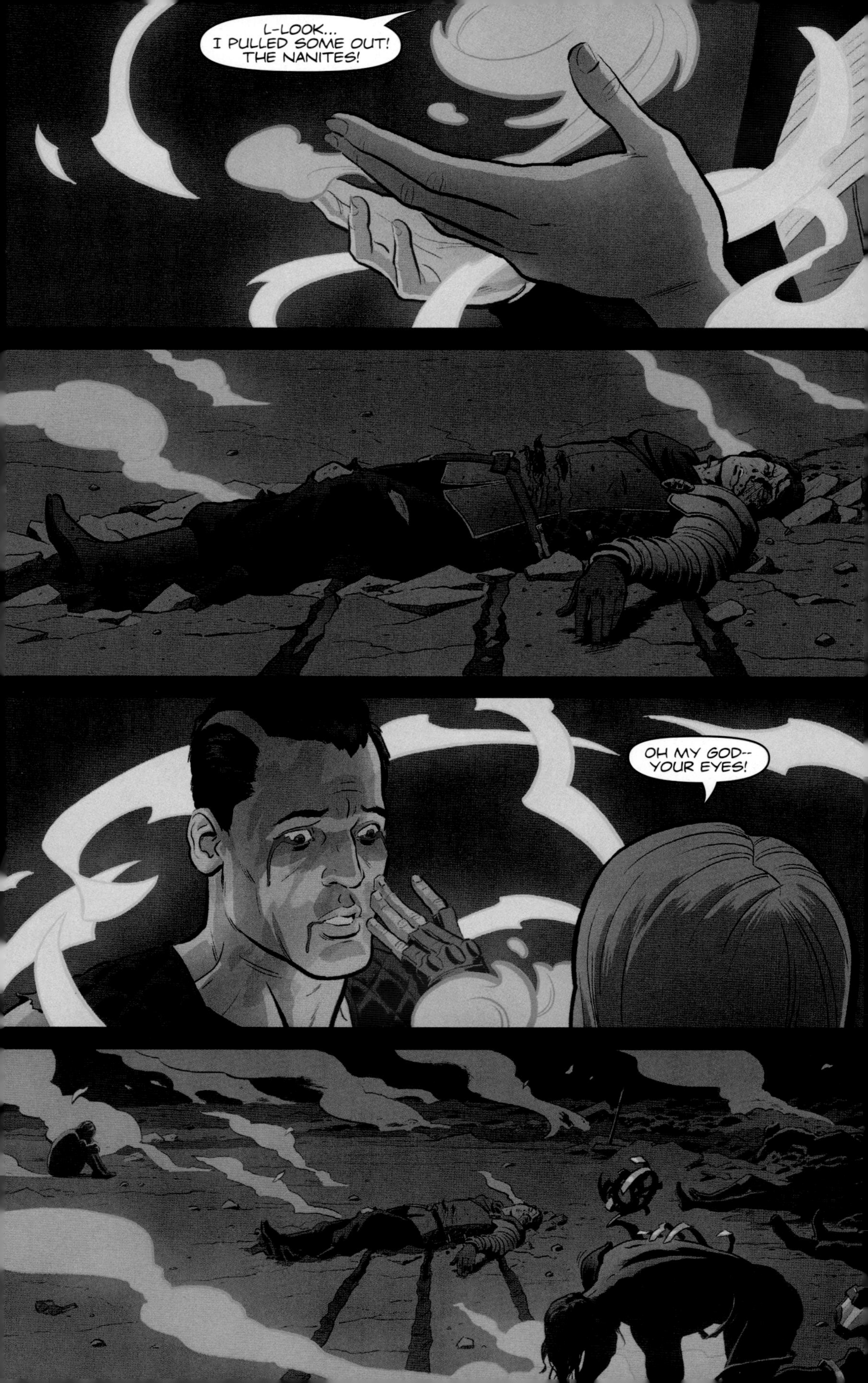
L-LOOK... I PULLED SOME OUT! THE NANITES!
OH MY GOD-- YOUR EYES!

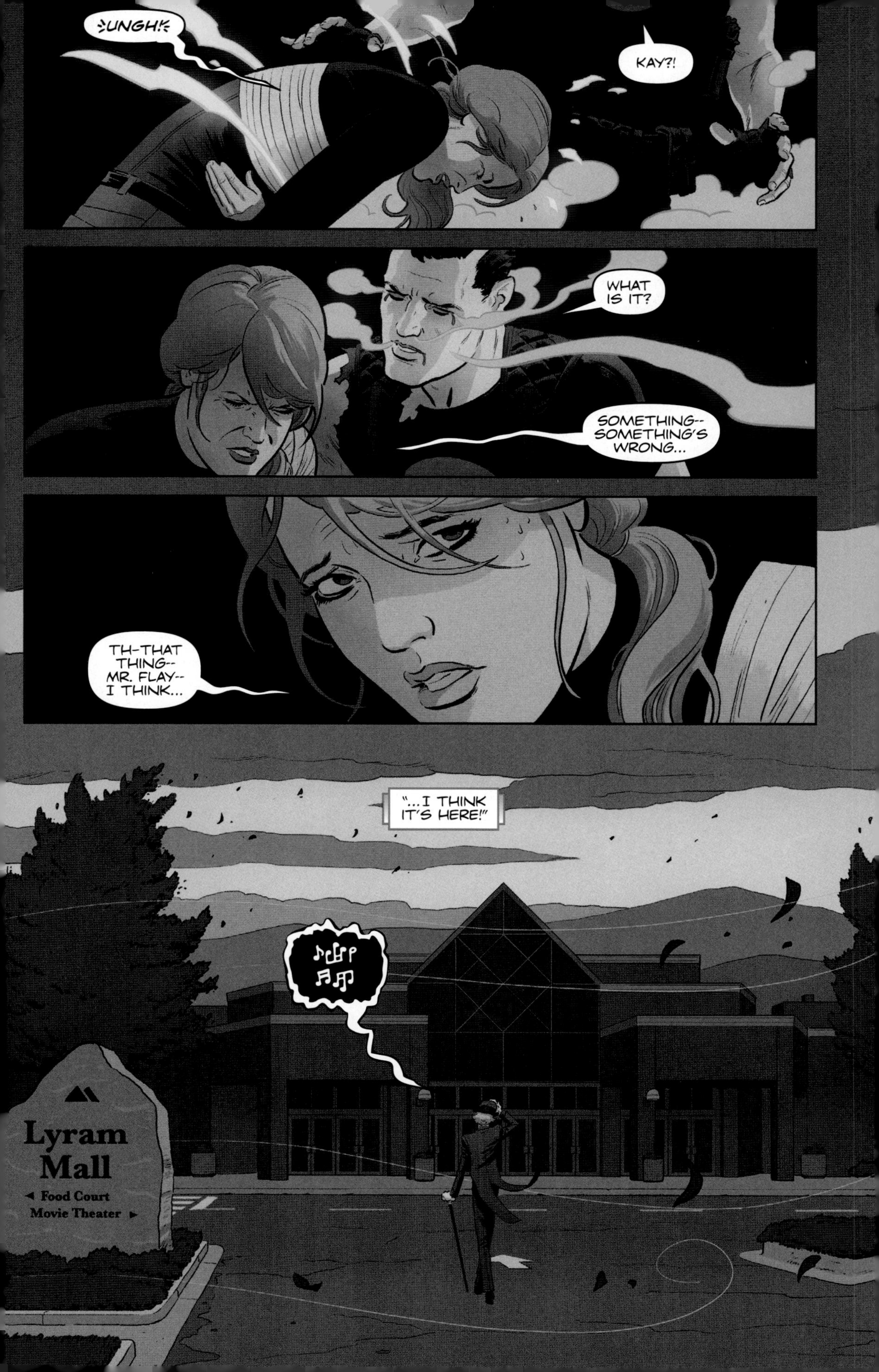
UNGH!
KAY?!
WHAT IS IT?
SOMETHING-- SOMETHING'S WRONG...
TH-THAT THING-- MR. FLAY-- I THINK...
"...I THINK IT'S HERE!"
Lyram Mall
◄ Food Court
Movie Theater ►

VALIANT
THE VALIANT
#4
JEFF LEMIR
MATT KIND
PAOLO RIVER
JOE RIVER

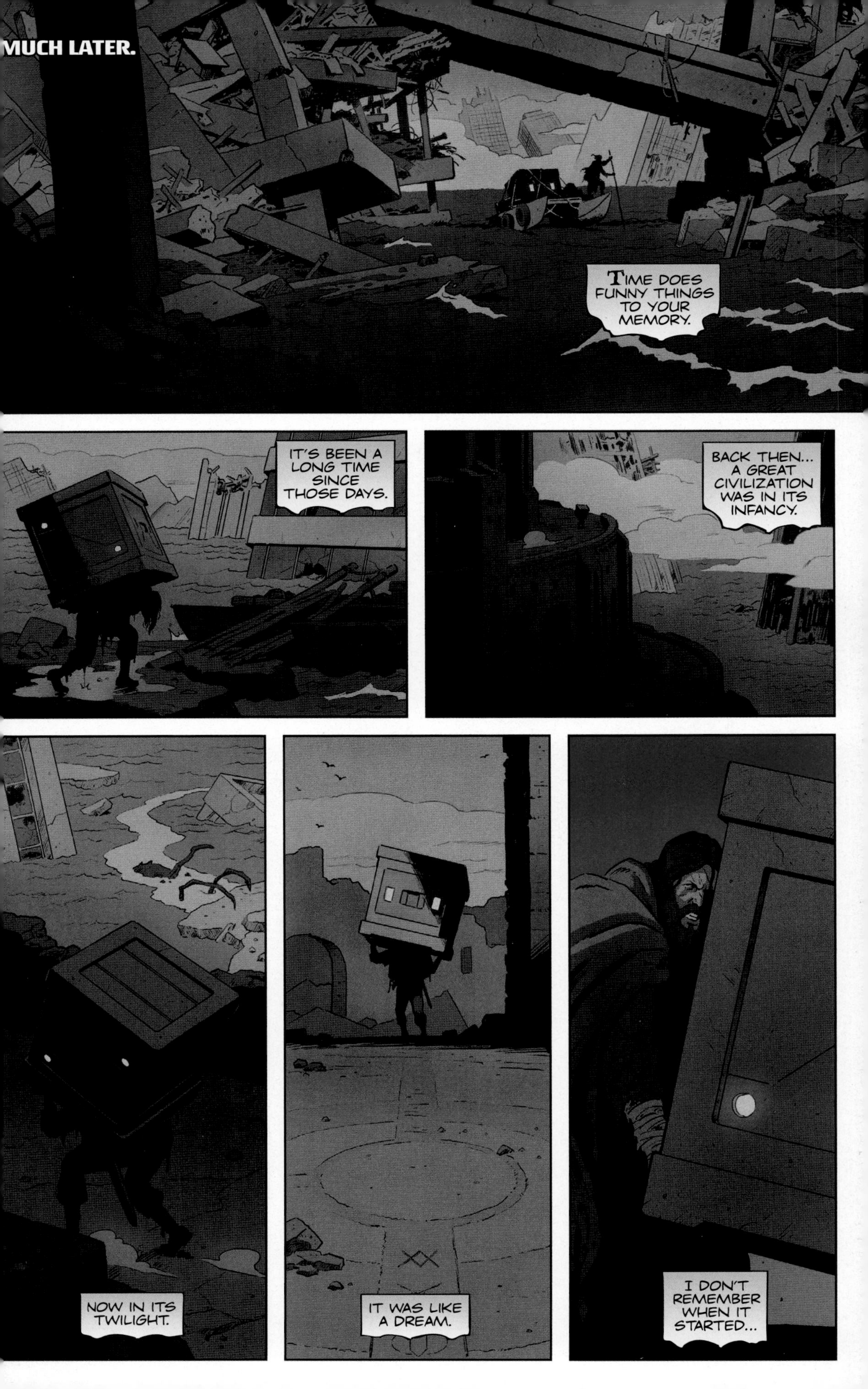
MUCH LATER.
TIME DOES FUNNY THINGS TO YOUR MEMORY.
IT'S BEEN A LONG TIME SINCE THOSE DAYS.
BACK THEN... A GREAT CIVILIZATION WAS IN ITS INFANCY.
NOW IN ITS TWILIGHT.
IT WAS LIKE A DREAM.
I DON'T REMEMBER WHEN IT STARTED...

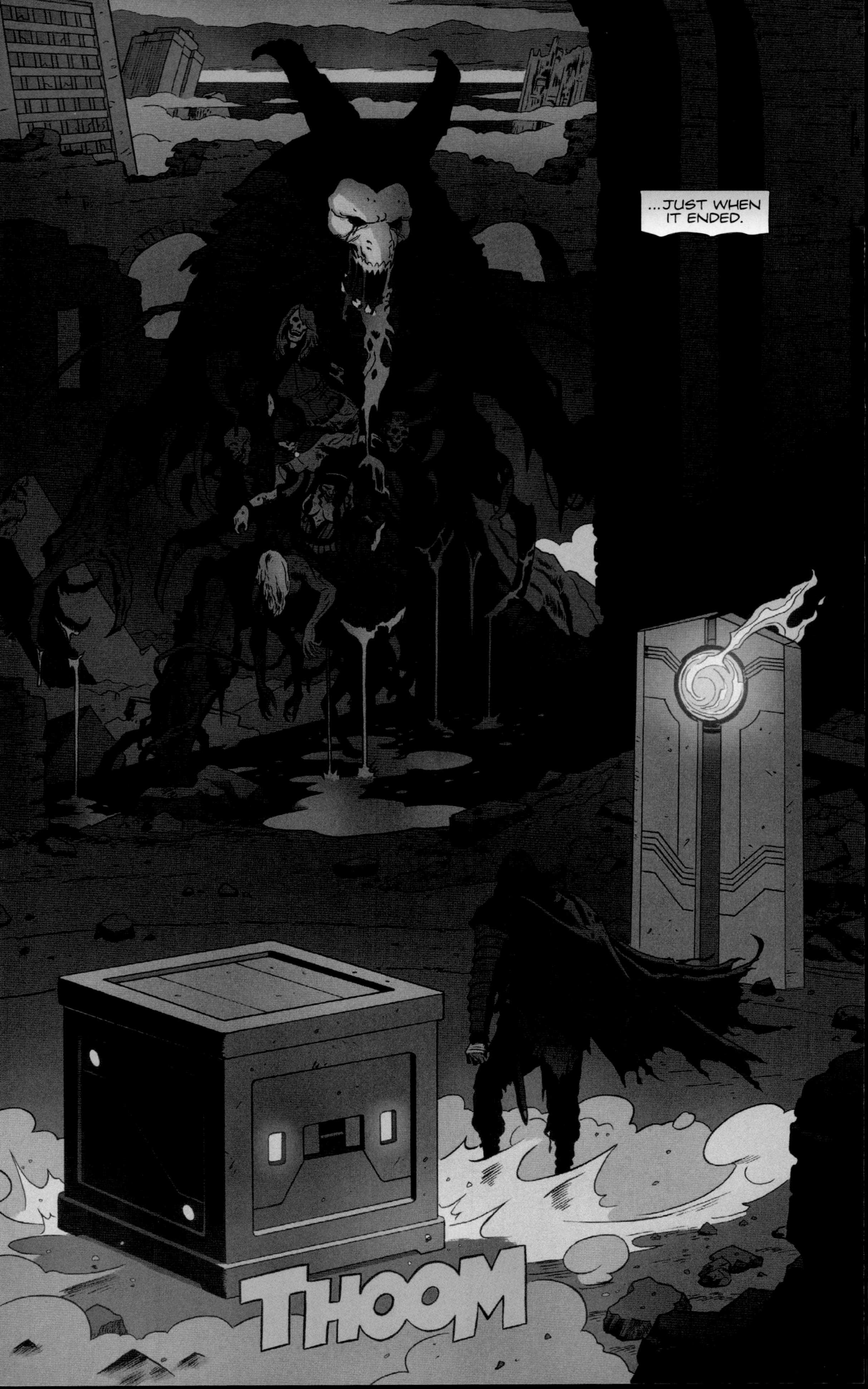
...JUST WHEN IT ENDED.
THOOM

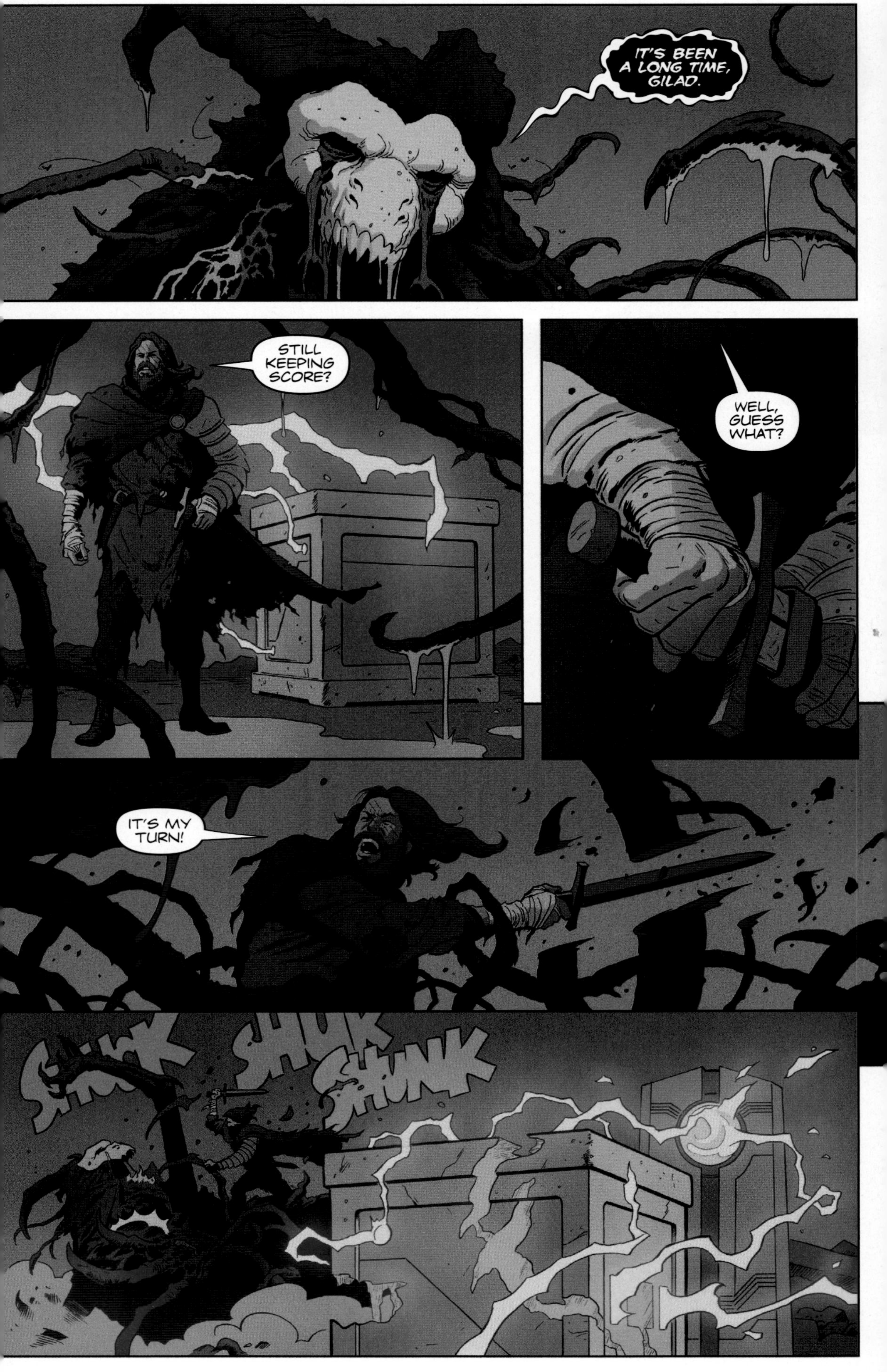
IT'S BEEN A LONG TIME, GILAD.
STILL KEEPING SCORE?
WELL, GUESS WHAT?
IT'S MY TURN!
SHUNK
SHUNK
SHUNK

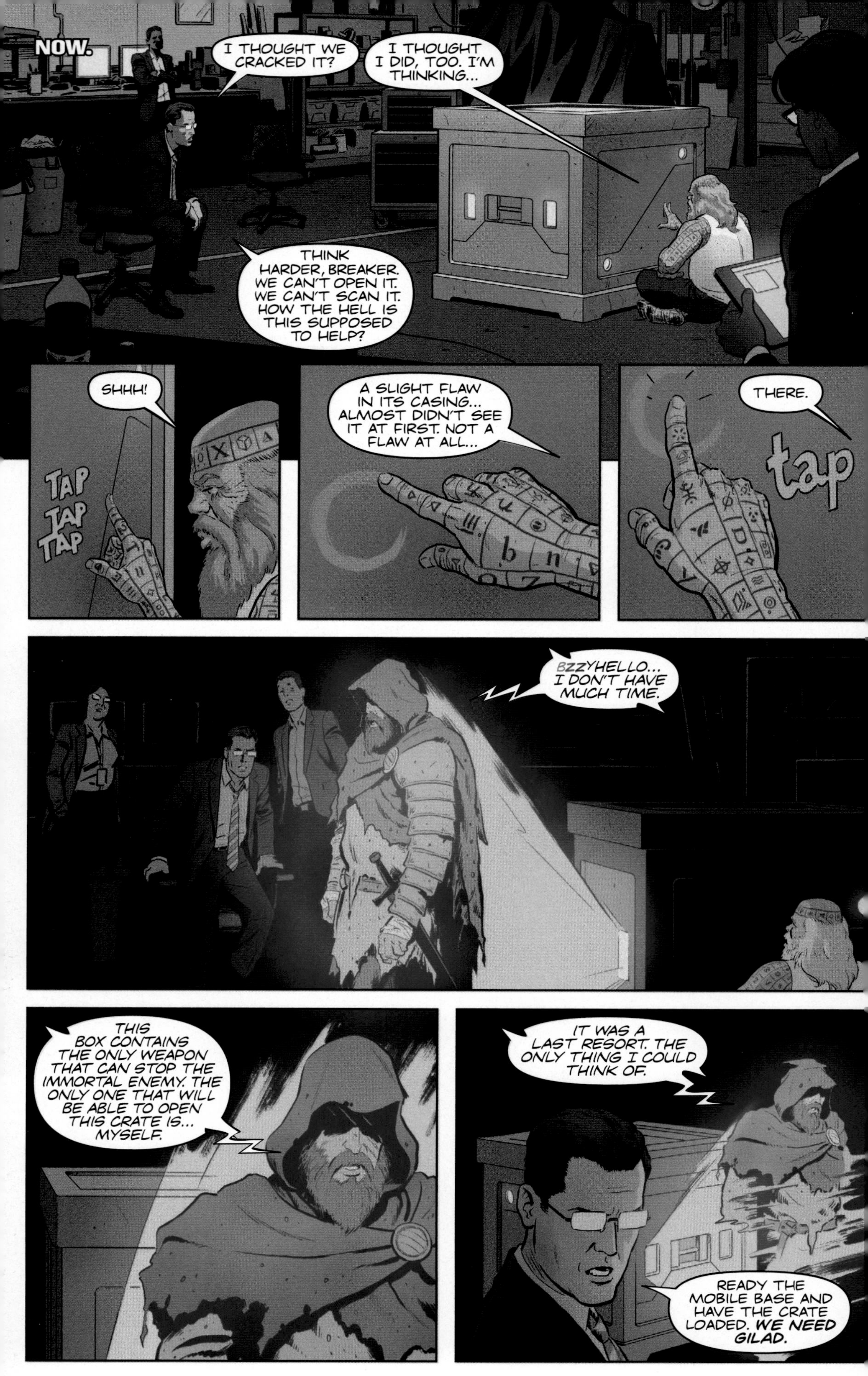
NOW.
I THOUGHT WE CRACKED IT?
I THOUGHT I DID, TOO. I'M THINKING...
THINK HARDER, BREAKER. WE CAN'T OPEN IT. WE CAN'T SCAN IT. HOW THE HELL IS THIS SUPPOSED TO HELP?
SHHH!
TAP TAP TAP
A SLIGHT FLAW IN ITS CASING... ALMOST DIDN'T SEE IT AT FIRST. NOT A FLAW AT ALL...
THERE.
tap
BZZYHELLO... I DON'T HAVE MUCH TIME.
THIS BOX CONTAINS THE ONLY WEAPON THAT CAN STOP THE IMMORTAL ENEMY. THE ONLY ONE THAT WILL BE ABLE TO OPEN THIS CRATE IS... MYSELF.
IT WAS A LAST RESORT. THE ONLY THING I COULD THINK OF.
READY THE MOBILE BASE AND HAVE THE CRATE LOADED. WE NEED GILAD.

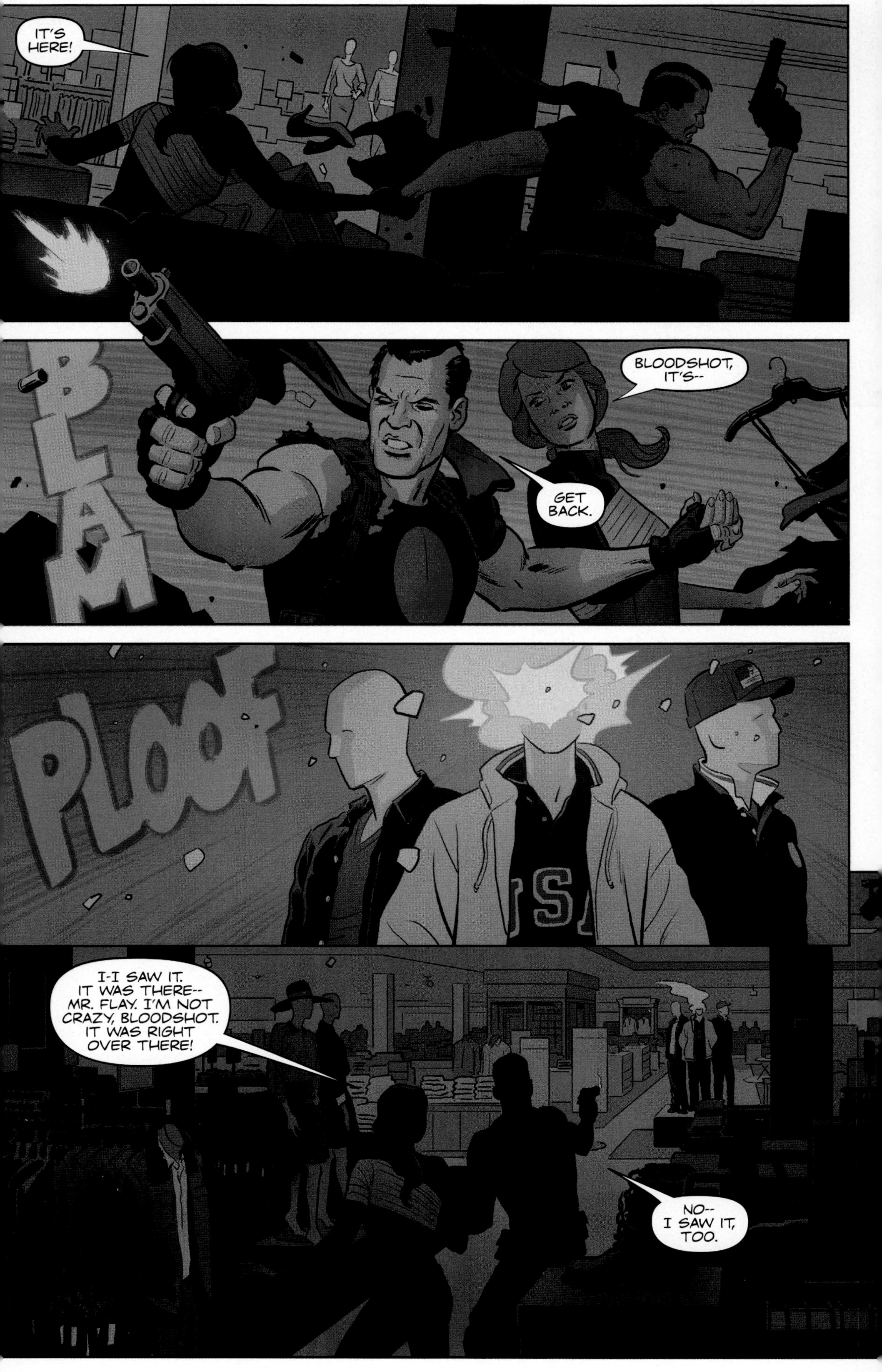
IT'S HERE!
BLAM
BLOODSHOT, IT'S--
GET BACK.
PLOOF
I-I SAW IT. IT WAS THERE-- MR. FLAY. I'M NOT CRAZY, BLOODSHOT. IT WAS RIGHT OVER THERE!
NO-- I SAW IT, TOO.

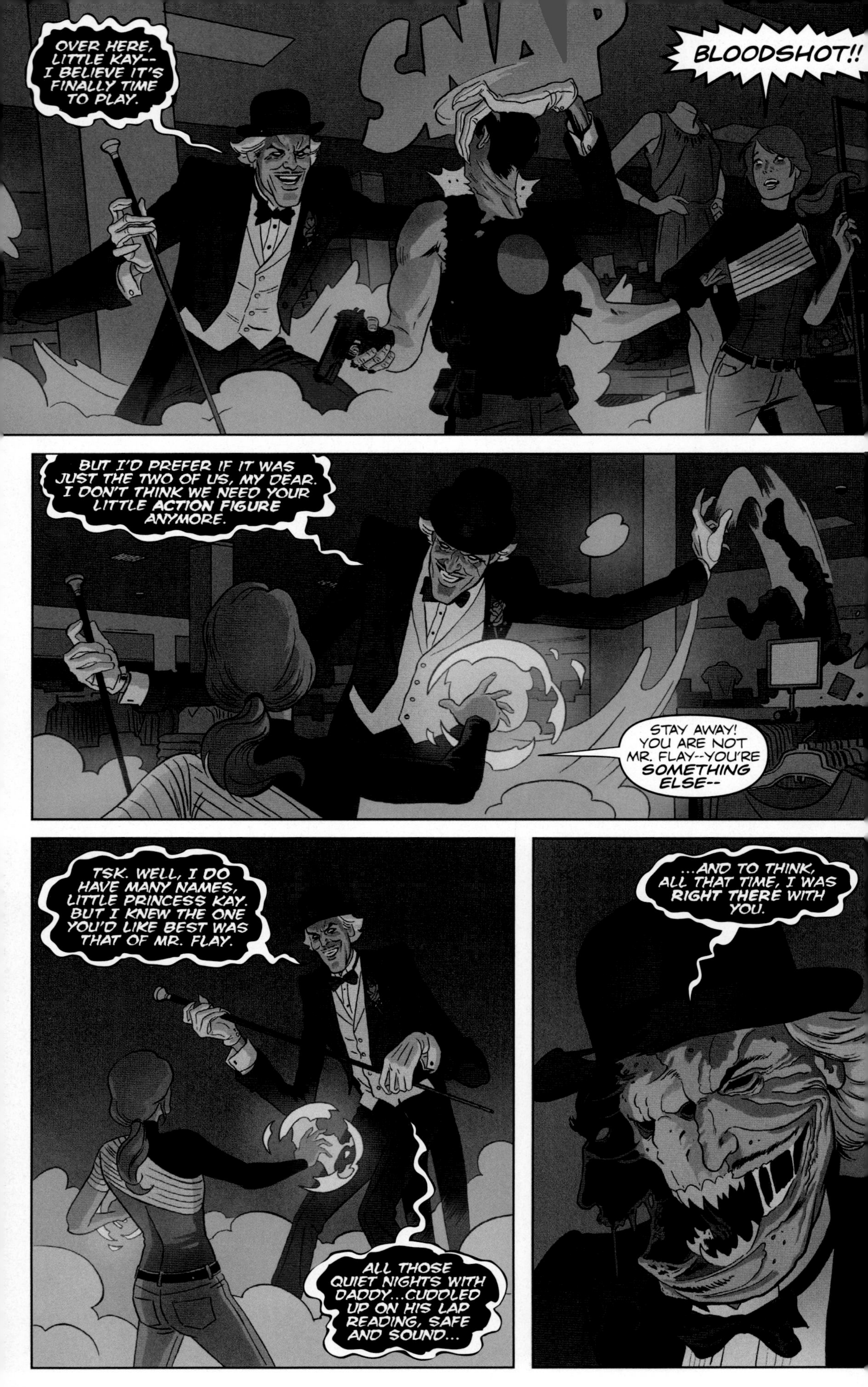
SNAP
OVER HERE, LITTLE KAY-- I BELIEVE IT'S FINALLY TIME TO PLAY.
BLOODSHOT!!
BUT I'D PREFER IF IT WAS JUST THE TWO OF US, MY DEAR. I DON'T THINK WE NEED YOUR LITTLE ACTION FIGURE ANYMORE.
STAY AWAY! YOU ARE NOT MR. FLAY--YOU'RE SOMETHING ELSE--
TSK. WELL, I DO HAVE MANY NAMES, LITTLE PRINCESS KAY. BUT I KNEW THE ONE YOU'D LIKE BEST WAS THAT OF MR. FLAY.
ALL THOSE QUIET NIGHTS WITH DADDY...CUDDLED UP ON HIS LAP READING, SAFE AND SOUND...
...AND TO THINK, ALL THAT TIME, I WAS RIGHT THERE WITH YOU.

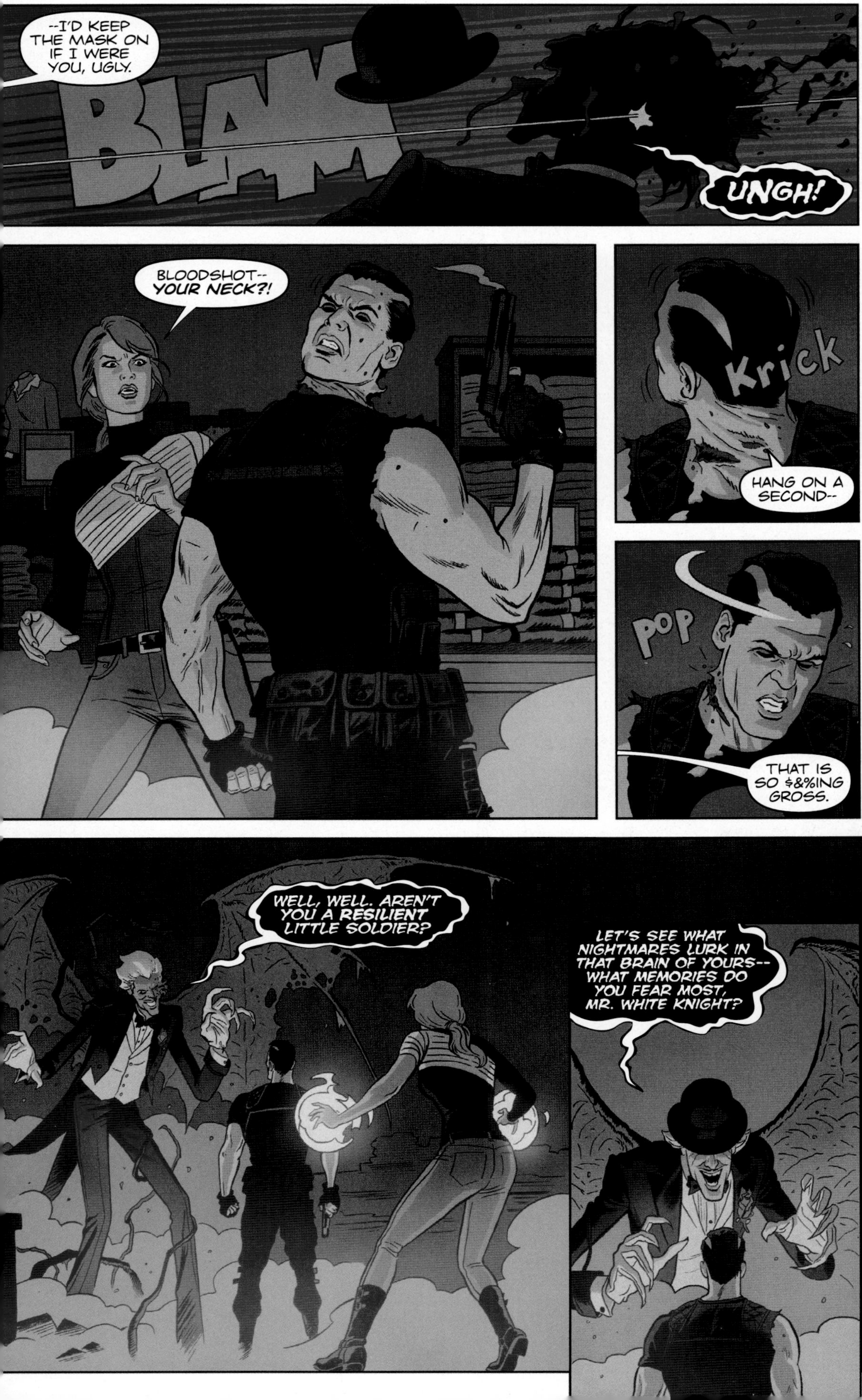
--I'D KEEP THE MASK ON IF I WERE YOU, UGLY.
BLAM
UNGH!
BLOODSHOT-- YOUR NECK?!
Krick
HANG ON A SECOND--
POP
THAT IS SO $&%ING GROSS.
WELL, WELL. AREN'T YOU A RESILIENT LITTLE SOLDIER?
LET'S SEE WHAT NIGHTMARES LURK IN THAT BRAIN OF YOURS-- WHAT MEMORIES DO YOU FEAR MOST, MR. WHITE KNIGHT?

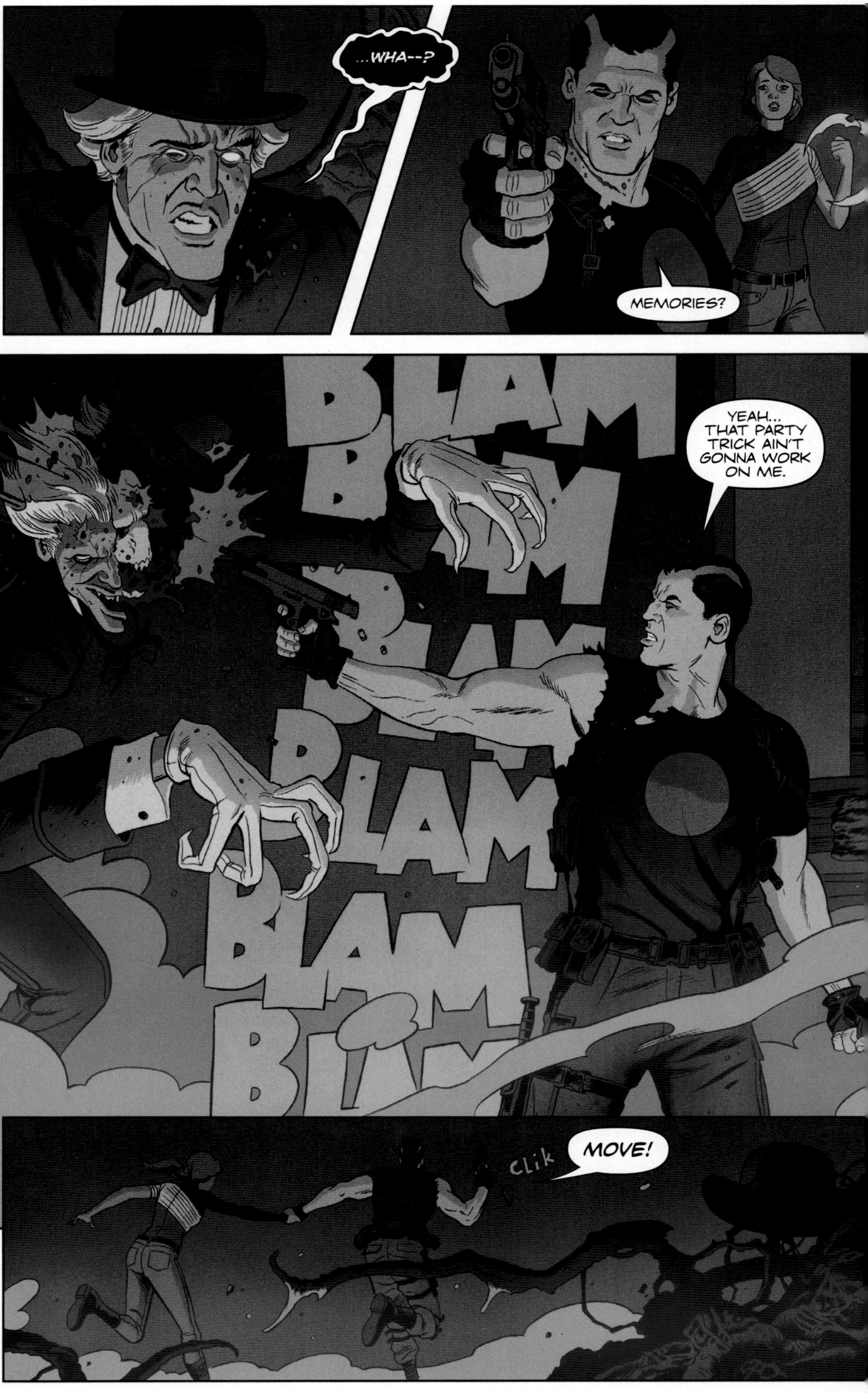
...WHA--?
MEMORIES?
BLAM BLAM BLAM BLAM BLAM BLAM BLAM
YEAH... THAT PARTY TRICK AIN'T GONNA WORK ON ME.
clik
MOVE!

WE MUST GO! WHOEVER CAN STILL FIGHT!

GILAD, WAIT!

NO! WE ARE RUNNING OUT OF TIME! *KAY* IS RUNNING OUT OF TIME!

LISTEN TO ME! NEVILLE IS EN ROUTE WITH THE CRATE. HE SAID-- HE SAID BREAKER WAS ABLE TO ACTIVATE IT AND THERE WAS A MESSAGE.

SO WHAT, NINJAK?! THIS IS IRRELEVANT NOW--WE HAVE TO FIGHT!

GILAD...THE MESSAGE WAS *FROM YOU.* FROM *THE FUTURE.*

YOU SAID IT CONTAINS THE ONLY WEAPON THAT WILL DEFEAT THAT THING. IT SAYS ONLY YOU CAN OPEN IT.

WHAT?! THAT'S IMPOSSIBLE. WE CAN'T WASTE ANY MORE TIME ON THIS NONSENSE! KAY IS IN DANGER. BLOODSHOT CAN'T STOP THAT THING. NOT ALONE.

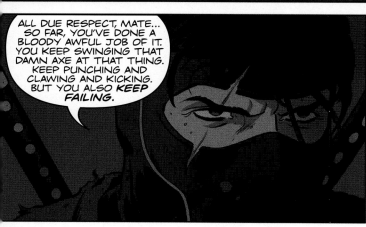

ALL DUE RESPECT, MATE... SO FAR, YOU'VE DONE A BLOODY AWFUL JOB OF IT. YOU KEEP SWINGING THAT DAMN AXE AT THAT THING. KEEP PUNCHING AND CLAWING AND KICKING. BUT YOU ALSO KEEP *FAILING.*

IF YOU WON'T LISTEN TO ME, *LISTEN TO YOURSELF.* IT'S TIME YOU TRIED A *DIFFERENT WAY.*

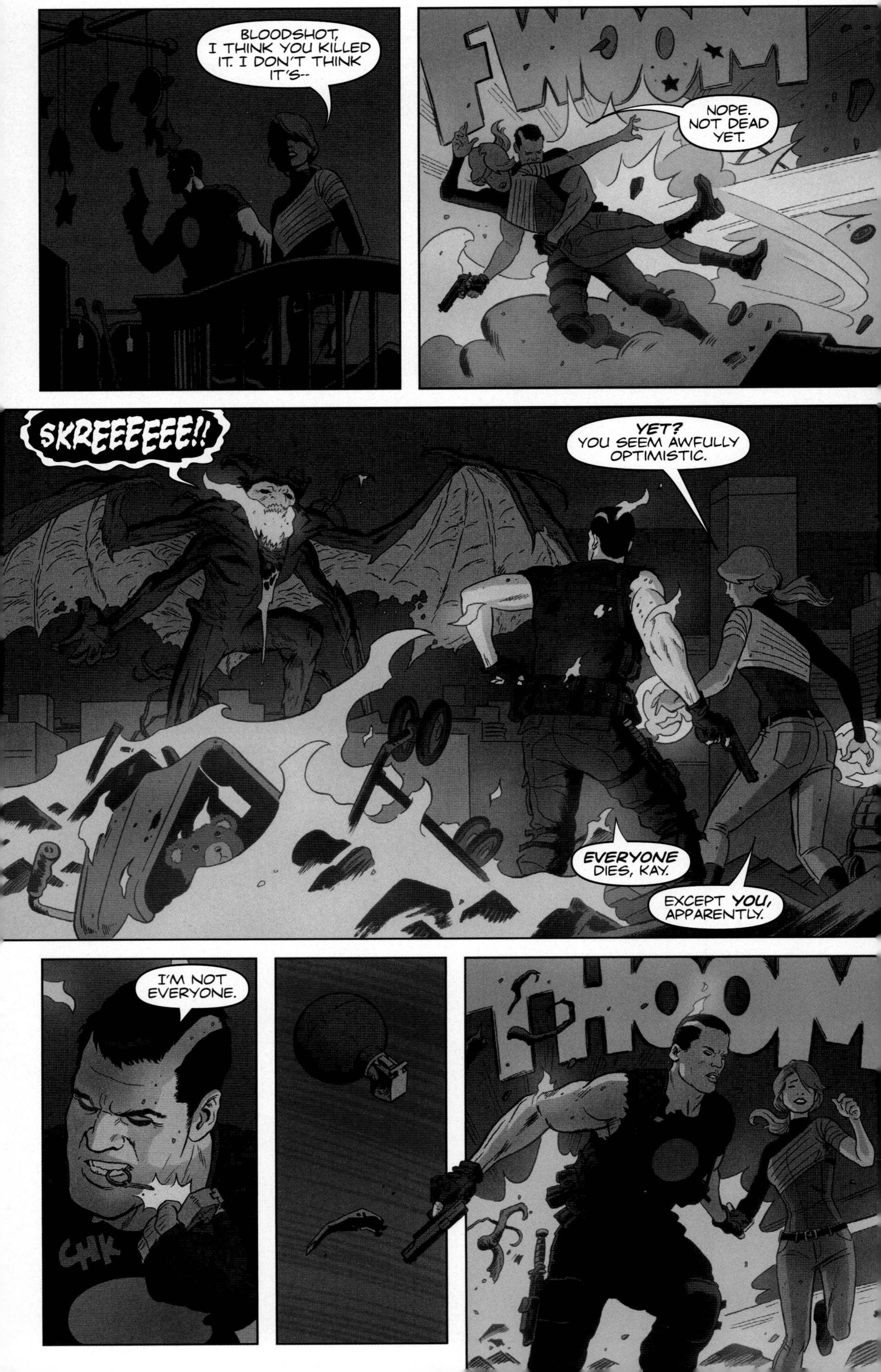
BLOODSHOT, I THINK YOU KILLED IT. I DON'T THINK IT'S--
FWOOM
NOPE. NOT DEAD YET.
SKREEEEEEE!!
YET? YOU SEEM AWFULLY OPTIMISTIC.
EVERYONE DIES, KAY.
EXCEPT YOU, APPARENTLY.
I'M NOT EVERYONE.
CHK
THOOM

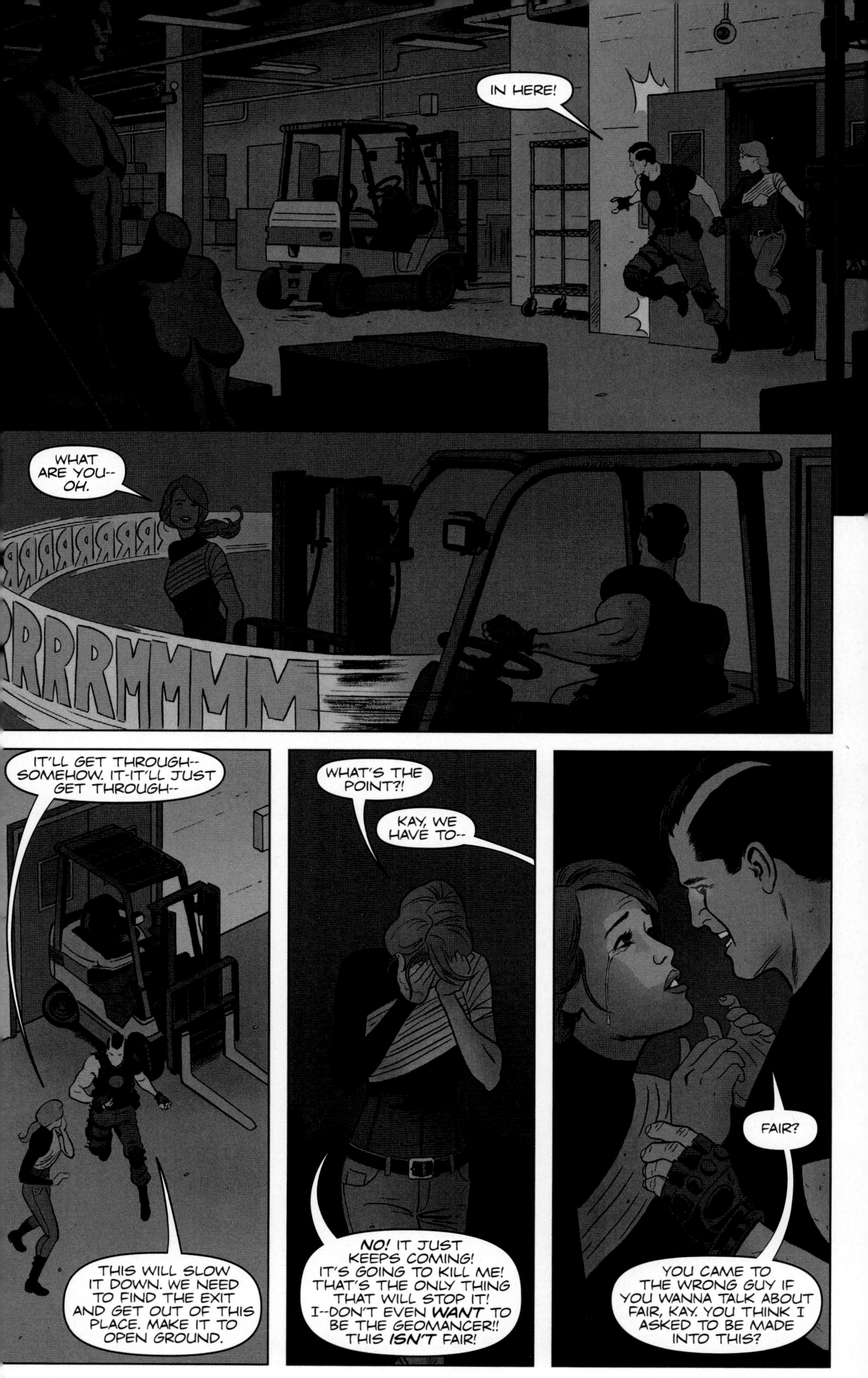
IN HERE!
WHAT ARE YOU-- OH.
RRRRRRRRRRRMMMMM
IT'LL GET THROUGH-- SOMEHOW. IT-IT'LL JUST GET THROUGH--
THIS WILL SLOW IT DOWN. WE NEED TO FIND THE EXIT AND GET OUT OF THIS PLACE. MAKE IT TO OPEN GROUND.
WHAT'S THE POINT?!
KAY, WE HAVE TO--
NO! IT JUST KEEPS COMING! IT'S GOING TO KILL ME! THAT'S THE ONLY THING THAT WILL STOP IT! I--DON'T EVEN WANT TO BE THE GEOMANCER!! THIS ISN'T FAIR!
FAIR?
YOU CAME TO THE WRONG GUY IF YOU WANNA TALK ABOUT FAIR, KAY. YOU THINK I ASKED TO BE MADE INTO THIS?

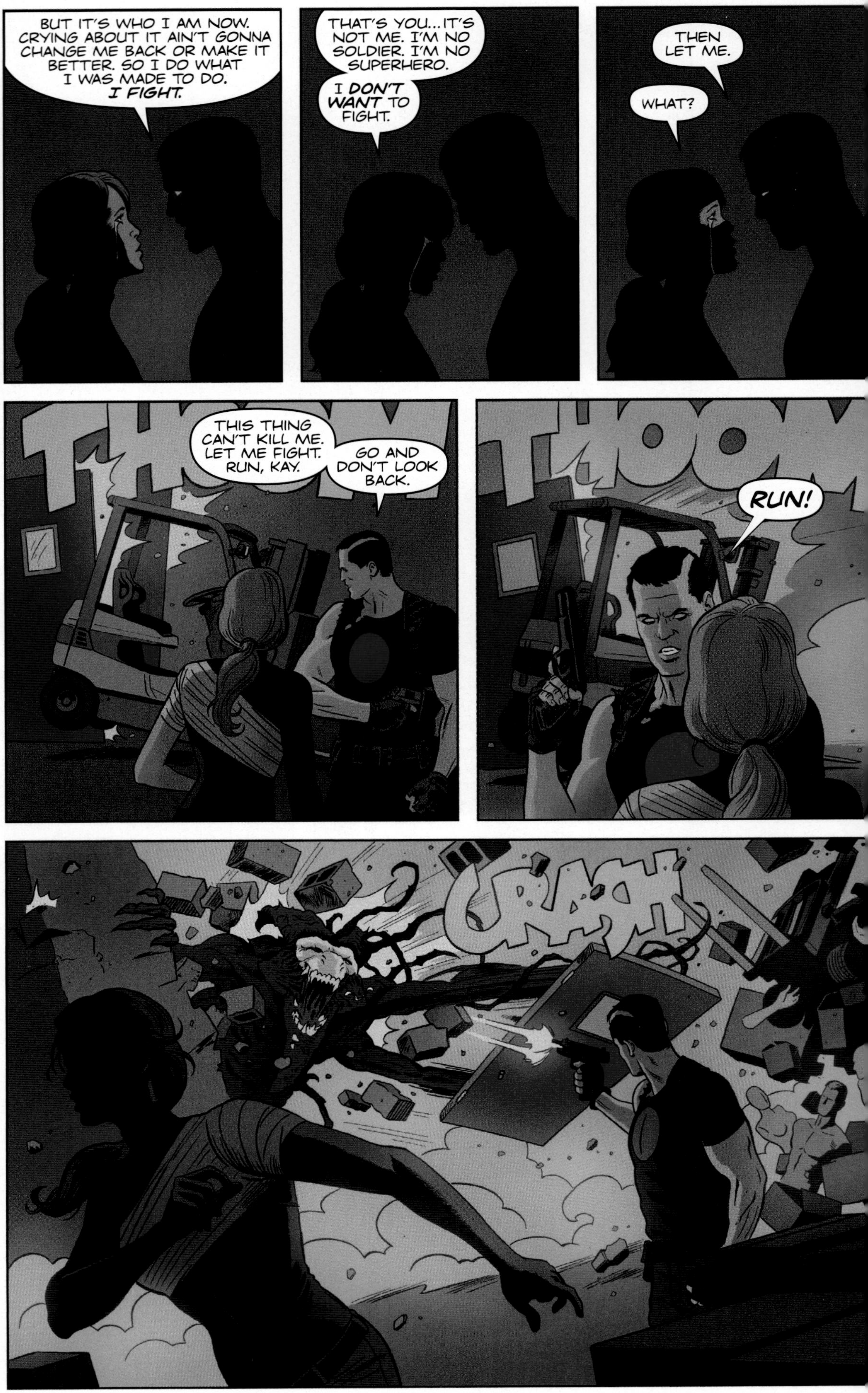
BUT IT'S WHO I AM NOW. CRYING ABOUT IT AIN'T GONNA CHANGE ME BACK OR MAKE IT BETTER. SO I DO WHAT I WAS MADE TO DO. I FIGHT.
THAT'S YOU...IT'S NOT ME. I'M NO SOLDIER. I'M NO SUPERHERO.
I DON'T WANT TO FIGHT.
THEN LET ME.
WHAT?
THOOM
THIS THING CAN'T KILL ME. LET ME FIGHT. RUN, KAY.
GO AND DON'T LOOK BACK.
THOOM
RUN!
CRASH

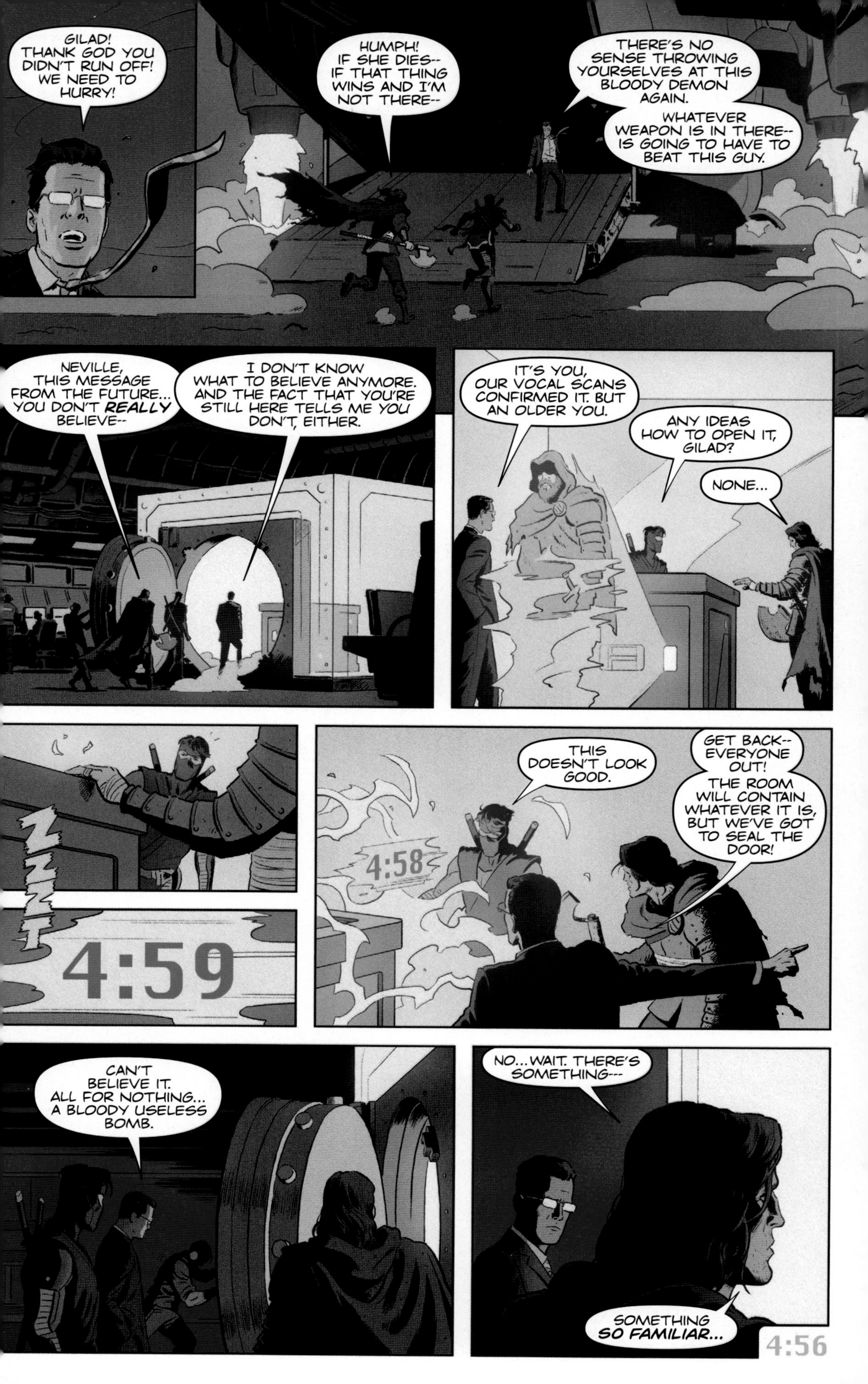
GILAD! THANK GOD YOU DIDN'T RUN OFF! WE NEED TO HURRY!
HUMPH! IF SHE DIES-- IF THAT THING WINS AND I'M NOT THERE--
THERE'S NO SENSE THROWING YOURSELVES AT THIS BLOODY DEMON AGAIN.
WHATEVER WEAPON IS IN THERE-- IS GOING TO HAVE TO BEAT THIS GUY.
NEVILLE, THIS MESSAGE FROM THE FUTURE... YOU DON'T REALLY BELIEVE--
I DON'T KNOW WHAT TO BELIEVE ANYMORE. AND THE FACT THAT YOU'RE STILL HERE TELLS ME YOU DON'T, EITHER.
IT'S YOU, OUR VOCAL SCANS CONFIRMED IT. BUT AN OLDER YOU.
ANY IDEAS HOW TO OPEN IT, GILAD?
NONE...
NNNT
4:59
4:58
THIS DOESN'T LOOK GOOD.
GET BACK-- EVERYONE OUT!
THE ROOM WILL CONTAIN WHATEVER IT IS, BUT WE'VE GOT TO SEAL THE DOOR!
CAN'T BELIEVE IT. ALL FOR NOTHING... A BLOODY USELESS BOMB.
NO...WAIT. THERE'S SOMETHING---
SOMETHING SO FAMILIAR...
4:56

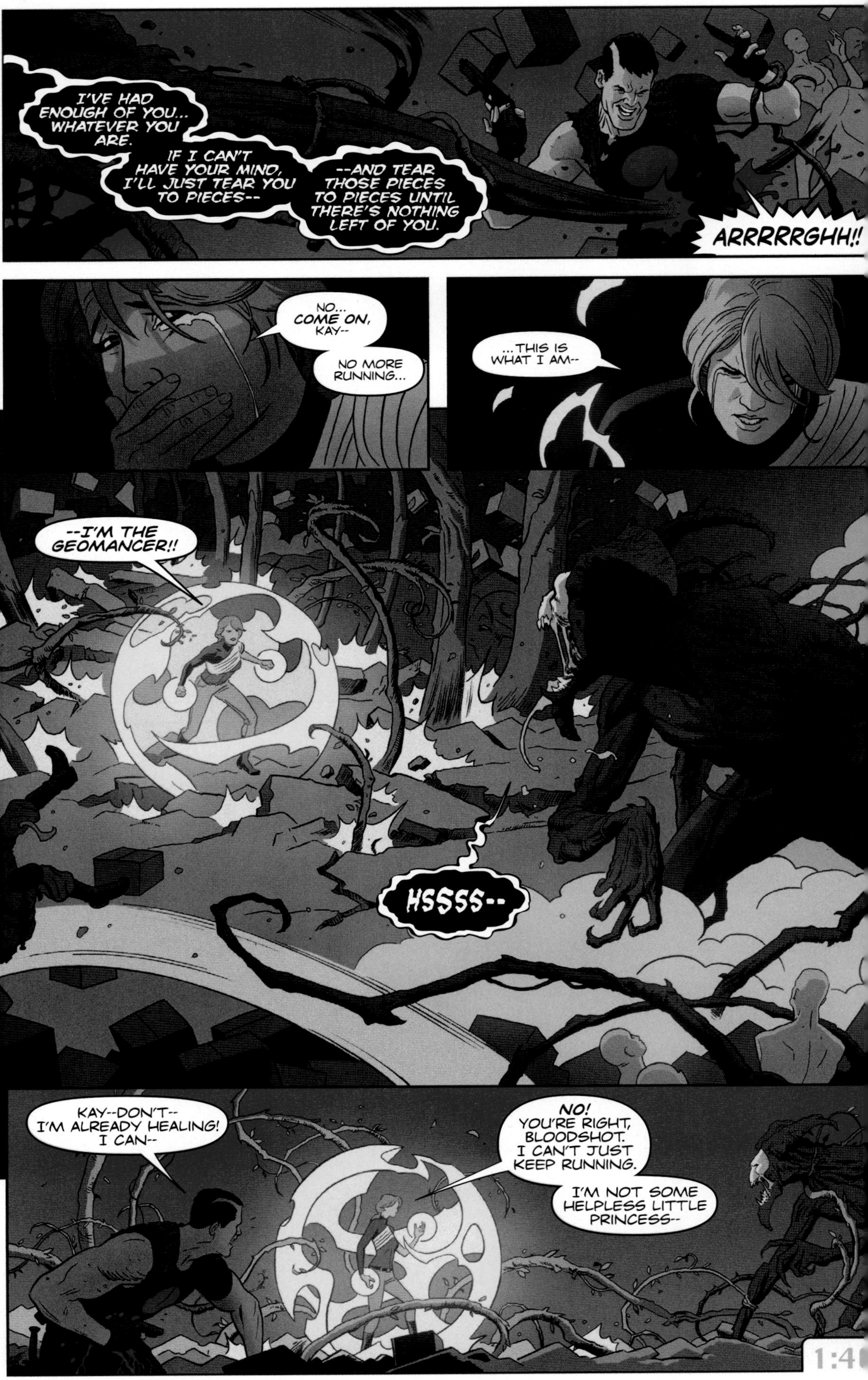
I'VE HAD ENOUGH OF YOU... WHATEVER YOU ARE.
IF I CAN'T HAVE YOUR MIND, I'LL JUST TEAR YOU TO PIECES--
--AND TEAR THOSE PIECES TO PIECES UNTIL THERE'S NOTHING LEFT OF YOU.
ARRRRRGHH!!
NO... COME ON, KAY--
NO MORE RUNNING...
...THIS IS WHAT I AM--
--I'M THE GEOMANCER!!
HSSSS--
KAY--DON'T-- I'M ALREADY HEALING! I CAN--
NO! YOU'RE RIGHT, BLOODSHOT. I CAN'T JUST KEEP RUNNING.
I'M NOT SOME HELPLESS LITTLE PRINCESS--

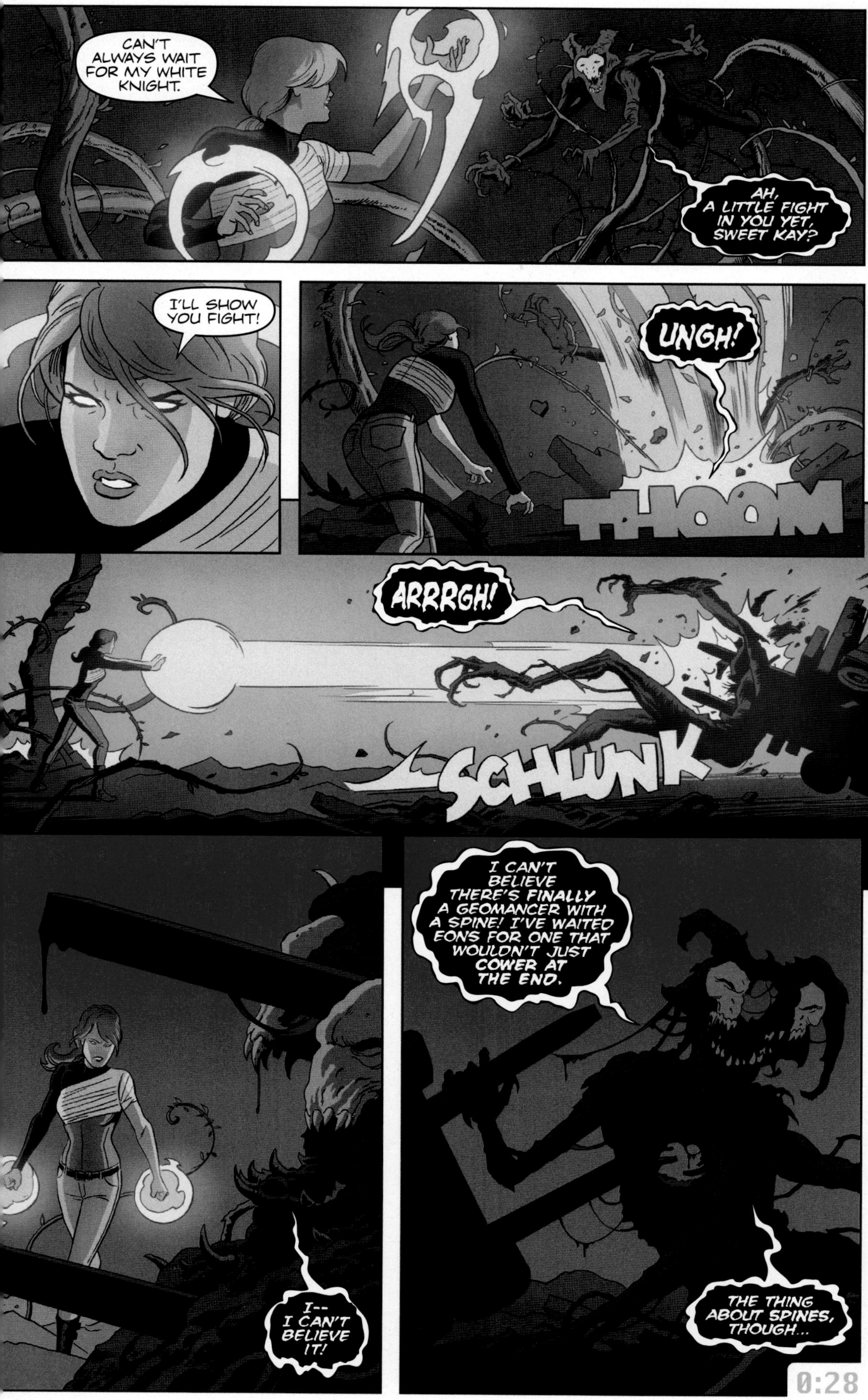
CAN'T ALWAYS WAIT FOR MY WHITE KNIGHT.
AH, A LITTLE FIGHT IN YOU YET, SWEET KAY?
I'LL SHOW YOU FIGHT!
UNGH!
THOOM
ARRRGH!
SCHLUNK
I-- I CAN'T BELIEVE IT!
I CAN'T BELIEVE THERE'S FINALLY A GEOMANCER WITH A SPINE! I'VE WAITED EONS FOR ONE THAT WOULDN'T JUST COWER AT THE END.
THE THING ABOUT SPINES, THOUGH...
0:28

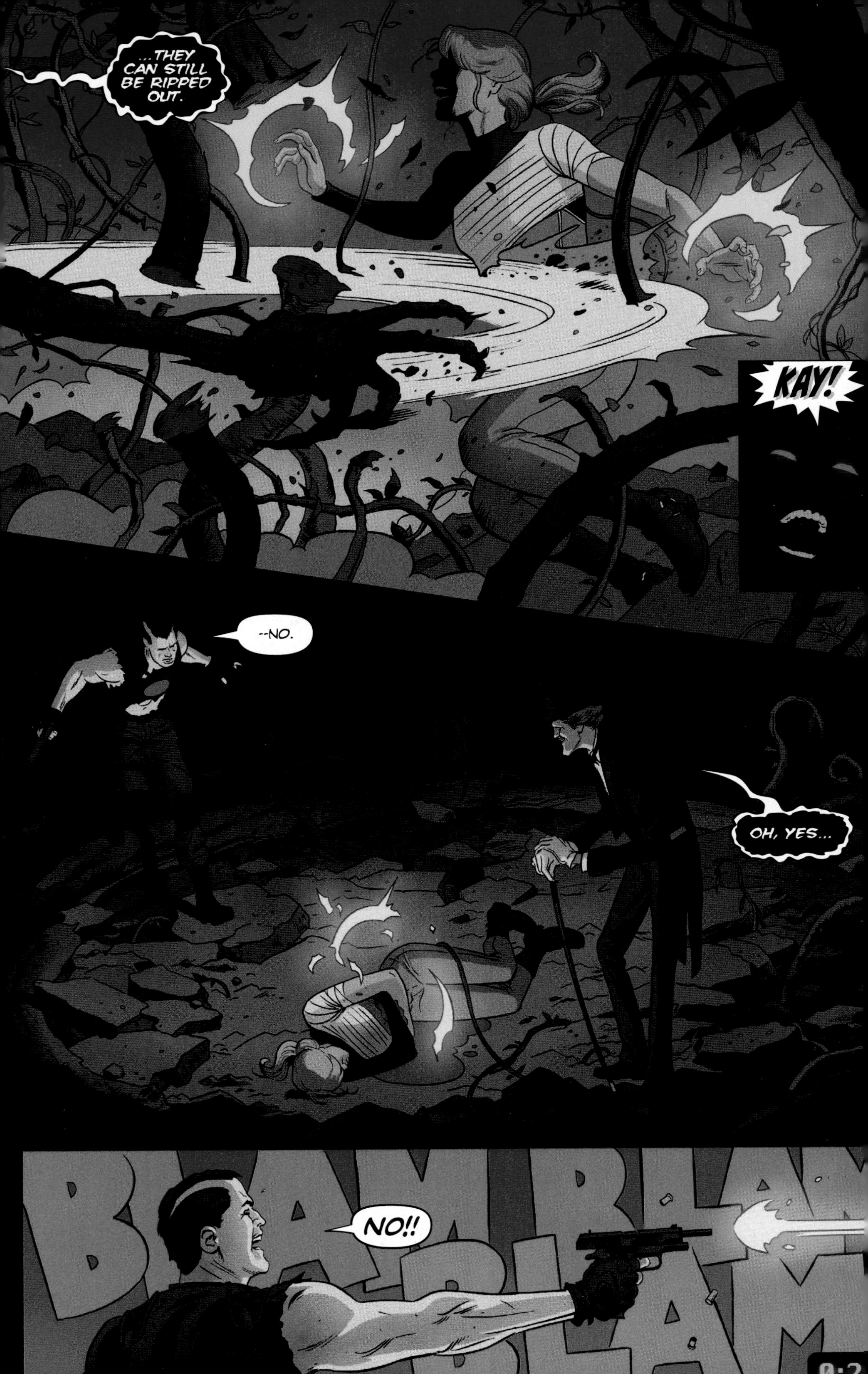
...THEY CAN STILL BE RIPPED OUT.
KAY!
--NO.
OH, YES...
NO!!
BLAM BLAM BLAM BLAM

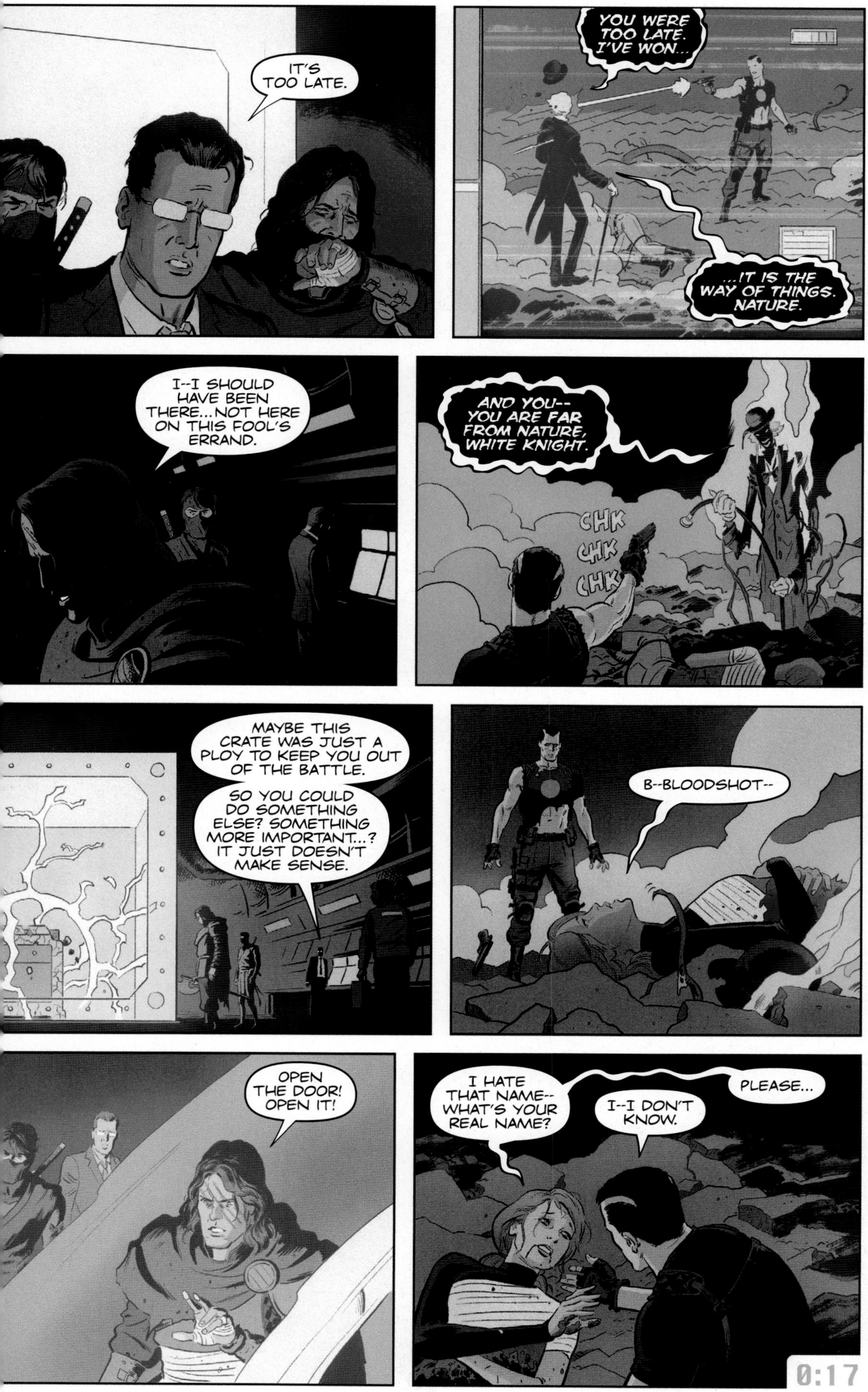
IT'S TOO LATE.
YOU WERE TOO LATE. I'VE WON...
...IT IS THE WAY OF THINGS. NATURE.
I--I SHOULD HAVE BEEN THERE...NOT HERE ON THIS FOOL'S ERRAND.
AND YOU-- YOU ARE FAR FROM NATURE, WHITE KNIGHT.
CHK
CHK
CHK
MAYBE THIS CRATE WAS JUST A PLOY TO KEEP YOU OUT OF THE BATTLE.
SO YOU COULD DO SOMETHING ELSE? SOMETHING MORE IMPORTANT...? IT JUST DOESN'T MAKE SENSE.
B--BLOODSHOT--
OPEN THE DOOR! OPEN IT!
I HATE THAT NAME-- WHAT'S YOUR REAL NAME?
PLEASE...
I--I DON'T KNOW.
0:17

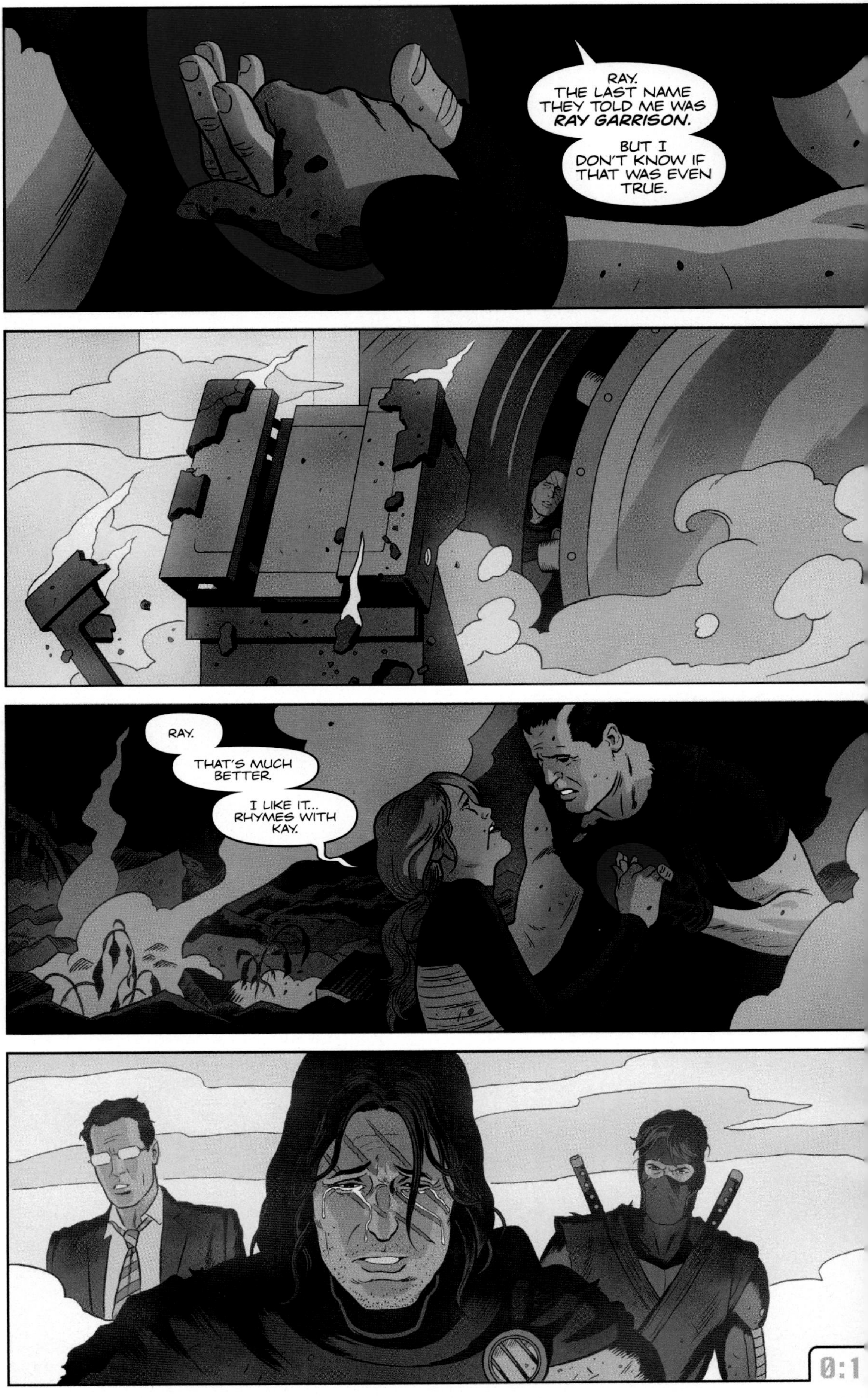
RAY.
THE LAST NAME THEY TOLD ME WAS **RAY GARRISON.**
BUT I DON'T KNOW IF THAT WAS EVEN TRUE.
RAY.
THAT'S MUCH BETTER.
I LIKE IT... RHYMES WITH KAY.

KAY, I-- I'M SORRY. I WAS SUPPOSED TO SAVE YOU...

NO... I DON'T THINK YOU WERE.

I TOLD YOU, I DON'T NEED A WHITE KNIGHT.

I THINK MAYBE THIS IS WHAT *HAD* TO HAPPEN--

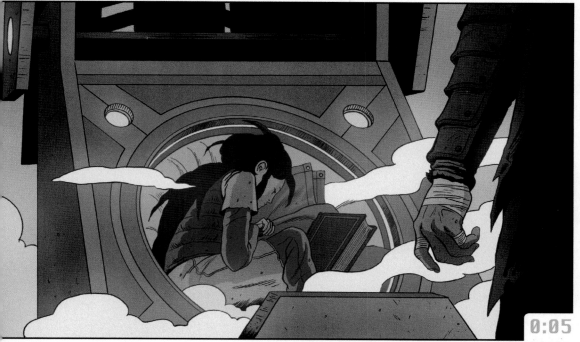

0:05

WHAT-- WHAT DO YOU MEAN?

ALL THOSE LITTLE ROBOTS--I CAN SEE THEM.

THEY SHOULDN'T BE THERE--

0:01

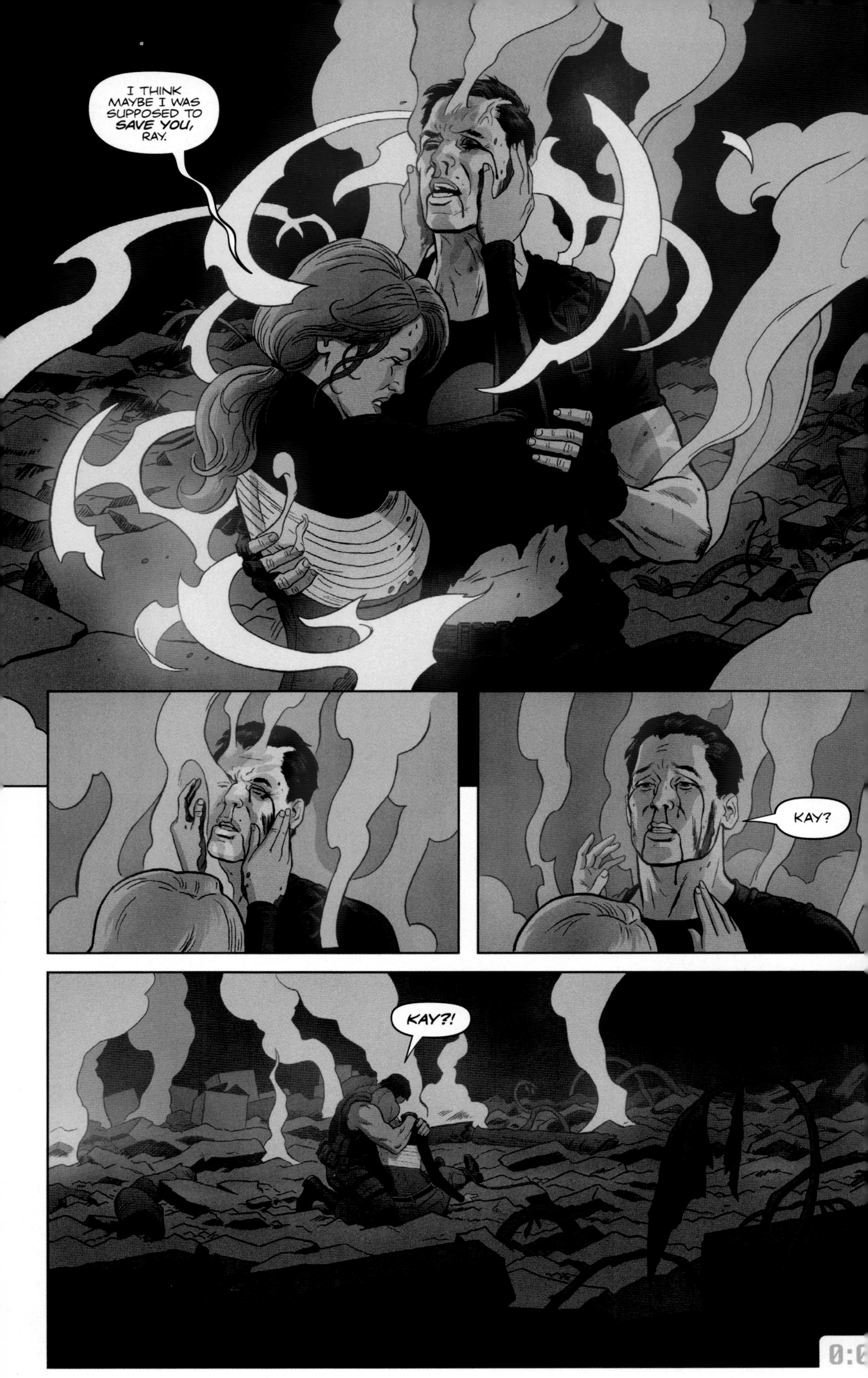
I THINK MAYBE I WAS SUPPOSED TO SAVE YOU, RAY.
KAY?
KAY?!

IS IT REALLY OVER?

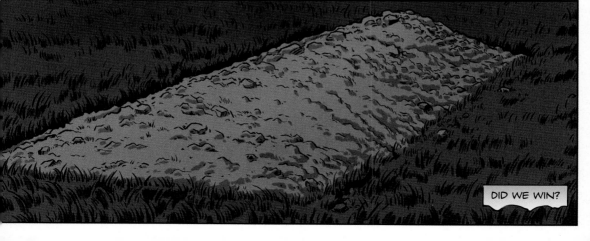

DID WE WIN?

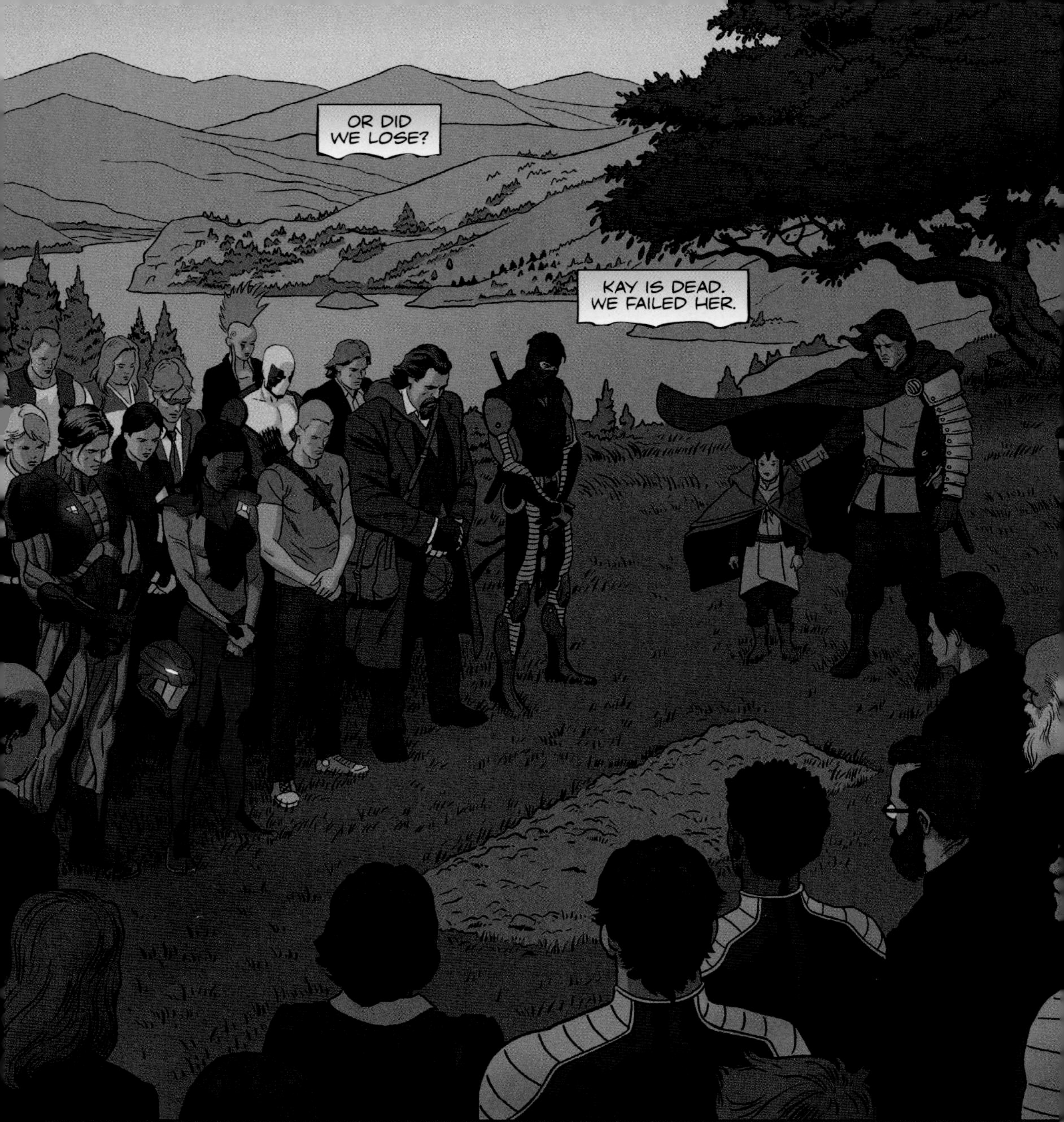
OR DID WE LOSE?
KAY IS DEAD. WE FAILED HER.

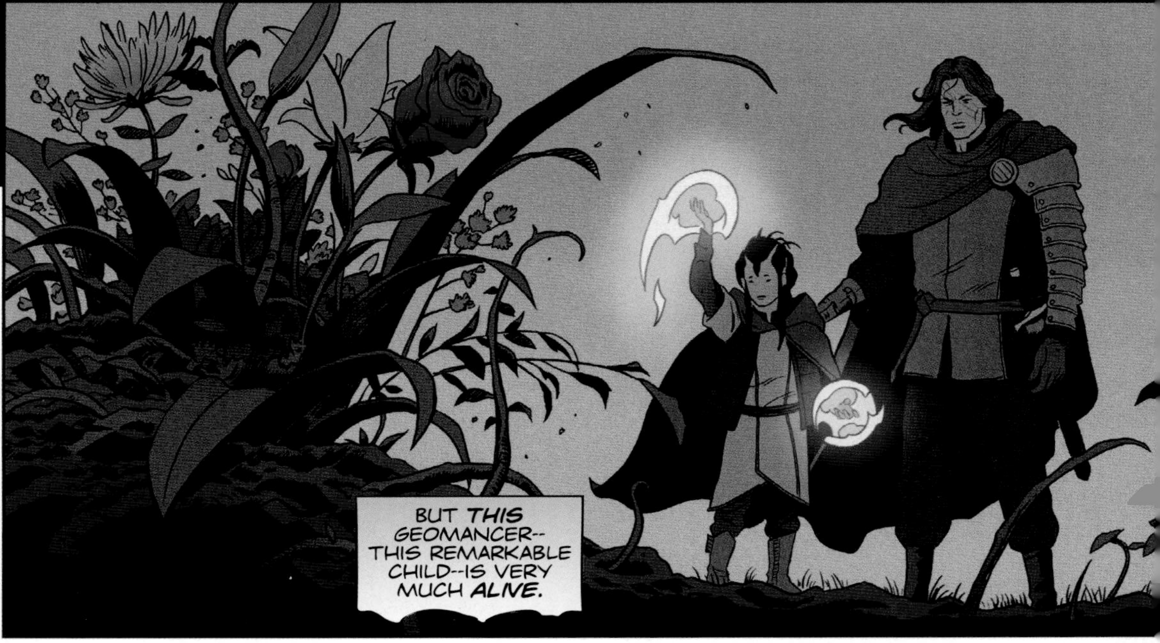
BUT THIS GEOMANCER-- THIS REMARKABLE CHILD--IS VERY MUCH ALIVE.

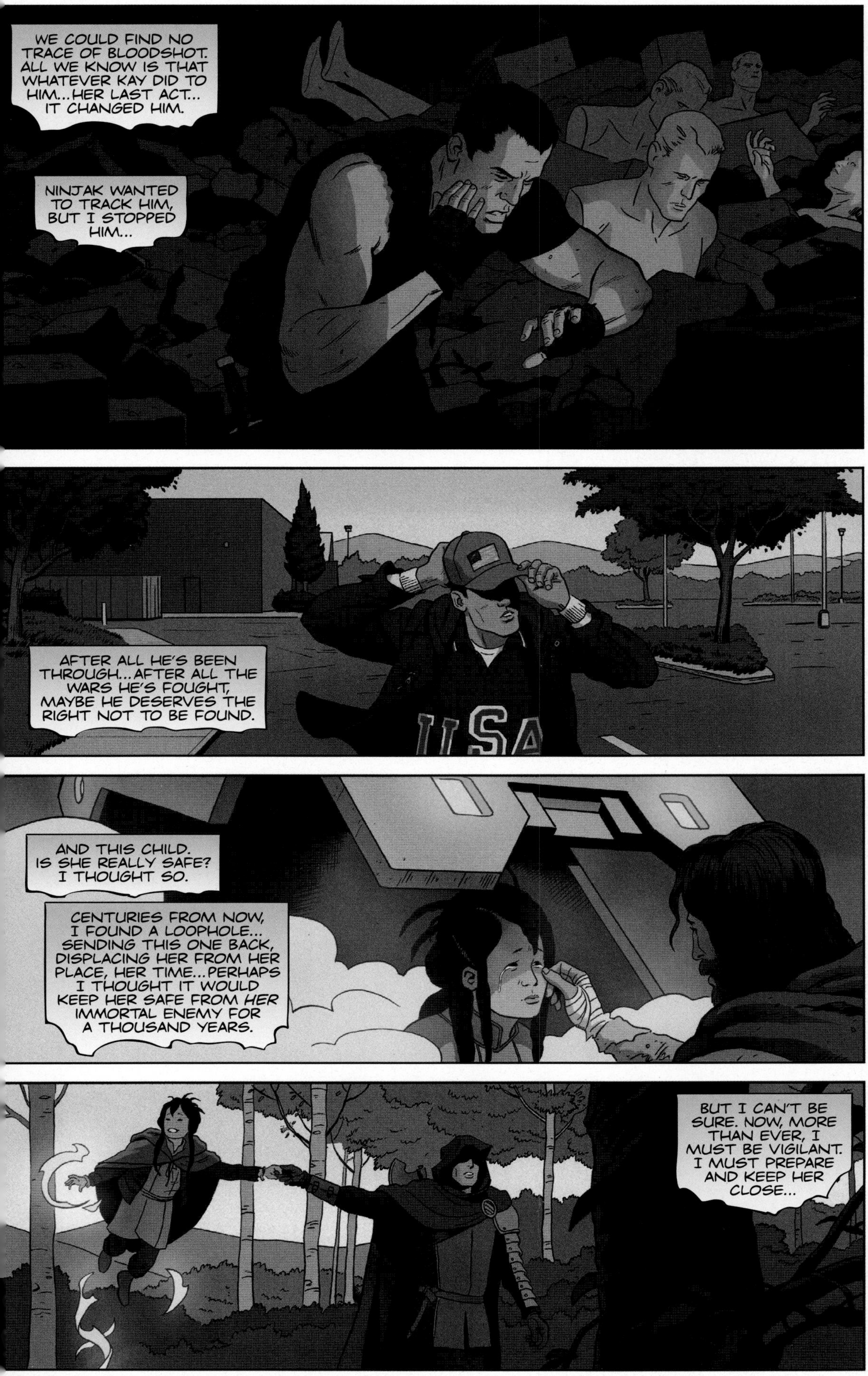
WE COULD FIND NO TRACE OF BLOODSHOT. ALL WE KNOW IS THAT WHATEVER KAY DID TO HIM...HER LAST ACT... IT CHANGED HIM.
NINJAK WANTED TO TRACK HIM, BUT I STOPPED HIM...
AFTER ALL HE'S BEEN THROUGH...AFTER ALL THE WARS HE'S FOUGHT, MAYBE HE DESERVES THE RIGHT NOT TO BE FOUND.
USA
AND THIS CHILD. IS SHE REALLY SAFE? I THOUGHT SO.
CENTURIES FROM NOW, I FOUND A LOOPHOLE... SENDING THIS ONE BACK, DISPLACING HER FROM HER PLACE, HER TIME...PERHAPS I THOUGHT IT WOULD KEEP HER SAFE FROM *HER* IMMORTAL ENEMY FOR A THOUSAND YEARS.
BUT I CAN'T BE SURE. NOW, MORE THAN EVER, I MUST BE VIGILANT. I MUST PREPARE AND KEEP HER CLOSE...

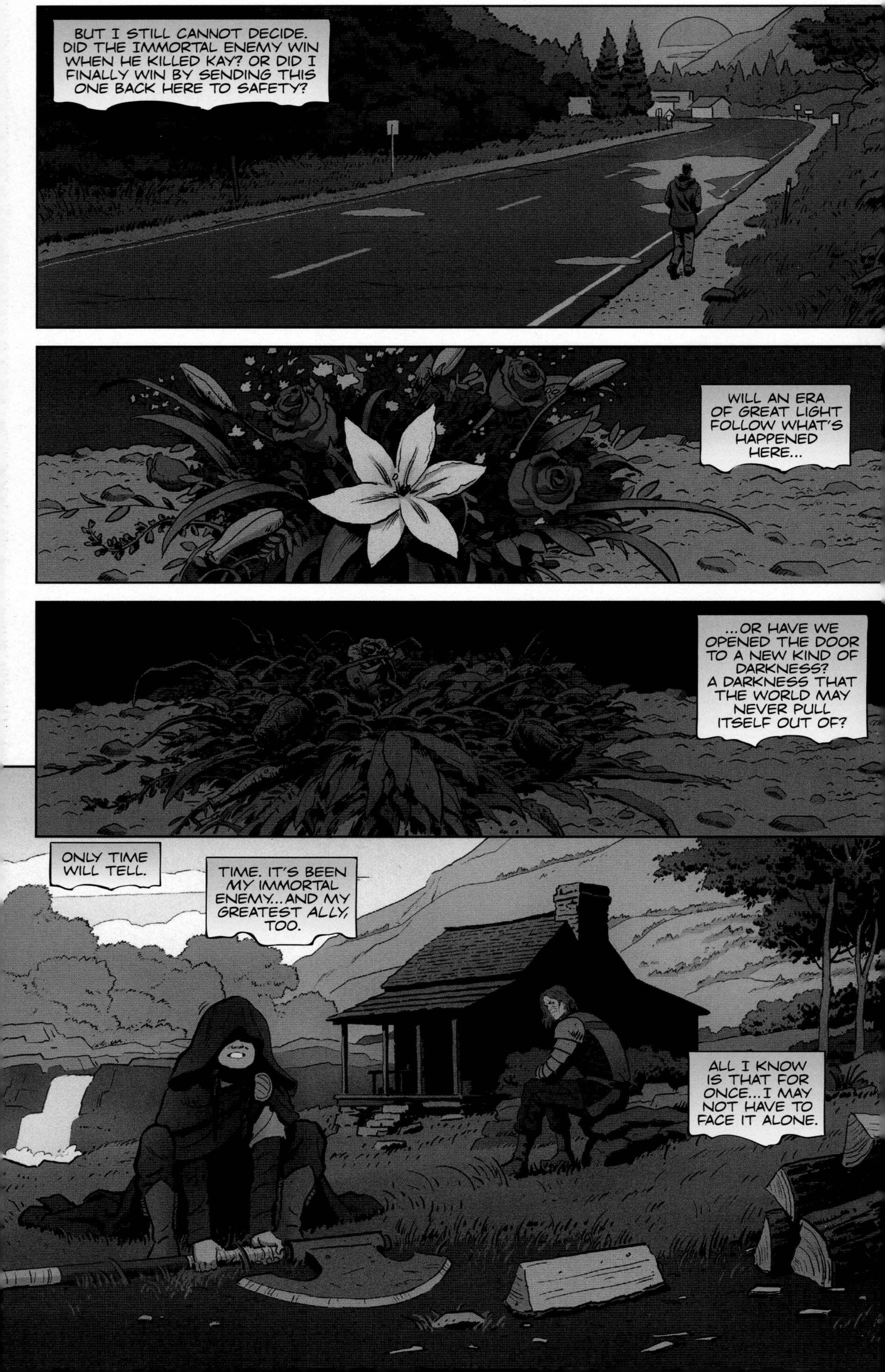
BUT I STILL CANNOT DECIDE. DID THE IMMORTAL ENEMY WIN WHEN HE KILLED KAY? OR DID I FINALLY WIN BY SENDING THIS ONE BACK HERE TO SAFETY?
WILL AN ERA OF GREAT LIGHT FOLLOW WHAT'S HAPPENED HERE...
...OR HAVE WE OPENED THE DOOR TO A NEW KIND OF DARKNESS? A DARKNESS THAT THE WORLD MAY NEVER PULL ITSELF OUT OF?
ONLY TIME WILL TELL.
TIME. IT'S BEEN MY IMMORTAL ENEMY...AND MY GREATEST ALLY, TOO.
ALL I KNOW IS THAT FOR ONCE...I MAY NOT HAVE TO FACE IT ALONE.

LAYOUTS | PENCILS | INKS | COLOR

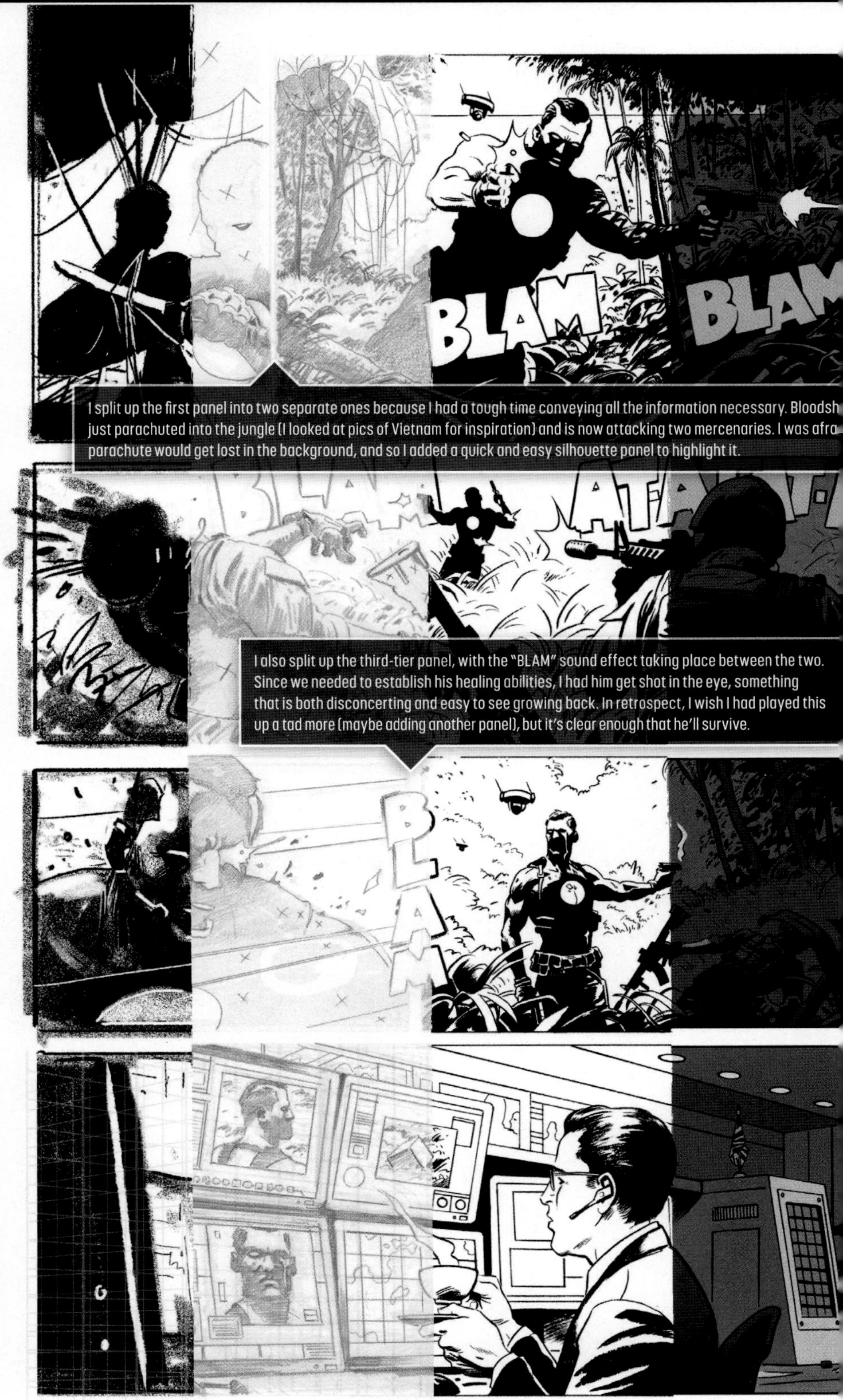
BLAM
BLAM
BLAM
BLAM

I split up the first panel into two separate ones because I had a tough time conveying all the information necessary. Bloodsh just parachuted into the jungle (I looked at pics of Vietnam for inspiration) and is now attacking two mercenaries. I was afra parachute would get lost in the background, and so I added a quick and easy silhouette panel to highlight it.

I also split up the third-tier panel, with the "BLAM" sound effect taking place between the two. Since we needed to establish his healing abilities, I had him get shot in the eye, something that is both disconcerting and easy to see growing back. In retrospect, I wish I had played this up a tad more (maybe adding another panel), but it's clear enough that he'll survive.

Double-page spreads are always fun, and this one didn't disappoint.

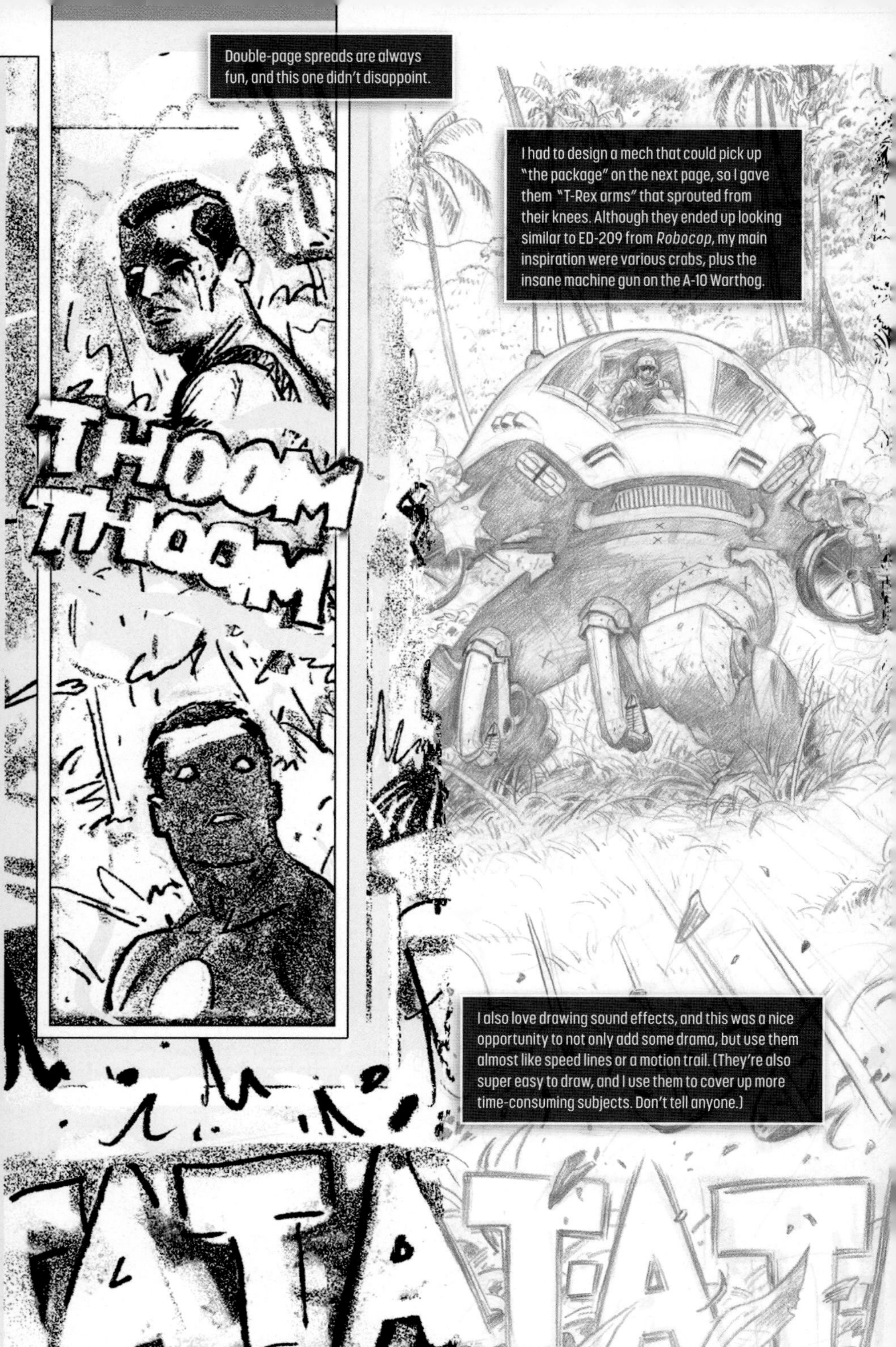
THOOM
THOOM
TATAT

I had to design a mech that could pick up "the package" on the next page, so I gave them "T-Rex arms" that sprouted from their knees. Although they ended up looking similar to ED-209 from *Robocop*, my main inspiration were various crabs, plus the insane machine gun on the A-10 Warthog.

I also love drawing sound effects, and this was a nice opportunity to not only add some drama, but use them almost like speed lines or a motion trail. (They're also super easy to draw, and I use them to cover up more time-consuming subjects. Don't tell anyone.)

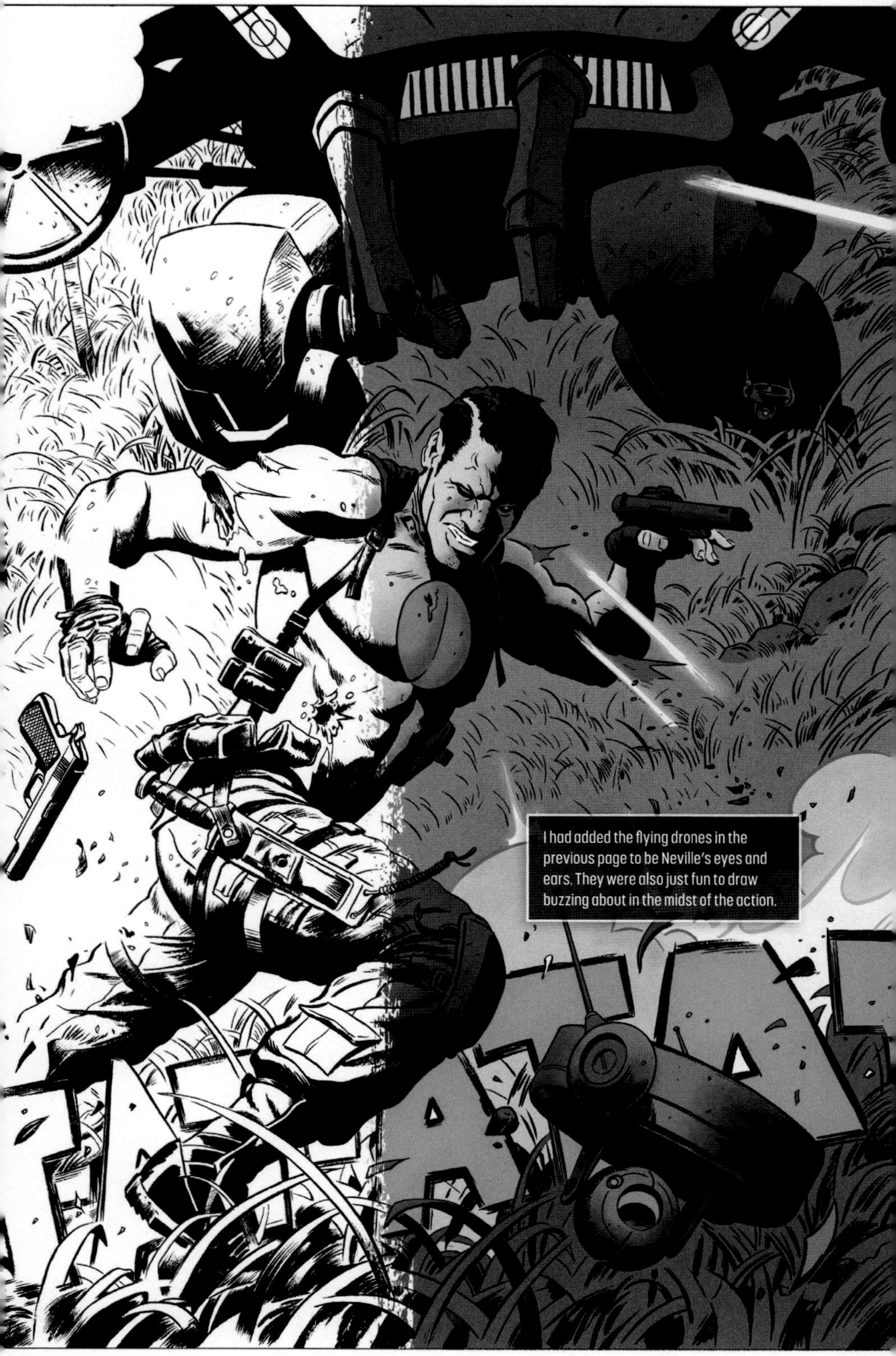

I had added the flying drones in the previous page to be Neville's eyes and ears. They were also just fun to draw buzzing about in the midst of the action.

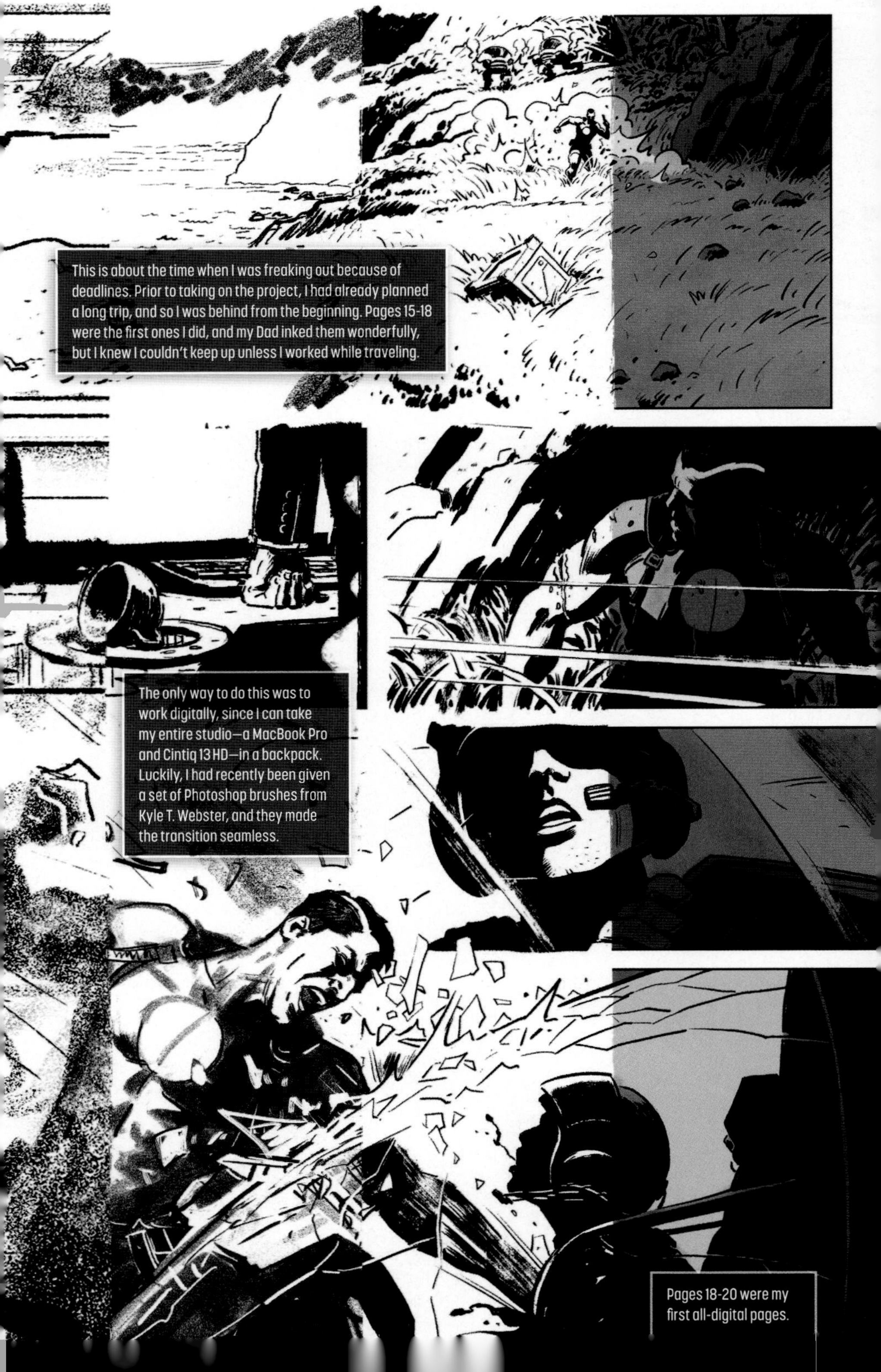

This is about the time when I was freaking out because of deadlines. Prior to taking on the project, I had already planned a long trip, and so I was behind from the beginning. Pages 15-18 were the first ones I did, and my Dad inked them wonderfully, but I knew I couldn't keep up unless I worked while traveling.

The only way to do this was to work digitally, since I can take my entire studio—a MacBook Pro and Cintiq 13 HD—in a backpack. Luckily, I had recently been given a set of Photoshop brushes from Kyle T. Webster, and they made the transition seamless.

Pages 18-20 were my first all-digital pages.

LAYOUTS | PENCILS | INKS | COLORS

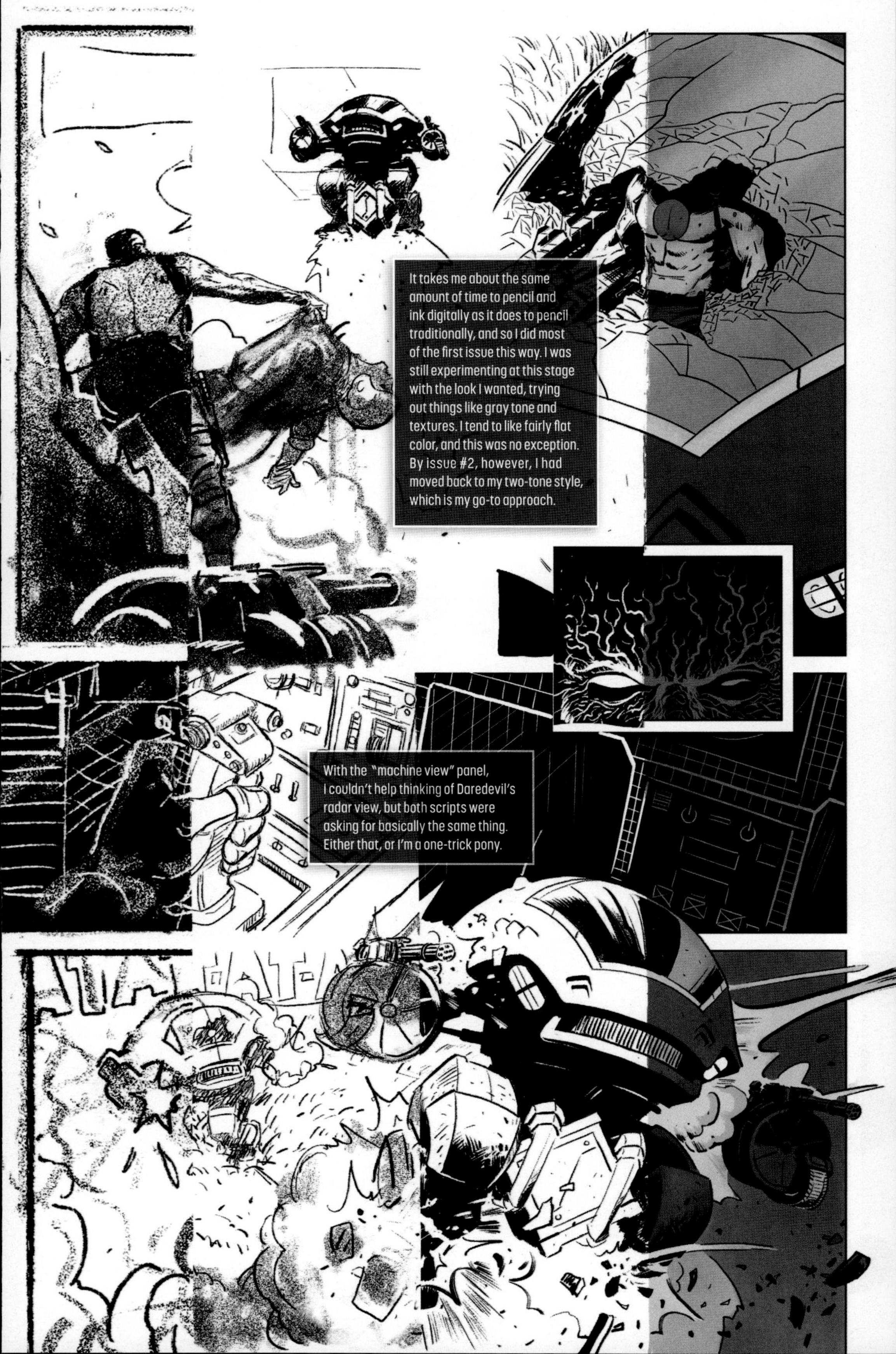

It takes me about the same amount of time to pencil and ink digitally as it does to pencil traditionally, and so I did most of the first issue this way. I was still experimenting at this stage with the look I wanted, trying out things like gray tone and textures. I tend to like fairly flat color, and this was no exception. By issue #2, however, I had moved back to my two-tone style, which is my go-to approach.

With the "machine view" panel, I couldn't help thinking of Daredevil's radar view, but both scripts were asking for basically the same thing. Either that, or I'm a one-trick pony.

THE VALIANT #2 COMMENTARY BY MATT KINDT

LAYOUTS | PENCILS | INKS | COLORS

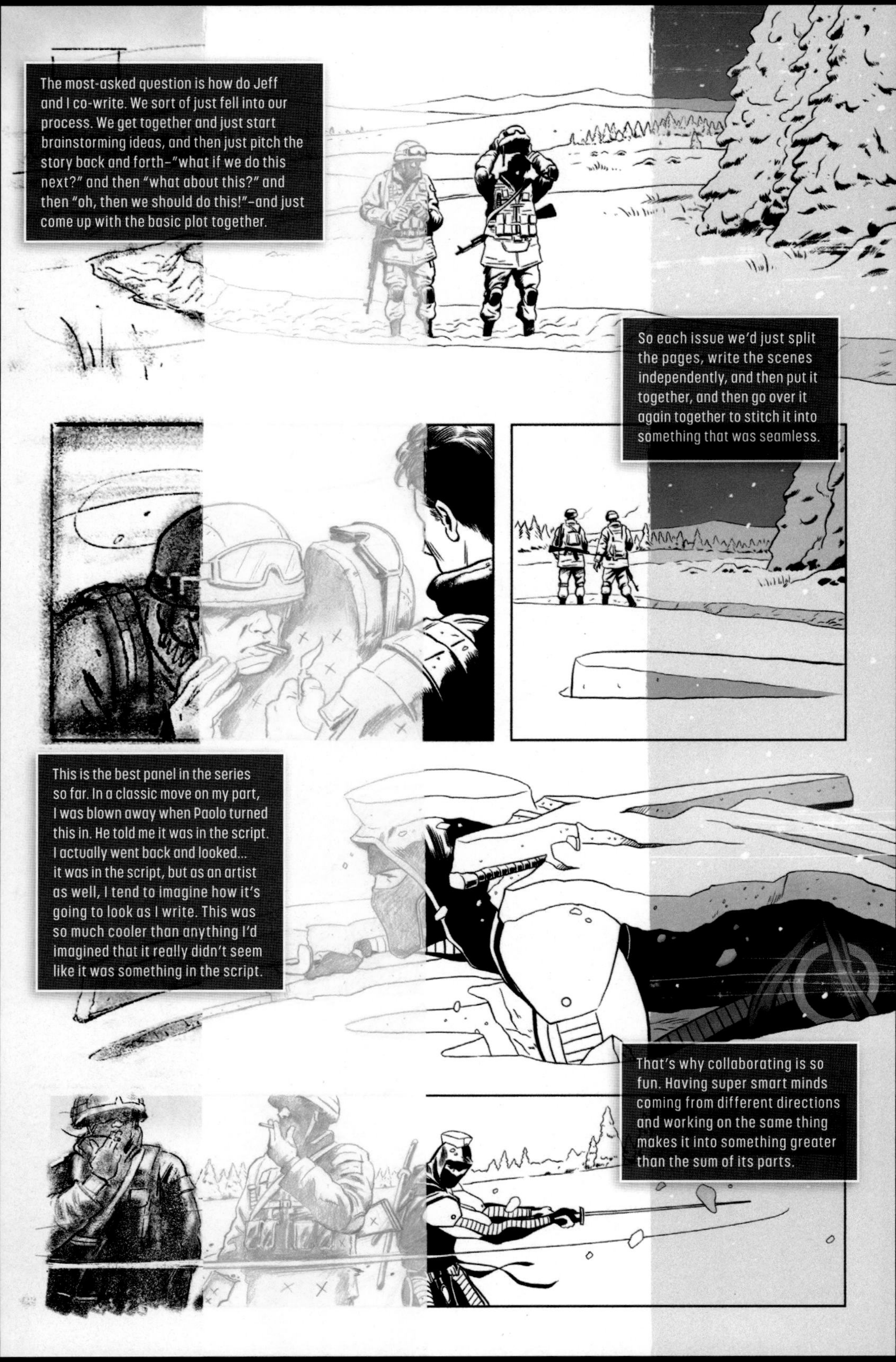

The most-asked question is how do Jeff and I co-write. We sort of just fell into our process. We get together and just start brainstorming ideas, and then just pitch the story back and forth–"what if we do this next?" and then "what about this?" and then "oh, then we should do this!"–and just come up with the basic plot together.

So each issue we'd just split the pages, write the scenes independently, and then put it together, and then go over it again together to stitch it into something that was seamless.

This is the best panel in the series so far. In a classic move on my part, I was blown away when Paolo turned this in. He told me it was in the script. I actually went back and looked... it was in the script, but as an artist as well, I tend to imagine how it's going to look as I write. This was so much cooler than anything I'd imagined that it really didn't seem like it was something in the script.

That's why collaborating is so fun. Having super smart minds coming from different directions and working on the same thing makes it into something greater than the sum of its parts.

GRAPHIC DESIGN BY DYLAN TODD

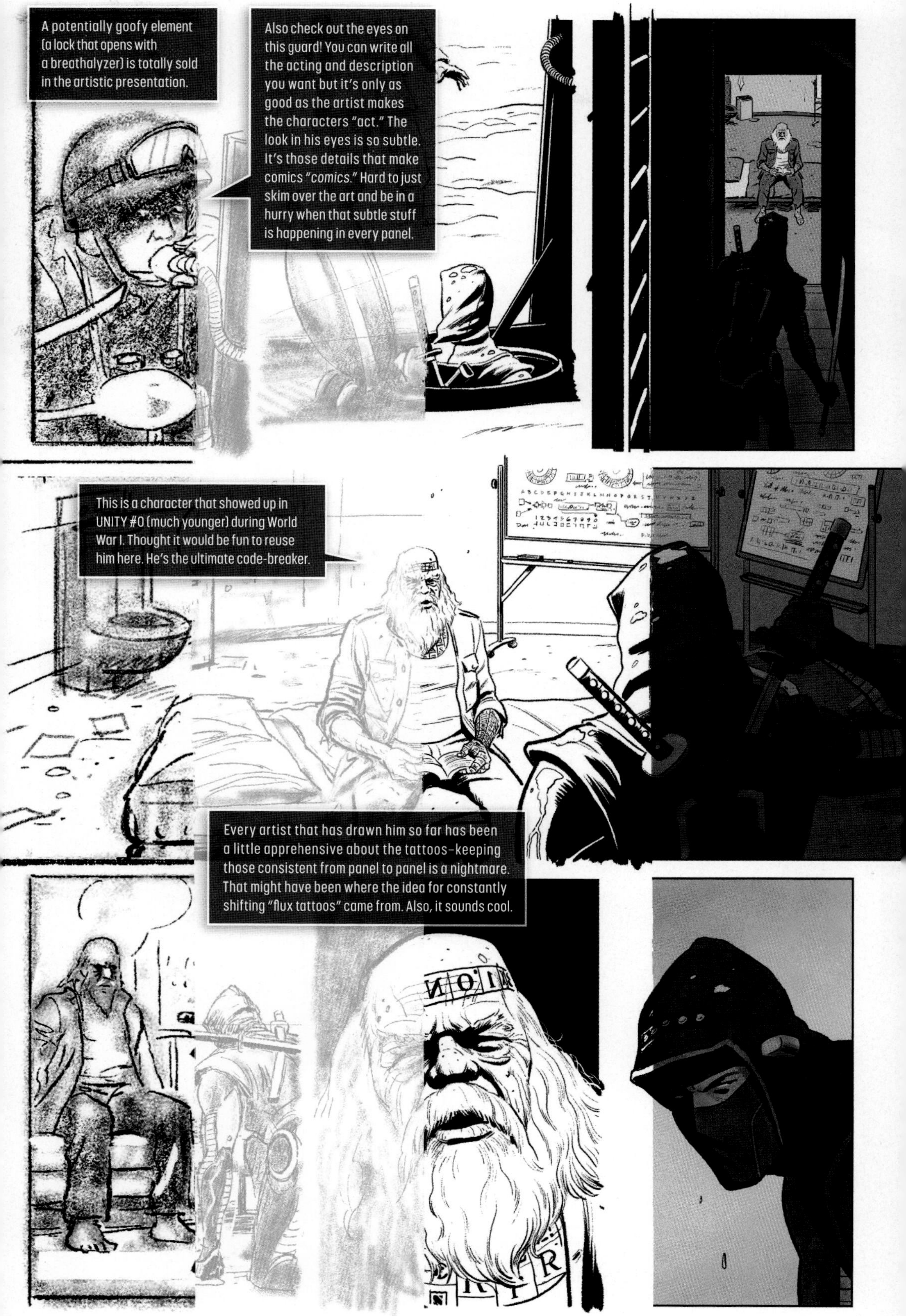

A potentially goofy element (a lock that opens with a breathalyzer) is totally sold in the artistic presentation.

Also check out the eyes on this guard! You can write all the acting and description you want but it's only as good as the artist makes the characters "act." The look in his eyes is so subtle. It's those details that make comics *"comics."* Hard to just skim over the art and be in a hurry when that subtle stuff is happening in every panel.

This is a character that showed up in UNITY #0 (much younger) during World War I. Thought it would be fun to reuse him here. He's the ultimate code-breaker.

Every artist that has drawn him so far has been a little apprehensive about the tattoos–keeping those consistent from panel to panel is a nightmare. That might have been where the idea for constantly shifting "flux tattoos" came from. Also, it sounds cool.

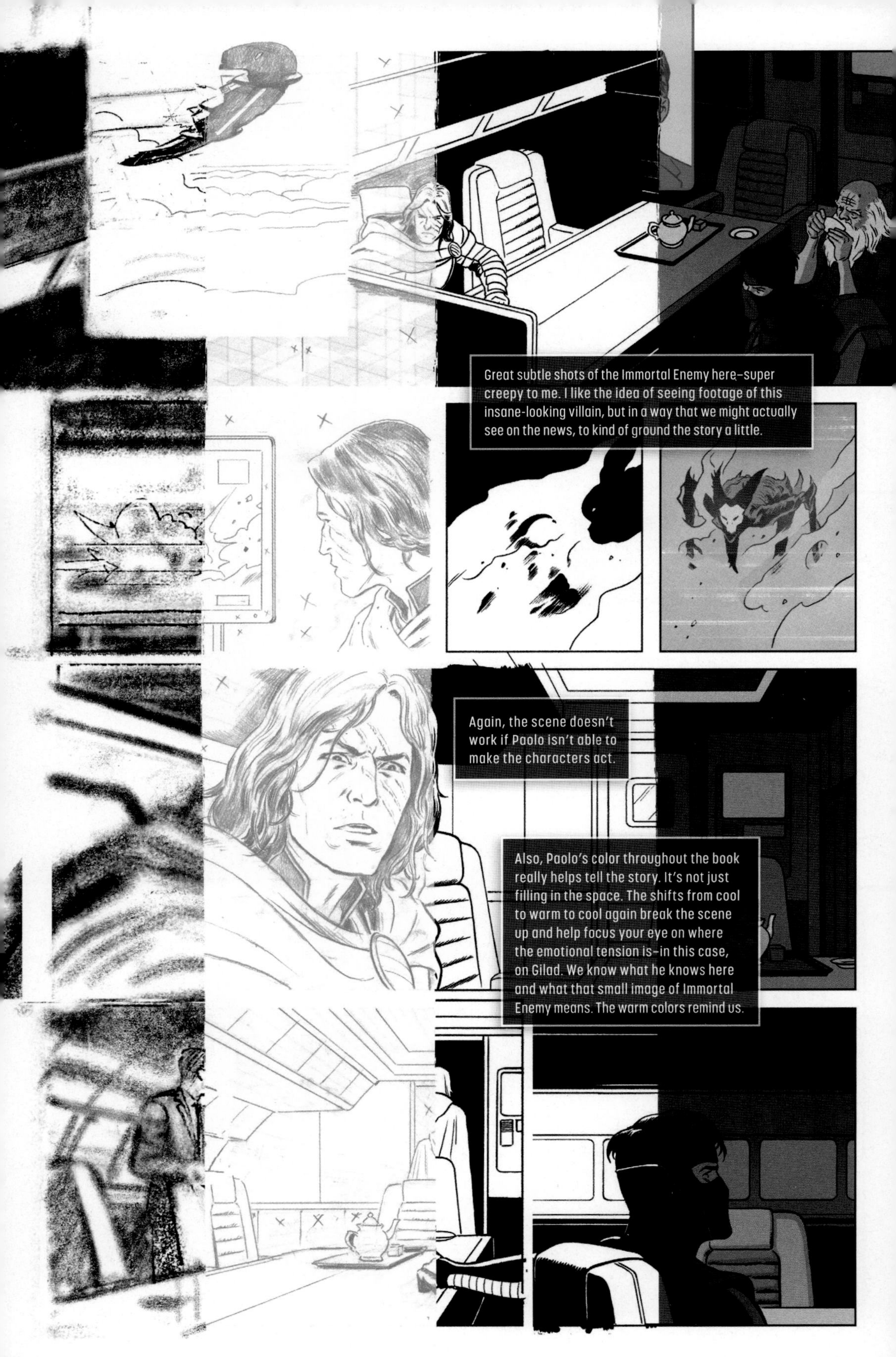

Great subtle shots of the Immortal Enemy here–super creepy to me. I like the idea of seeing footage of this insane-looking villain, but in a way that we might actually see on the news, to kind of ground the story a little.

Again, the scene doesn't work if Paolo isn't able to make the characters act.

Also, Paolo's color throughout the book really helps tell the story. It's not just filling in the space. The shifts from cool to warm to cool again break the scene up and help focus your eye on where the emotional tension is–in this case, on Gilad. We know what he knows here and what that small image of Immortal Enemy means. The warm colors remind us.

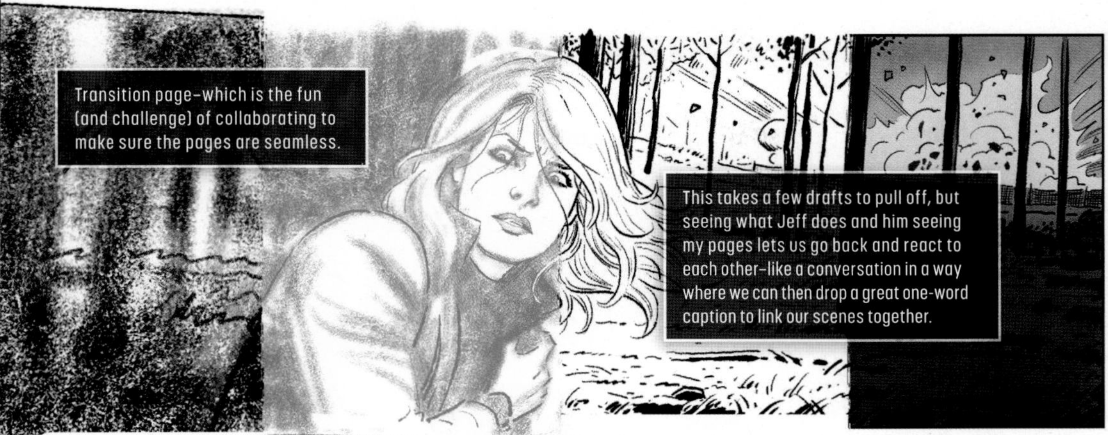

Transition page–which is the fun (and challenge) of collaborating to make sure the pages are seamless.

This takes a few drafts to pull off, but seeing what Jeff does and him seeing my pages lets us go back and react to each other–like a conversation in a way where we can then drop a great one-word caption to link our scenes together.

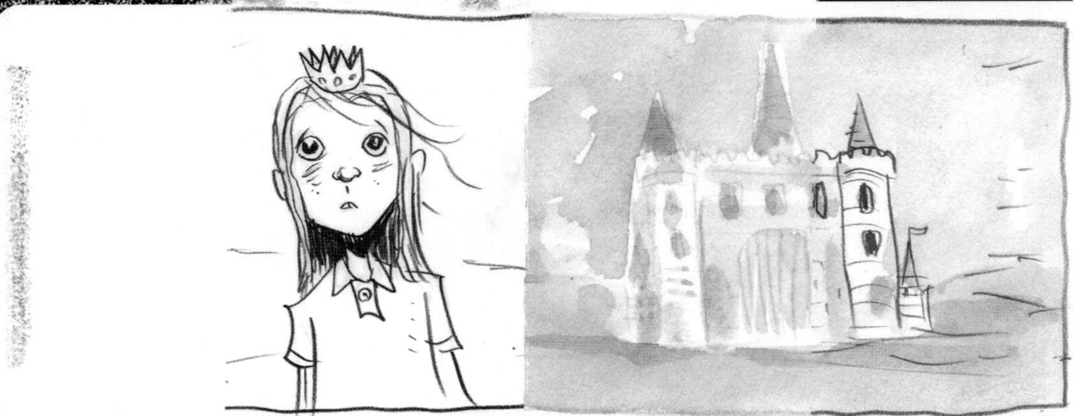

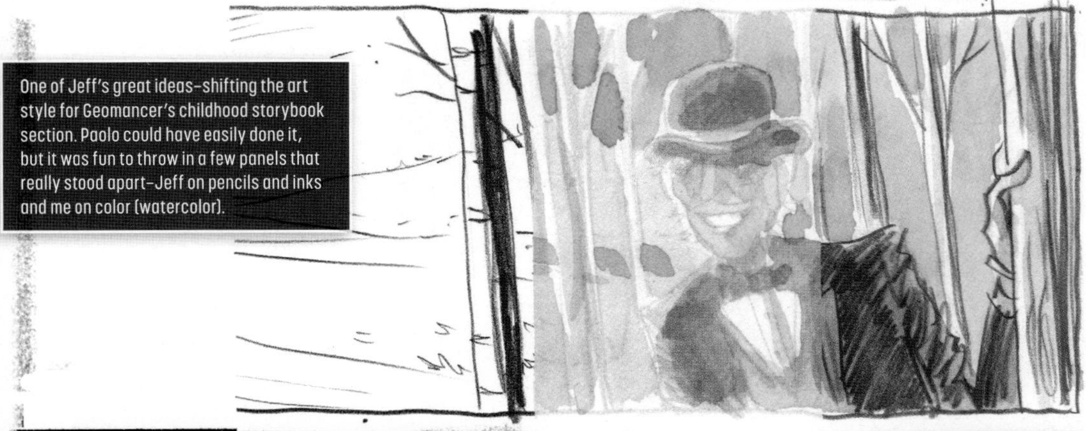

One of Jeff's great ideas–shifting the art style for Geomancer's childhood storybook section. Paolo could have easily done it, but it was fun to throw in a few panels that really stood apart–Jeff on pencils and inks and me on color (watercolor).

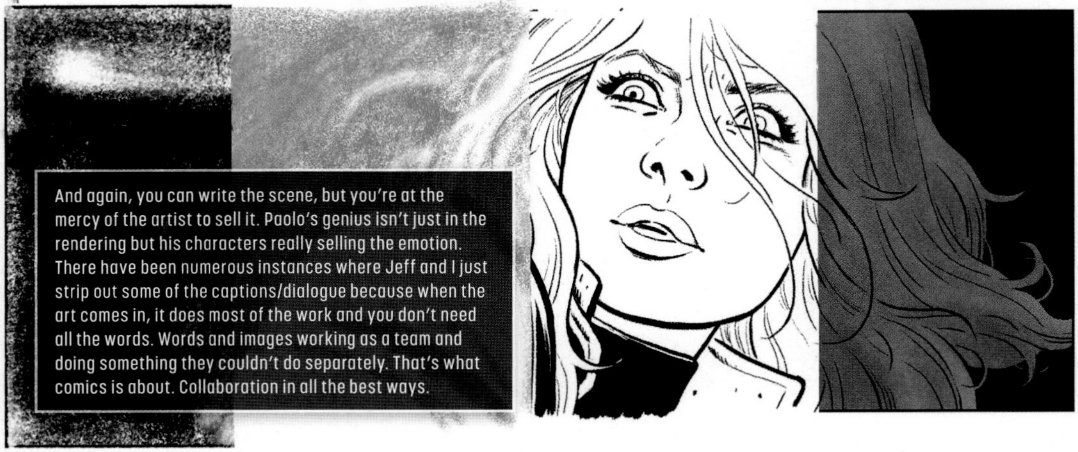

And again, you can write the scene, but you're at the mercy of the artist to sell it. Paolo's genius isn't just in the rendering but his characters really selling the emotion. There have been numerous instances where Jeff and I just strip out some of the captions/dialogue because when the art comes in, it does most of the work and you don't need all the words. Words and images working as a team and doing something they couldn't do separately. That's what comics is about. Collaboration in all the best ways.

THE VALIANT #3 COMMENTARY BY JEFF LEMIRE

LAYOUTS | PENCILS | INKS | COLORS

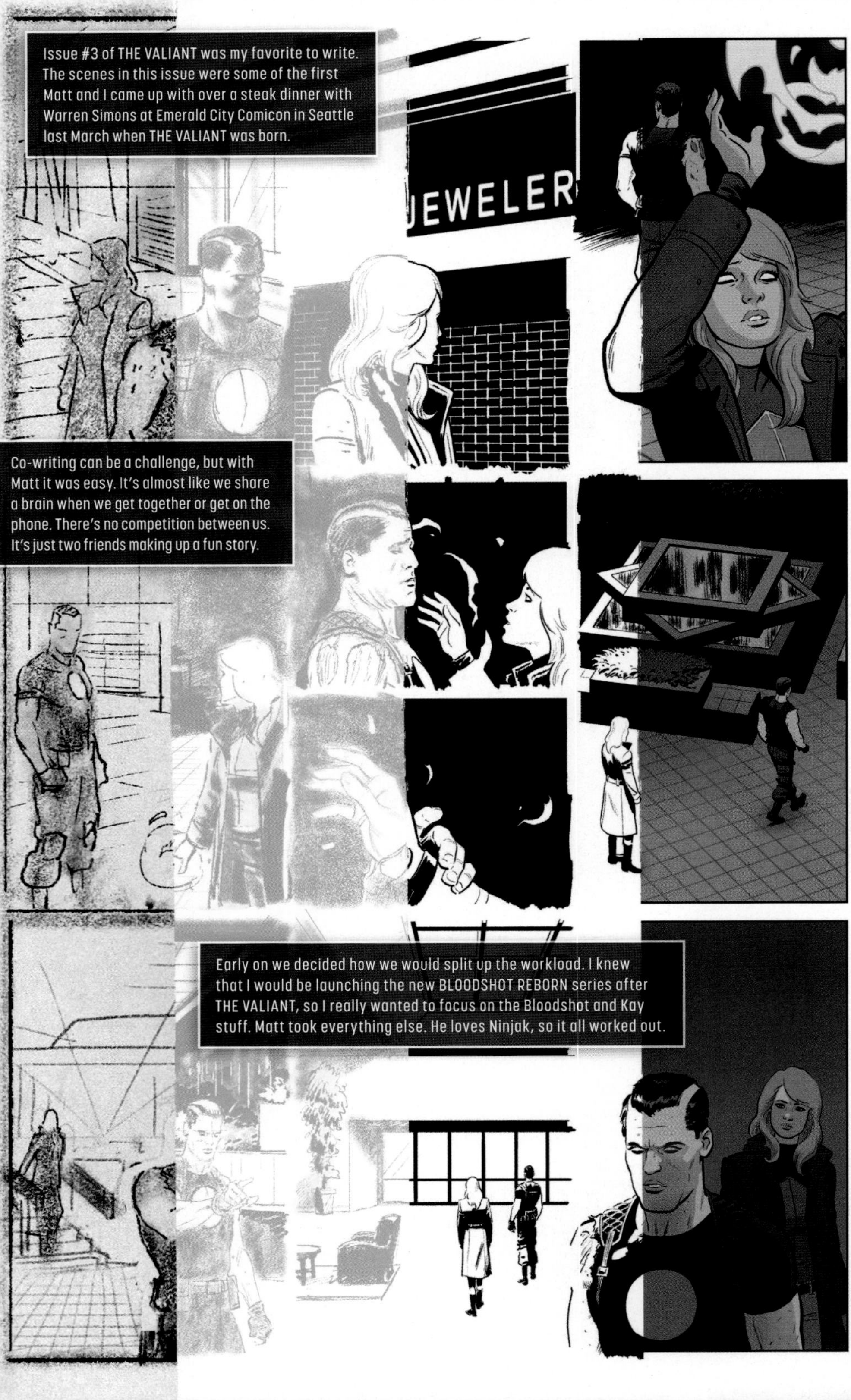
JEWELER

Issue #3 of THE VALIANT was my favorite to write. The scenes in this issue were some of the first Matt and I came up with over a steak dinner with Warren Simons at Emerald City Comicon in Seattle last March when THE VALIANT was born.

Co-writing can be a challenge, but with Matt it was easy. It's almost like we share a brain when we get together or get on the phone. There's no competition between us. It's just two friends making up a fun story.

Early on we decided how we would split up the workload. I knew that I would be launching the new BLOODSHOT REBORN series after THE VALIANT, so I really wanted to focus on the Bloodshot and Kay stuff. Matt took everything else. He loves Ninjak, so it all worked out.

GRAPHIC DESIGN BY DYLAN TODD

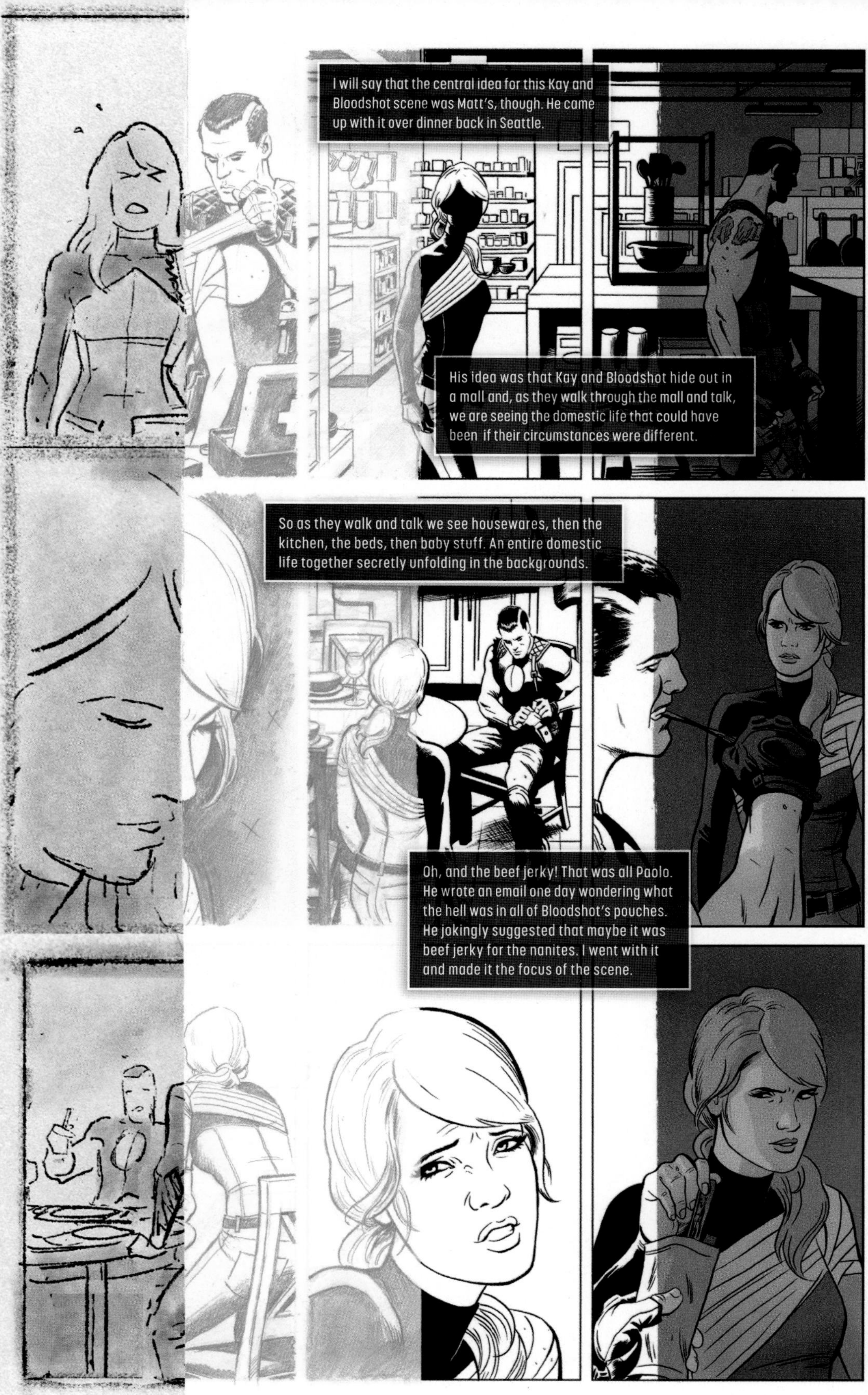
I will say that the central idea for this Kay and Bloodshot scene was Matt's, though. He came up with it over dinner back in Seattle.
His idea was that Kay and Bloodshot hide out in a mall and, as they walk through the mall and talk, we are seeing the domestic life that could have been if their circumstances were different.
So as they walk and talk we see housewares, then the kitchen, the beds, then baby stuff. An entire domestic life together secretly unfolding in the backgrounds.
Oh, and the beef jerky! That was all Paolo. He wrote an email one day wondering what the hell was in all of Bloodshot's pouches. He jokingly suggested that maybe it was beef jerky for the nanites. I went with it and made it the focus of the scene.

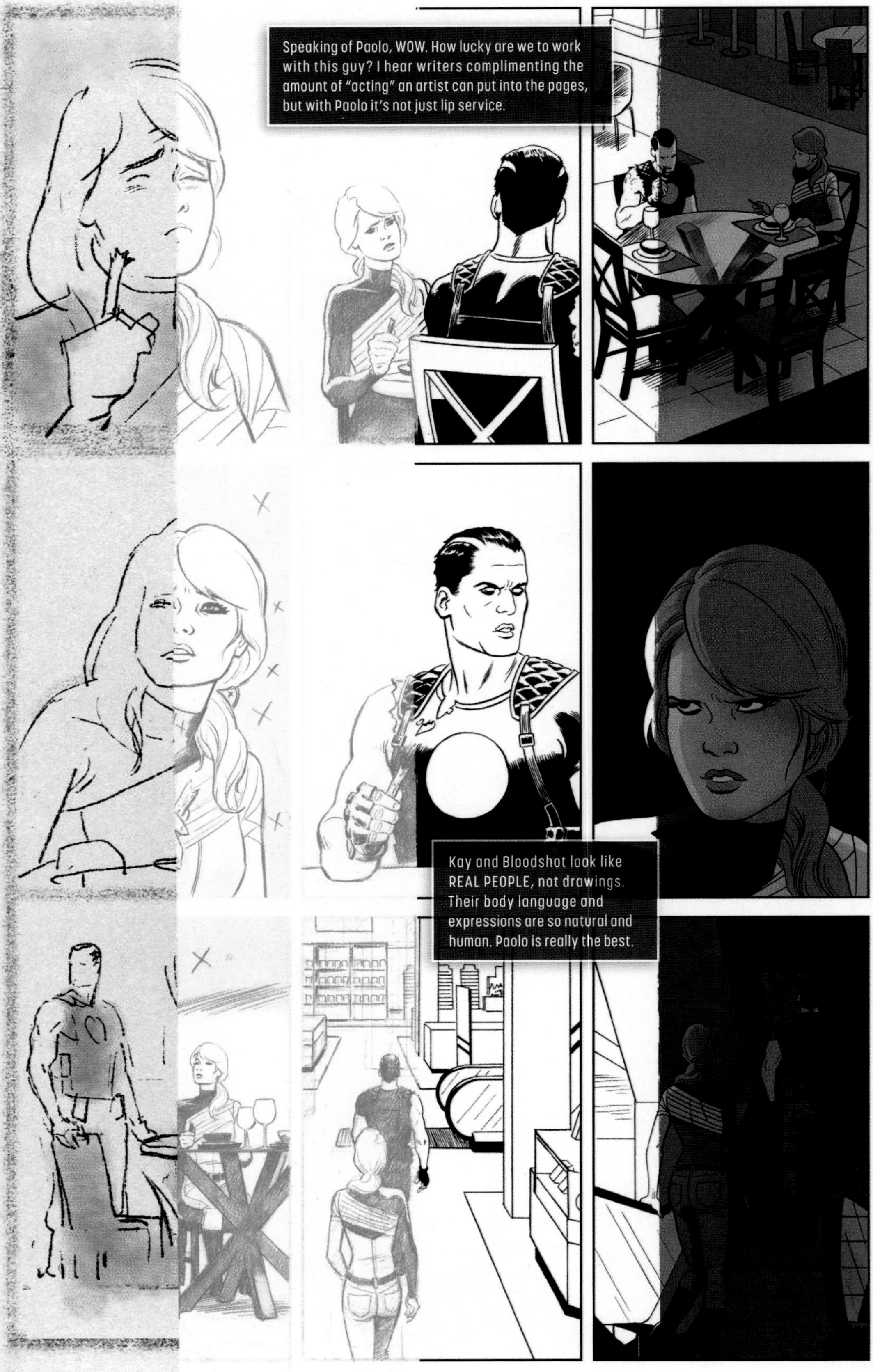
Speaking of Paolo, WOW. How lucky are we to work with this guy? I hear writers complimenting the amount of "acting" an artist can put into the pages, but with Paolo it's not just lip service.
Kay and Bloodshot look like REAL PEOPLE, not drawings. Their body language and expressions are so natural and human. Paolo is really the best.

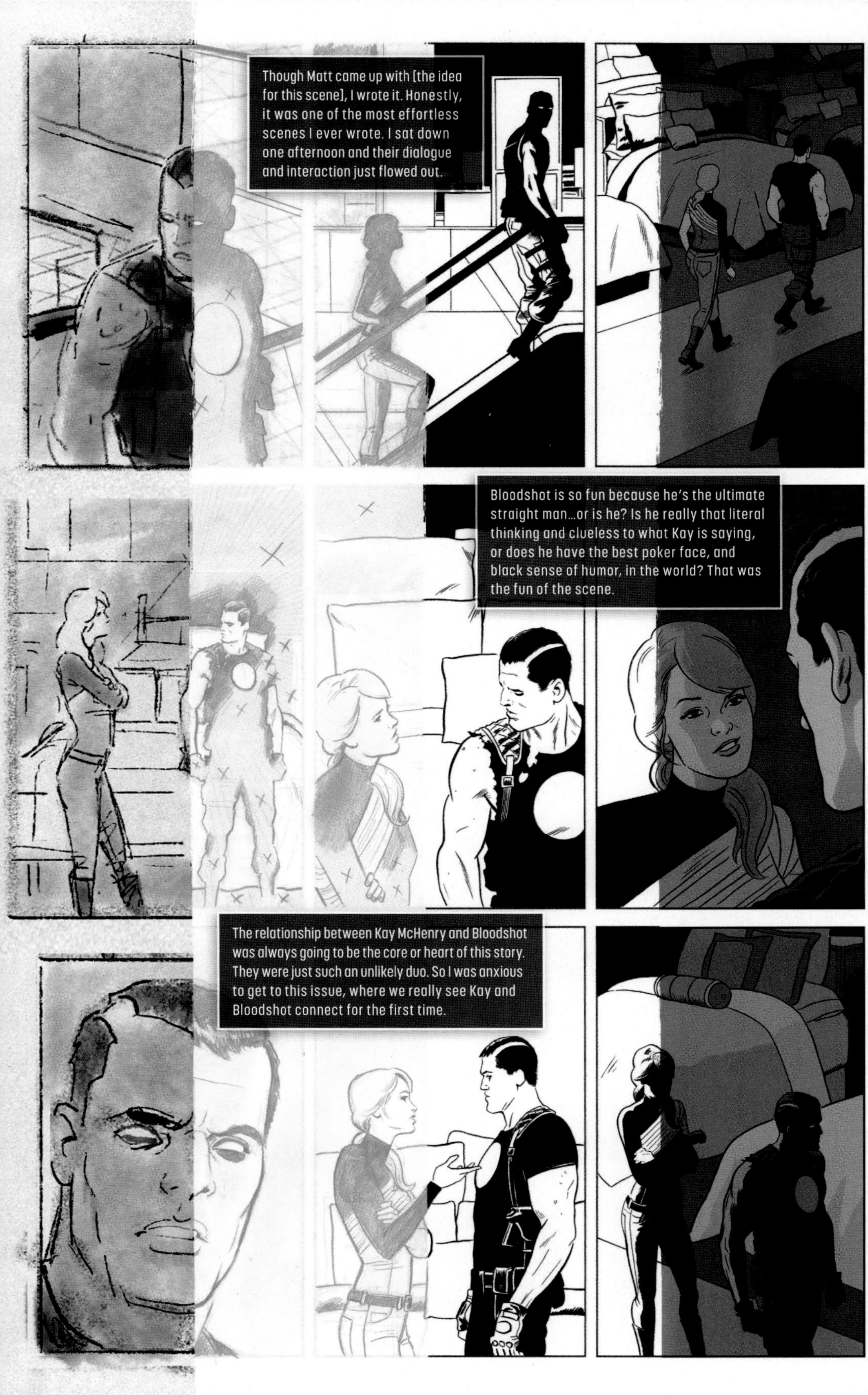
Though Matt came up with [the idea for this scene], I wrote it. Honestly, it was one of the most effortless scenes I ever wrote. I sat down one afternoon and their dialogue and interaction just flowed out.
Bloodshot is so fun because he's the ultimate straight man...or is he? Is he really that literal thinking and clueless to what Kay is saying, or does he have the best poker face, and black sense of humor, in the world? That was the fun of the scene.
The relationship between Kay McHenry and Bloodshot was always going to be the core or heart of this story. They were just such an unlikely duo. So I was anxious to get to this issue, where we really see Kay and Bloodshot connect for the first time.

LAYOUTS | PENCILS | INKS | COLORS

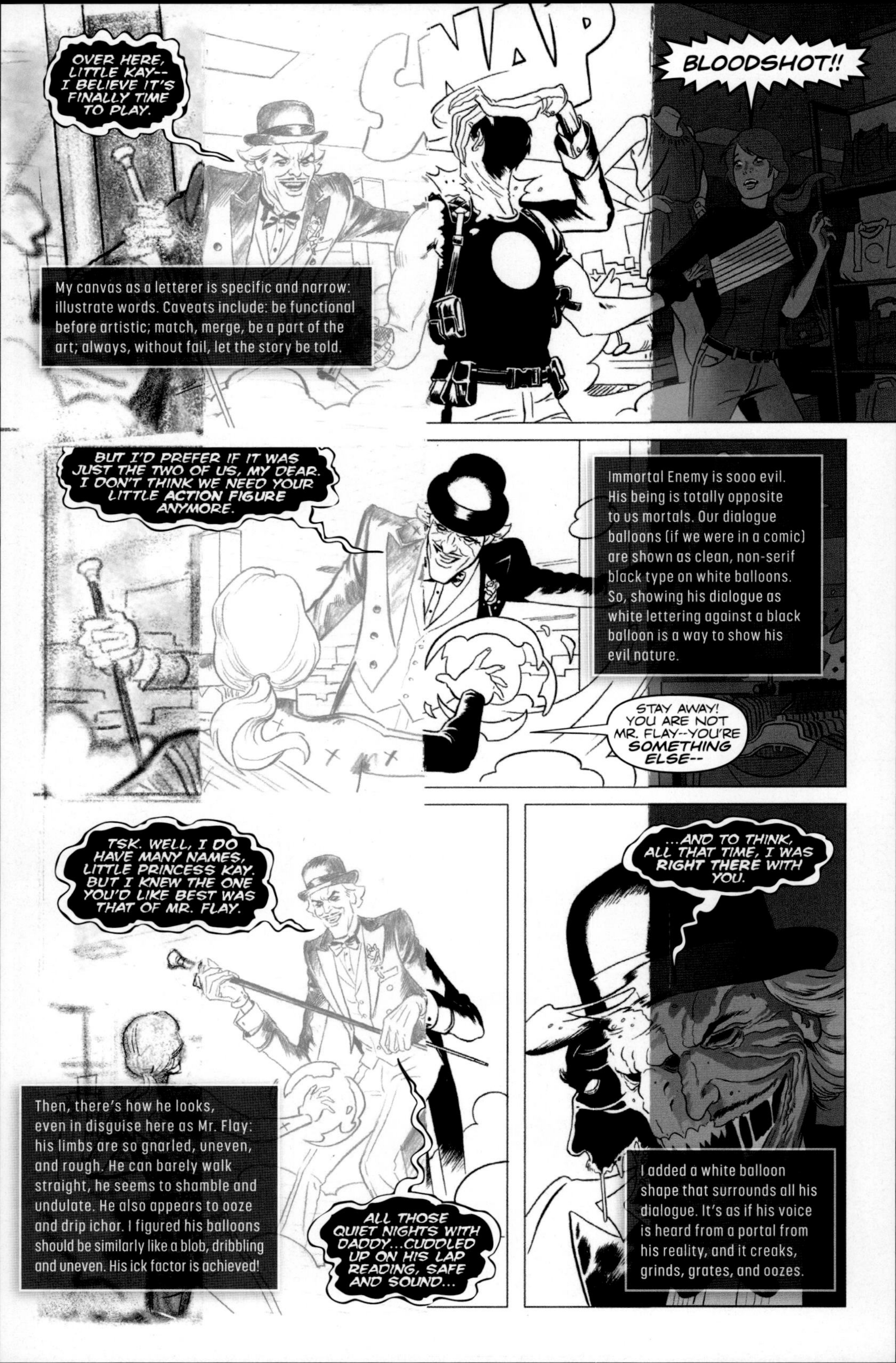
OVER HERE, LITTLE KAY-- I BELIEVE IT'S FINALLY TIME TO PLAY.
SNAP
BLOODSHOT!!
BUT I'D PREFER IF IT WAS JUST THE TWO OF US, MY DEAR. I DON'T THINK WE NEED YOUR LITTLE ACTION FIGURE ANYMORE.
STAY AWAY! YOU ARE NOT MR. FLAY--YOU'RE SOMETHING ELSE--
TSK. WELL, I DO HAVE MANY NAMES, LITTLE PRINCESS KAY. BUT I KNEW THE ONE YOU'D LIKE BEST WAS THAT OF MR. FLAY.
ALL THOSE QUIET NIGHTS WITH DADDY...CUDDLED UP ON HIS LAP READING, SAFE AND SOUND...
...AND TO THINK, ALL THAT TIME, I WAS RIGHT THERE WITH YOU.

My canvas as a letterer is specific and narrow: illustrate words. Caveats include: be functional before artistic; match, merge, be a part of the art; always, without fail, let the story be told.

Immortal Enemy is sooo evil. His being is totally opposite to us mortals. Our dialogue balloons (if we were in a comic) are shown as clean, non-serif black type on white balloons. So, showing his dialogue as white lettering against a black balloon is a way to show his evil nature.

Then, there's how he looks, even in disguise here as Mr. Flay: his limbs are so gnarled, uneven, and rough. He can barely walk straight, he seems to shamble and undulate. He also appears to ooze and drip ichor. I figured his balloons should be similarly like a blob, dribbling and uneven. His ick factor is achieved!

I added a white balloon shape that surrounds all his dialogue. It's as if his voice is heard from a portal from his reality, and it creaks, grinds, grates, and oozes.

LAYOUTS | PENCILS | INKS | COLORS

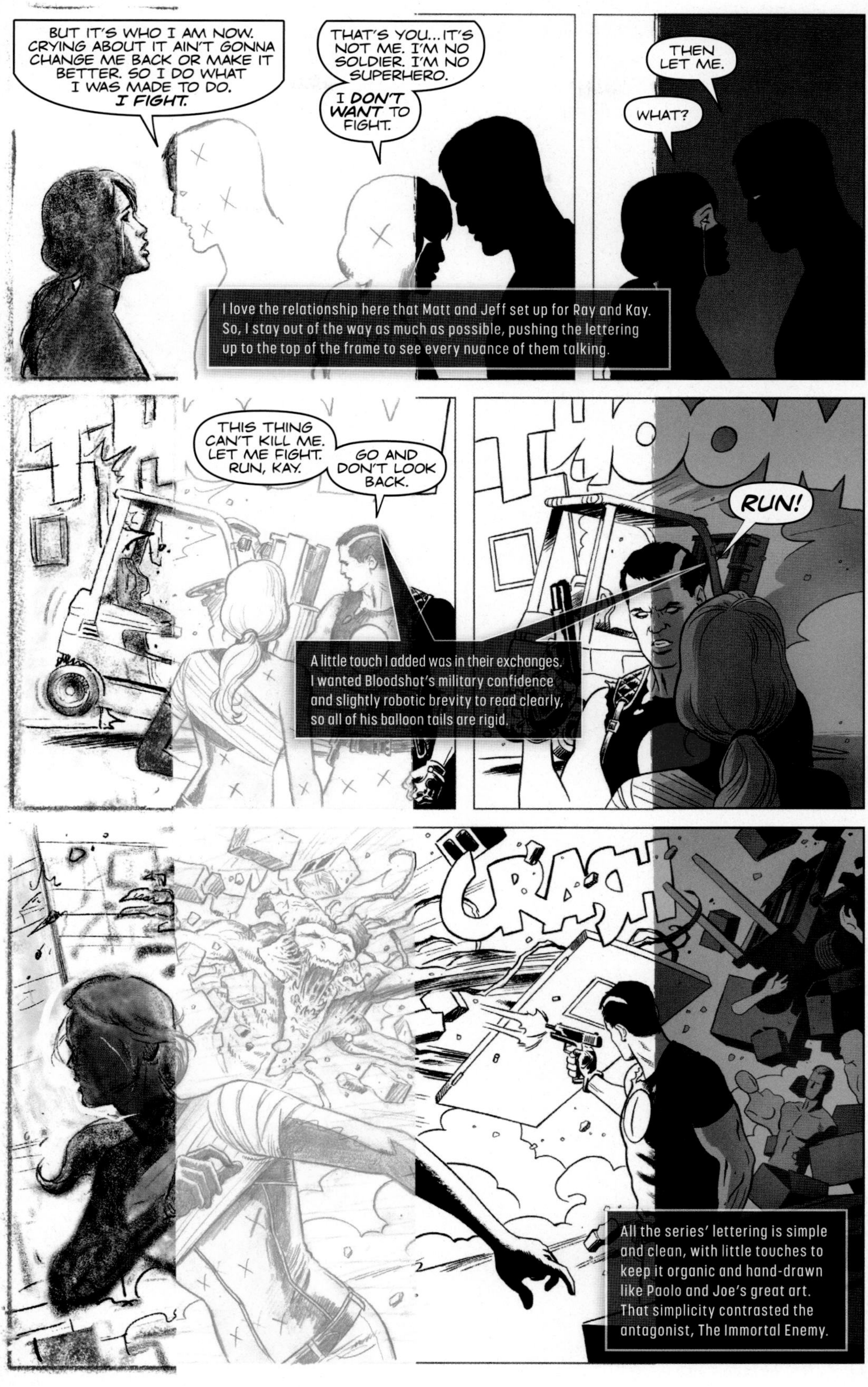
BUT IT'S WHO I AM NOW. CRYING ABOUT IT AIN'T GONNA CHANGE ME BACK OR MAKE IT BETTER. SO I DO WHAT I WAS MADE TO DO. *I FIGHT.*
THAT'S YOU... IT'S NOT ME. I'M NO SOLDIER. I'M NO SUPERHERO.
I *DON'T WANT* TO FIGHT.
THEN LET ME.
WHAT?
THIS THING CAN'T KILL ME. LET ME FIGHT. RUN, KAY.
GO AND DON'T LOOK BACK.
RUN!
CRASH

I love the relationship here that Matt and Jeff set up for Ray and Kay. So, I stay out of the way as much as possible, pushing the lettering up to the top of the frame to see every nuance of them talking.

A little touch I added was in their exchanges. I wanted Bloodshot's military confidence and slightly robotic brevity to read clearly, so all of his balloon tails are rigid.

All the series' lettering is simple and clean, with little touches to keep it organic and hand-drawn like Paolo and Joe's great art. That simplicity contrasted the antagonist, The Immortal Enemy.

GALLERY

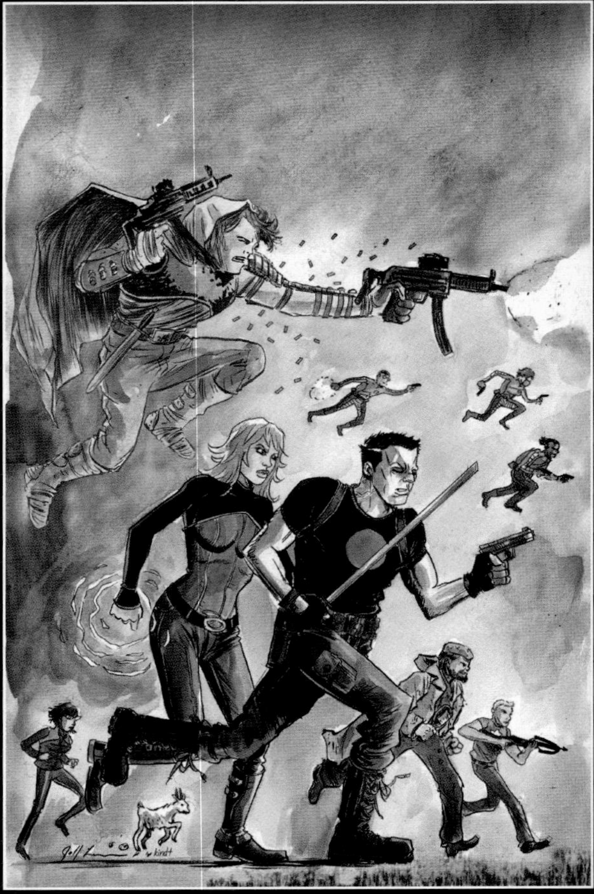

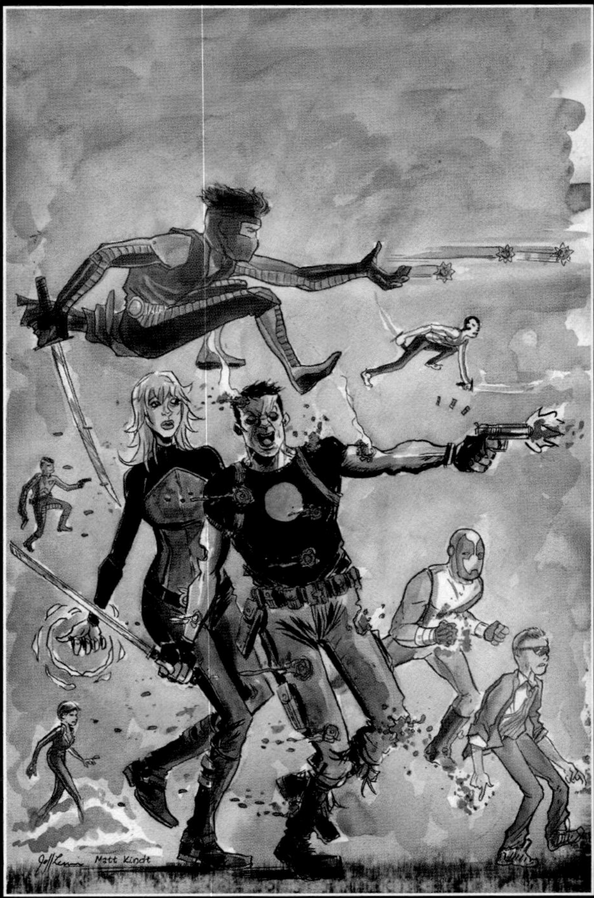

THE VALIANT #1 and #2 VARIANT COVERS
Art by JEFF LEMIRE and MATT KINDT

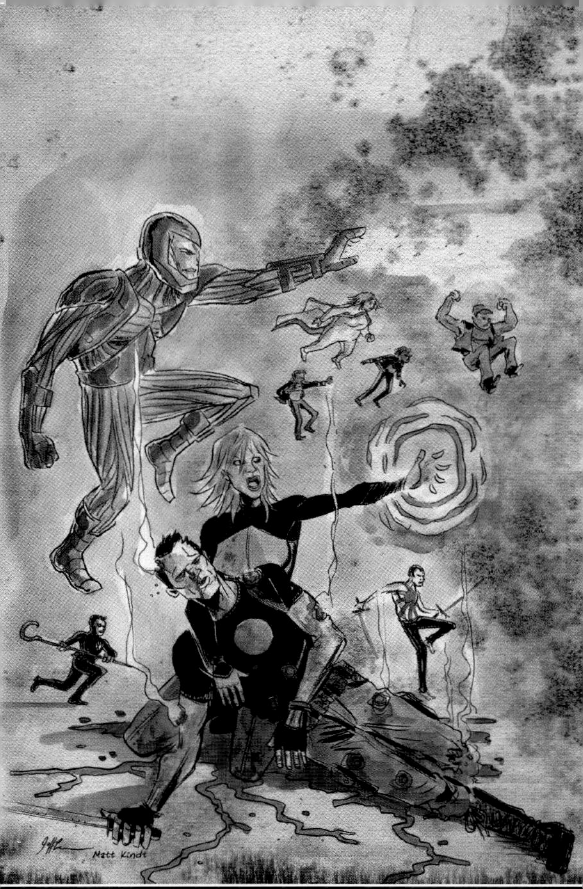
Matt Kindt

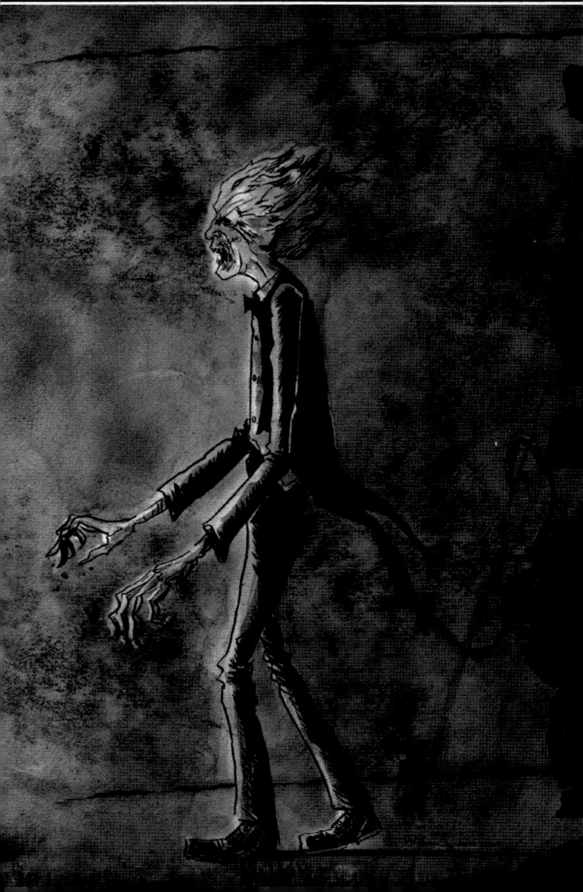

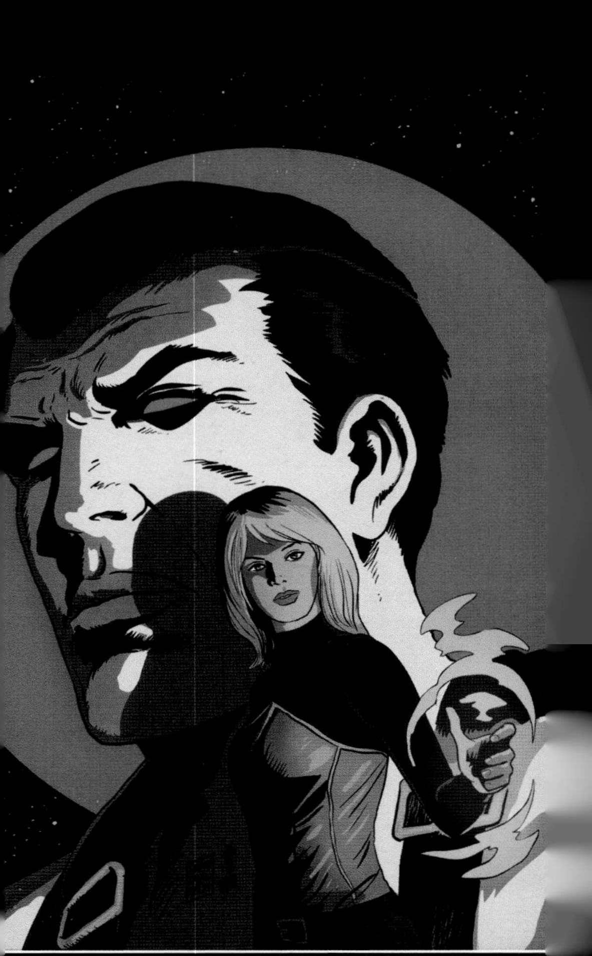

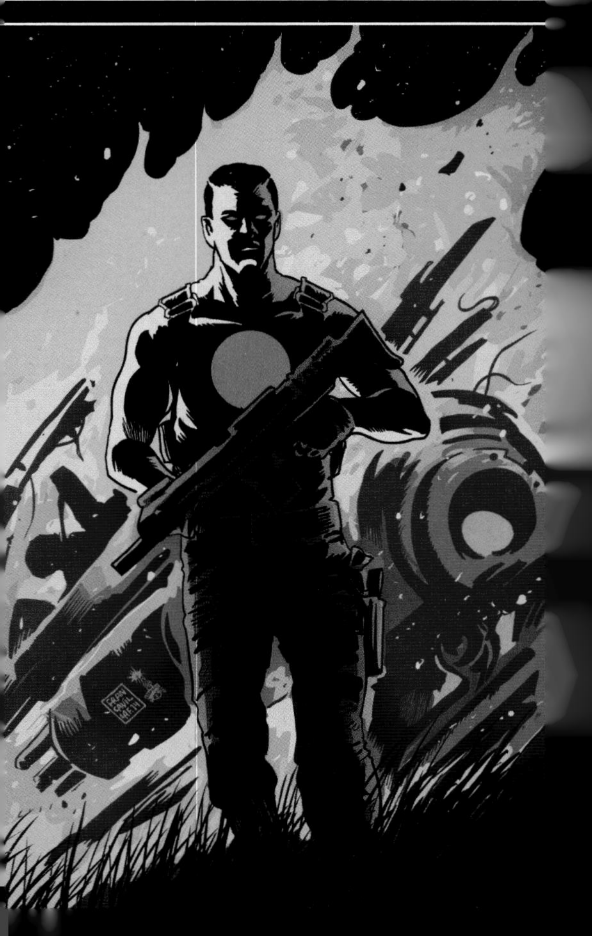

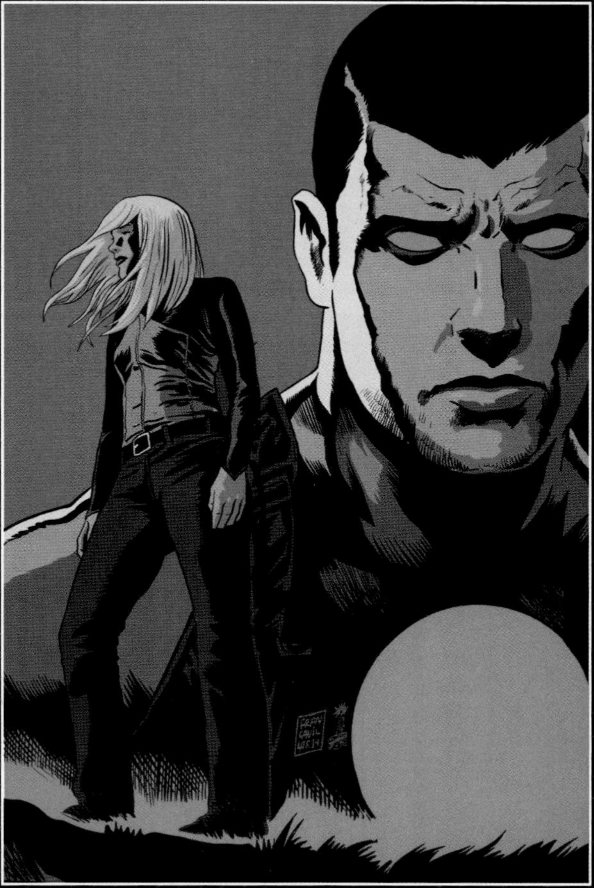

THE VALIANT #3 VARIANT
Cover by FRANCESCO FRANCAV

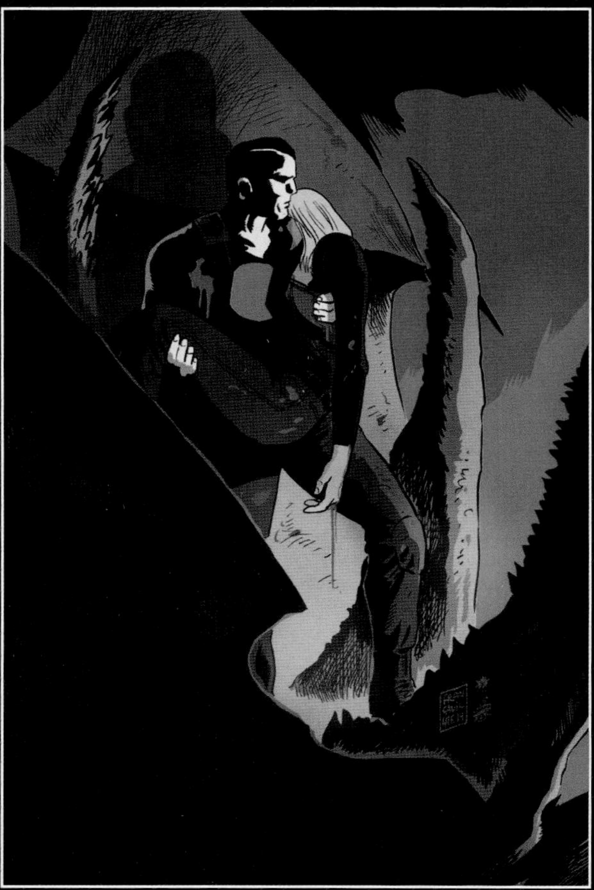

THE VALIANT #4 VARIANT
Cover by FRANCESCO FRANCAV

EXPLORE THE VALIANT UNIVERSE

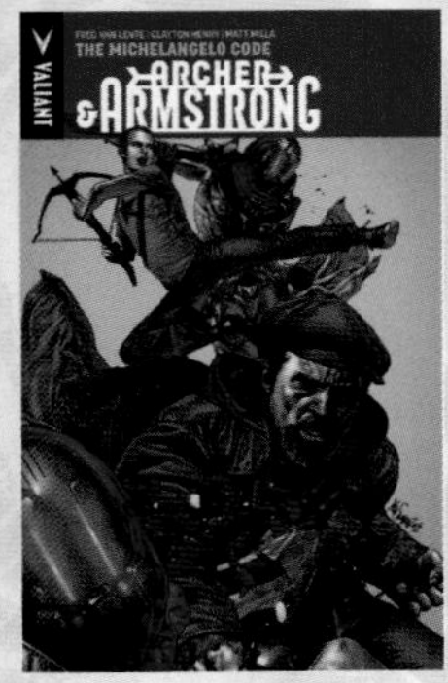
VALIANT
THE MICHELANGELO CODE
ARCHER & ARMSTRONG

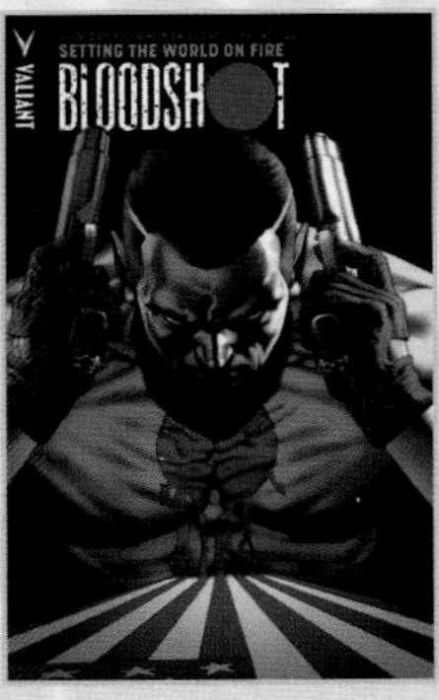
VALIANT
SETTING THE WORLD ON FIRE
BLOODSHOT

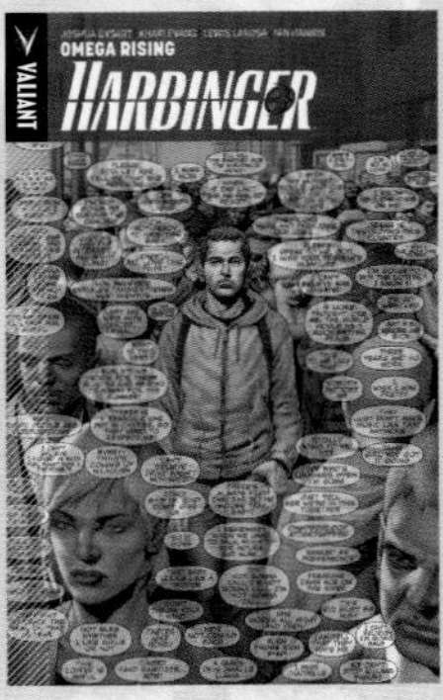
VALIANT
OMEGA RISING
HARBINGER

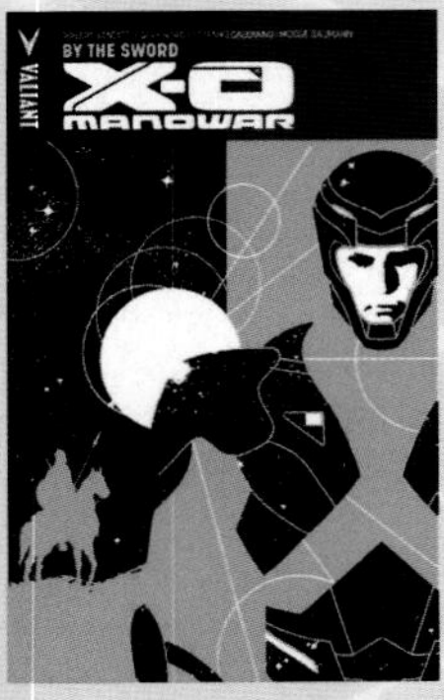
VALIANT
BY THE SWORD
X-O MANOWAR

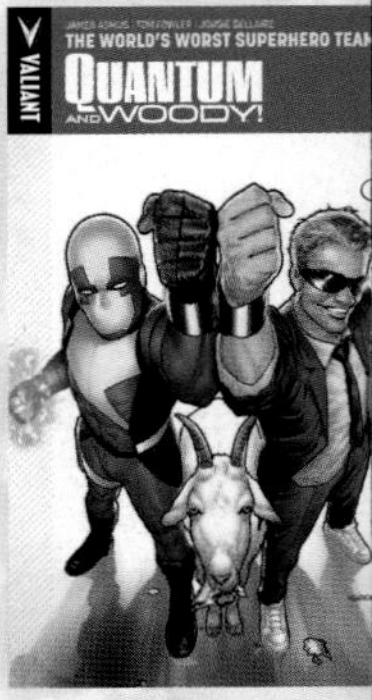
VALIANT
THE WORLD'S WORST SUPERHERO TEAM
QUANTUM AND WOODY!

ARCHER & ARMSTRONG

Volume 1: The Michelangelo Code
ISBN: 9780979640988

Volume 2: Wrath of the Eternal Warrior
ISBN: 9781939346049

Volume 3: Far Faraway
ISBN: 9781939346148

Volume 4: Sect Civil War
ISBN: 9781939346254

Volume 5: Mission: Improbable
ISBN: 9781939346353

Volume 6: American Wasteland
ISBN: 9781939346421

ARMOR HUNTERS

Armor Hunters
ISBN: 9781939346452

Armor Hunters: Bloodshot
ISBN: 9781939346469

Armor Hunters: Harbinger
ISBN: 9781939346506

Unity Vol. 3: Armor Hunters
ISBN: 9781939346445

X-O Manowar Vol. 7: Armor Hunters
ISBN: 9781939346476

BLOODSHOT

Volume 1: Setting the World on Fire
ISBN: 9780979640964

Volume 2: The Rise and the Fall
ISBN: 9781939346032

Volume 3: Harbinger Wars
ISBN: 9781939346124

Volume 4: H.A.R.D. Corps
ISBN: 9781939346193

Volume 5: Get Some!
ISBN: 9781939346315

Volume 6: The Glitch and Other Tales
ISBN: 9781939346711

THE DEATH-DEFYING DOCTOR MIRAGE

The Death-Defying Dr. Mirage
ISBN: 9781939346490

THE DELINQUENTS

The Delinquents
ISBN: 9781939346513

ETERNAL WARRIOR

Volume 1: Sword of the Wild
ISBN: 9781939346209

Volume 2: Eternal Emperor
ISBN: 9781939346292

Eternal Warrior: Days of Steel
ISBN: 9781939346742

HARBINGER

Volume 1: Omega Rising
ISBN: 9780979640957

Volume 2: Renegades
ISBN: 9781939346025

Volume 3: Harbinger Wars
ISBN: 9781939346117

Volume 4: Perfect Day
ISBN: 9781939346155

Volume 5: Death of a Renegade
ISBN: 9781939346339

Volume 6: Omegas
ISBN: 9781939346384

HARBINGER WARS

Harbinger Wars
ISBN: 9781939346094

Bloodshot Vol. 3: Harbinger Wars
ISBN: 9781939346124

Harbinger Vol. 3: Harbinger Wars
ISBN: 9781939346117

QUANTUM AND WOODY!

Volume 1: The World's Worst Superhero Team
ISBN: 9781939346186

Volume 2: In Security
ISBN: 9781939346230

Volume 3: Crooked Pasts, Present Tense
ISBN: 9781939346391

Volume 4: Quantum and Woody Must Die!
ISBN: 9781939346629
COMING SOON

EXPLORE THE VALIANT UNIVERSE

KICK ME
UANTUM AND WOODY
BY PRIEST & BRIGHT
L 1: KLANG

VALIANT
BATTLE FOR NEW JAPAN
RAI

VALIANT
THE VALIANT

VALIANT
THE DEATH-DEFYING
DOCTOR MIRAGE

VALIANT
VALIANT ZEROES ORIGINS

UANTUM AND WOODY BY PRIEST & BRIGHT

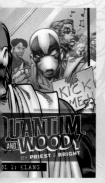

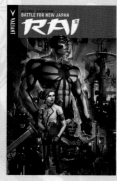

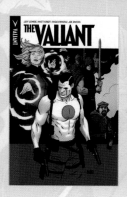

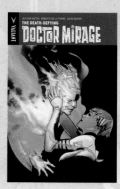

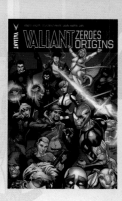

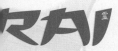

me 1: Klang
: 9781939346780
ING SOON

RAI

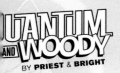

me 1: Welcome to New Japan
: 9781939346414

me 2: Battle for New Japan
: 9781939346612
ING SOON

HADOWMAN

me 1: Birth Rites
: 9781939346001

me 2: Darque Reckoning
: 9781939346056

me 3: Deadside Blues
: 9781939346162

me 4: Fear, Blood, And Shadows
: 9781939346278

me 5: End Times
: 9781939346377

Ivar, Timewalker

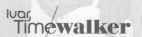

Volume 1: Making History
ISBN: 9781939346636
COMING SOON

UNITY

Volume 1: To Kill a King
ISBN: 9781939346261

Volume 2: Trapped by Webnet
ISBN: 9781939346346

Volume 3: Armor Hunters
ISBN: 9781939346445

Volume 4: The United
ISBN: 9781939346544

Volume 5: Homefront
ISBN: 9781939346797

THE VALIANT

The Valiant
ISBN: 9781939346605
COMING SOON

VALIANT ZEROES AND ORIGINS

Valiant: Zeroes and Origins
ISBN: 9781939346582
COMING SOON

X-O MANOWAR

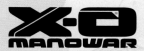

Volume 1: By the Sword
ISBN: 9780979640940

Volume 2: Enter Ninjak
ISBN: 9780979640995

Volume 3: Planet Death
ISBN: 9781939346087

Volume 4: Homecoming
ISBN: 9781939346179

Volume 5: At War With Unity
ISBN: 9781939346247

Volume 6: Prelude to Armor Hunters
ISBN: 9781939346407

Volume 7: Armor Hunters
ISBN: 9781939346476

Volume 8: Enter: Armorines
ISBN: 9781939346551

Volume 9: Dead Hand
ISBN: 9781939346650

VALIANT
HARBINGER
DELUXE EDITION 2

OMNIBUSES

Quantum and Woody: The Complete Classic Omnibus
ISBN: 9781939346360
Collecting QUANTUM AND WOODY (1997) #0, 1-21 and #32, THE GOAT: H.A.E.D.U.S. #1, and X-O MANOWAR (1996) #16

X-O Manowar Classic Omnibus Vol. 1
ISBN: 9781939346308
Collecting X-O MANOWAR (1992) #0-30, ARMORINES #0, X-O DATABASE #1, as well as material from SECRETS OF THE VALIANT UNIVERSE #1

DELUXE EDITIONS

Archer & Armstrong Deluxe Edition Book 1
ISBN: 9781939346223
Collecting ARCHER & ARMSTRONG #0-13

VALIANT
ARMOR HUNTERS
DELUXE EDITION

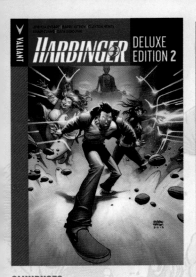

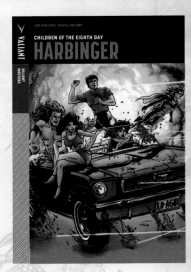

Armor Hunters Deluxe Edition
ISBN: 9781939346728
Collecting ARMOR HUNTERS #1-4, ARMOR HUNTERS: AFTERMATH #1, ARMOR HUNTERS: BLOODSHOT #1-3, ARMOR HUNTERS: HARBINGER #1-3, UNITY #8-11 and X-O MANOWAR #23-29

Bloodshot Deluxe Edition Book 1
ISBN: 9781939346216
Collecting BLOODSHOT #1-13

Harbinger Deluxe Edition Book 1
ISBN: 9781939346131
Collecting HARBINGER #0-14

Harbinger Deluxe Edition Book 2
ISBN: 9781939346773
Collecting HARBINGER #15-25, HARBINGER: OMEGAS #1-3, and HARBINGER: BLEEDING MONK #0

Harbinger Wars Deluxe Edition
ISBN: 9781939346322
Collecting HARBINGER WARS #1-4, HARBINGER #11-14, and BLOODSHOT #10-13

Quantum and Woody Deluxe Edition Book 1
ISBN: 9781939346681
Collecting QUANTUM AND WOODY #1-12 and QUANTUM AND WOODY: THE GOAT #0

Q2: The Return of Quantum and Woody Deluxe Edition
ISBN: 9781939346568
Collecting Q2: THE RETURN OF QUANTUM AND WOODY #1-5

JAMES ASMUS | TOM FOWLER | MING DOYLE
KANO | JORDIE BELLAIRE | DAVE LANPHEAR
VALIANT
QUANTUM AND WOODY!
DELUXE EDITION 1
MEH!

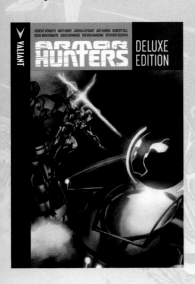

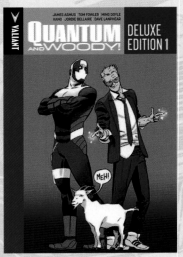

Shadowman Deluxe Edition Book 1
ISBN: 9781939346438
Collecting SHADOWMAN #0-10

X-O Manowar Deluxe Edition Book 1
ISBN: 9781939346100
Collecting X-O MANOWAR #1-14

X-O Manowar Deluxe Edition Book 2
ISBN: 9781939346520
Collecting X-O MANOWAR #15-22, and UNITY #1-4

JIM SHOOTER | DAVID LAPHAM
VALIANT
CHILDREN OF THE EIGHTH DAY
HARBINGER
VALIANT MASTERS

VALIANT MASTERS

Bloodshot Vol. 1 - Blood of the Machine
ISBN: 9780979640933

H.A.R.D. Corps Vol. 1 - Search and Destroy
ISBN: 9781939346285

Harbinger Vol. 1 - Children of the Eighth Day
ISBN: 9781939346483

Ninjak Vol. 1 - Black Water
ISBN: 9780979640971

Rai Vol. 1 - From Honor to Strength
ISBN: 9781939346070

Shadowman Vol. 1 - Spirits Within
ISBN: 9781939346018

KEVIN VANHOOK | DON PERLIN
VALIANT
BLOOD OF THE MACHINE
BLOODSHOT
VALIANT MASTERS

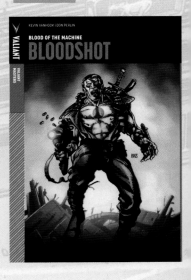

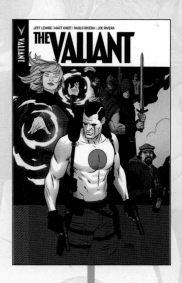

BLOODSHOT REBORN®

VOLUME ONE: **COLORADO**

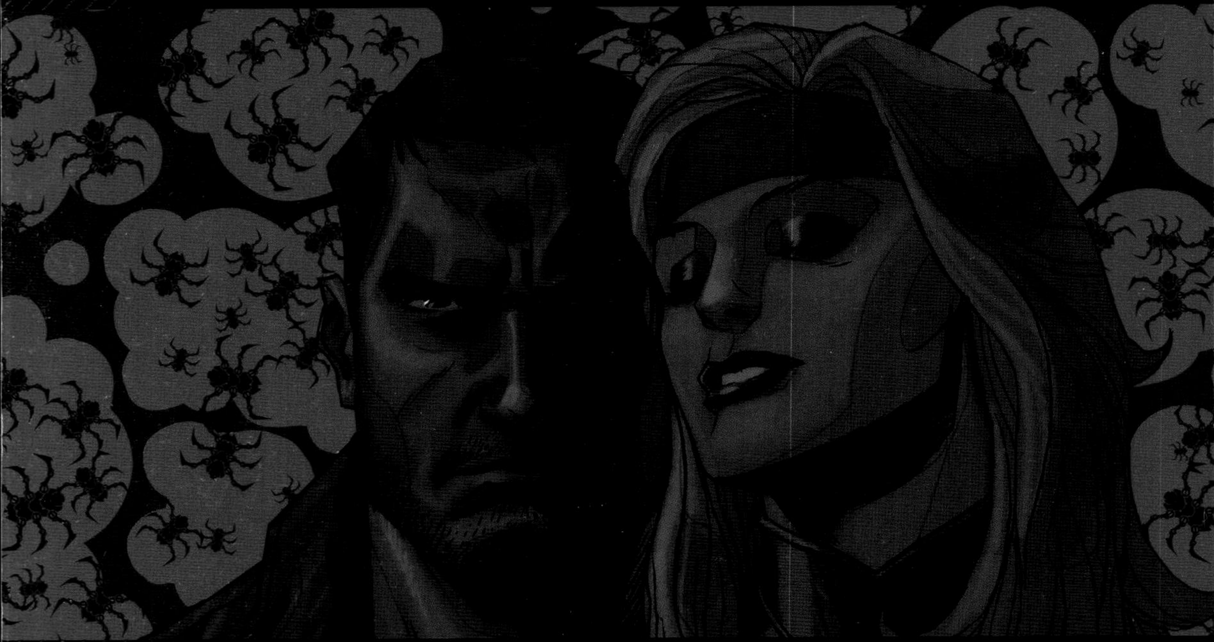

NEW YORK TIMES BEST-SELLING WRITER JEFF LEMIRE (THE VALIANT, *Green Arrow*) AND RED-HOT RISING STAR MICO SUAYAN (HARBINGER, *Moon Knight*) DELIVER AN ALL-NEW ONGOING SERIES FOR VALIANT'S MOST UNRELENTING HERO!

Bloodshot's nanites made him a nearly unstoppable killing machine. His enhanced strength, speed, endurance, and healing made him the perfect weapon, and he served his masters at Project Rising Spirit - a private contractor trafficking in violence - very well.

Now, Bloodshot is a shadow of his former self. He lives in self-imposed exile, reeling from the consequences of his past life and the recent events that nearly drove him mad. But when a rash of shootings by gunmen who appear to look just like Bloodshot begin, his guilt will send him on a mission to stop the killers, even if it means diving headlong into the violence that nearly destroyed him.

Start reading here as visionary creators Jeff Lemire and Mico Suayan kick off a brand-new beginning for the cutting-edge commando called Bloodshot...and plunge him to his darkest, bloodiest, most mind-bending depths yet. Collecting BLOODSHOT REBORN #1-5.

TRADE PAPERBACK
ISBN: 978-1-939346-82-7

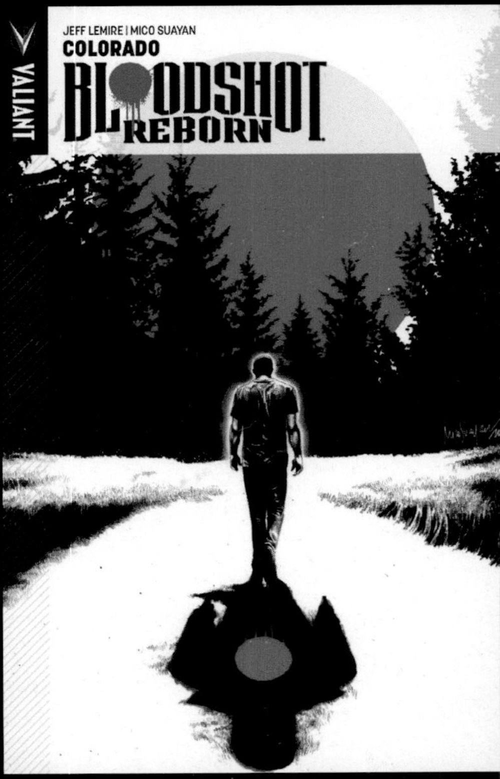
VALIANT
JEFF LEMIRE | MICO SUAYAN
COLORADO
BLOODSHOT REBORN